Architectural Office Standards and Practices: A Practical Users Guide

Architectural Office Standards and Practices: A Practical Users Guide

Office Practice Committee
Denver Chapter
American Institute of Architects

Larry D. Jenks
Chair, Office Practice Committee
Principal, Klipp Colussy Jenks DuBois Architects, P.C.
Denver, Colorado

McGraw-Hill, Inc.
New York   San Francisco   Washington, D.C.   Auckland   Bogota
Caracas   Lisbon   London   Madrid   Mexico City   Milan
Montreal   New Delhi   San Juan   Singapore
Sydney   Tokyo   Toronto

Library of Congress Cataloging-in-Publication Data

Jenks, Larry D.
    Architectural office standards and practices : a practical user's
guide / Larry D. Jenks.
        p. cm.
    Includes biographical references.
    ISBN 0-07-001533-3
    1. Architectural practice—Standards.   I. Title.
NA1996.J461995
720' .68--dc20   95-18881
                                                    CIP

1 2 3 4 5 6 7 8 9 0 K G P / K G P 9 0 0 9 8 7 6 5

ISBN 0-07-001533-3

*The sponsoring editor for this book was Joel Stein, the editing supervisor was
Bernard Onken, and the production supervisor was Suzanne Rapcavage.
It was set in Helvetica by Larry D. Jenks.*

Printed and bound by Quebecor/Kingsport.

McGraw-Hill books are available at special quantity discounts to use as premi-
ums and sales promotions, or for use in corporate training programs. For more
information, please write to the Director of Special Sales, McGraw-Hill, Inc., 11
West 19th Street, New York, NY 10011. Or contact your local bookstore.

This book is printed on recycled, acid-free paper containing a minimum of 50%
recycled de-inked fiber.

Table of Contents

The policies, procedures, information, and forms that appear in this manual were prepared for an imaginary office. Hopefully, your office will bear enough resemblance to this imaginary office that you will be able to use many of them just as they are. If you do not already have a policy or procedure for something included here, consider adopting the one shown. Where necessary, modify the language so that it reflects the actuals conditions or methodology of your office.

ACKNOWLEDGEMENTS

This manual was almost never completed, and would not have been completed without the undying commitment, hard work, and commitment of time and talent of the following people:

Editor, Committee Chairman, and Principal Author
  Larry D. Jenks

Contributing Authors and Steering Committee
  Bruce Bollenbach
  Laurie Jessen
  Mark McClelland
  Ben Wilking

Contributing Authors
  Eric Bartczak
  Curt Dale
  Cornelius R. (Kin) DuBois
  L. Brand Gould
  David Lay
  Joe Levi
  Jeff von Breitenfeld

Creative Consultants
  Bruce Bollenbach
  Marianne Garehime
  Warren Lange
  John Maus
  Elizabeth Rehfeld
  Lance Sherwood
  Maureen Troy

Graphics and Drawings
  Bruce Bollenbach
  Bill Campbell
  Mark Carvalho
  Larry Jenks
  Mark McClelland
  Lance Sherwood
  Ben Wilking

Text Processing
  Jane Jennings
  Kim Pierce

Text Formatting and Manipulation
  Larry Jenks
  Maureen Troy

We also want to thank those firms who contributed their Procedures Manuals for reference:

- Anderson/Mason/Dale, P.C.
- Klipp Colussy Jenks DuBois Architects, P.C.
- Fisher Reece and Johnson
- RNL

And those firms that have supported our efforts:

- Hoover Berg Desmond
- Anderson/Mason/Dale, P.C.
- Klipp Colussy Jenks DuBois Architects, P.C.
- Fisher, Reece and Johnson
- OZ Architecture
- Eric Bartczak, Architect
- David Owen Tryba, Architect
- MCB Architects

We extend our special thanks to Elizabeth (Betsy) Boudreau of Denver Chapter AIA for guidance, encouragement, and motivation.

We would like to offer a special acknowledgement to the Northern California Chapter of AIA for providing the inspiration for this effort. The POP (Professional Office Practice) Manual published in 1980 was the first comprehensive effort we could find that served the needs of the profession in the area of production standards, conventions, and methodologies. We will be forever grateful to them for that landmark publication, and we can only hope that this manual will be as useful to architects somewhere as that one has been for us.

Production of working drawings is the most time-consuming part of architectural design services.

It's the most expensive part of design service.

It requires the most office space, resources, labor, and supervisory time.

And it's the phase of design most fraught with liability risks.

From that perspective, you would expect the subject to receive lots of respectful attention by professionals and educators. And, as everybody knows, it doesn't.

Last year I reviewed a list of the skills that the National Architectural Accrediting Board expected schools to convey to students. I could not find the words "drafting," "production," or "working drawings" anywhere. No surprise: You won't find such subjects taught in most institutions of higher architectural education.

So how are people supposed to learn it?

On the job.

From whom?

From bosses and supervisors who are too busy getting their own work done to offer anything resembling systematic training or formal education.

So employees just have to sort of "pick it up." And they do. Pretty much.

With this piecemeal approach to technical education, it's a wonder that things aren't much worse.

How bad is it?

The average sheet of working drawings has from four to six major coordination errors. Almost every year, one out of four insured design firms suffers claims for errors or omissions. Contractors are now trained how to seek out and charge extra costs from errors in working drawings — a profit center for them. Building failures, big and small, are epidemic across the United States, and most of those building failures are traceable to flawed documents.

The seeds for all this were planted in the 50s and 60s with a movement to "professionalize" architectural education. That meant middle-class and upper-class kids would go to the university and become designers, managers, and licensed professionals. Working-class kids would go to technical schools and become drafters, spec writers, and construction contract administrators. That meant the end of any vestige of prestige or respect for the "technical" side of practice. It was not to be something that "better" people did or thought about. It was a dumb idea and Fascist to boot, but it became the unwritten law of the land. Now we pay the price.

The price is too high and the profession must change. How does change start? What do we do first?

What will be done about it is that the nation's most concerned professionals will start to pull together to make up for the deficiencies of the schools. They'll create reference manuals like this one — *Architectural Office Standards and Practices* — which is a major effort towards creating a ready-made production management manual that most offices can use as is. They'll set new standards for enlightened education and ongoing training of design professionals.

Larry Jenks and the fine professionals he has brought together have assembled solid, practical, much needed information on production standards. And more important, they've provided great information on how to cut drudgery and eliminate some of the more absurd timewasters in working drawing production.

You'll find this *Architectural Office Standards and Practices* manual to be enormously beneficial to your office and I endorse it wholeheartedly. I see it as an important step toward larger, long-overdue reform throughout the profession.

Fred Stitt, Editor/Publisher, *Guidelines*. Director, San Francisco Institute of Architecture.

Author of *Production Systems for Architects and Designers, The Architect's Detail Library, Architect's Room Design Data Handbook, Design Office Handbook*, and other related books, manuals, and newsletters.

PURPOSE

Numerous books have been written about communicating meaning through architecture. Christian Norburg-Schulz, Niels Luning Prak, Christopher Alexander, Charles Jencks, and others too numerous to mention have provided us with superb works about how and why built form communicates its meaning to us. Other books take a perceptual / psychological / behavioral perspective (Hall or Sommer) and suggest ways in which we can more intentionally and more effectively shape and direct the actions of those who use our buildings. Still other books speak to our social conscience, criticizing the way traditional architecture has tacitly reinforced the oppression of entire segments of our society and admonishing us as a profession for our lack of concern for the role architecture can take in helping to alleviate society's woes, insisting that there are more noble tasks at hand than minimizing "cost per square foot" or improving a building's net-to-gross floor area. These are all praiseworthy books.

This book is also about communication.

Its premise is that all completed architectural works, whether "good" or "bad" in terms of design, whether socially responsible or irresponsible, whether complex or simple in their content — each and every one must first be effectively communicated to contractors, masons, steel erectors, plasterers, and painters before they can ever begin to communicate on a more significant, philosophical level. If we ever hope to see our designs realized, we must clearly, completely, and competently explain precisely what it is we want done.

While analogies can be risky, what we are doing in preparing a set of construction contract documents is not unlike a composer scoring an orchestral piece. Just as the composer knows and can hear inside his own mind the particular sound or feeling he may want played, if his notes are written incorrectly (or sloppily), if his time signatures conflict, if there are other technical problems with the piece as scored, it will never be played properly and may never be heard either by the listener or, perhaps worse, by the composer himself. Of course, very few composers are sued for not preparing a coherent score.

In contrast, much of what we do *does* have legal significance. I remember as a young graduate architect being nearly paralyzed by one partner's impassioned warning that "each and every line we drew, *each* word, *each* letter" had ominous legal ramifications. His plea was so dramatic but earnest that for a while afterward, examining every working drawing I completed was like surveying some abandoned mine field—supposedly cleared, but impossible to cross without the utmost caution. Since then, the world has become more, not less, lawsuit-happy, and I have to wonder if my mentor of that day has made it through without suffering a total nervous collapse.

As said earlier, this book is about communication. It is about how we can prepare our construction contract documents in a manner that will facilitate both communication and construction. It is about how we can improve, even streamline, the way we prepare construction drawings, and the ways in which others use them.

One doesn't have to fight a lawsuit or suffer through a protracted arbitration hearing to fully appreciate the need for clarity in our contract documents. Simply experience that uncomfortable conversation with a client where you try to explain the concept of "value received" and why drawings are not necessarily perfect and why she needs to pay an additional $251.36 for a light switch that from her perspective "should have been in there anyway." These are simple enough and common enough experiences to make one want and need to do a better job during this phase of our work. While the use of these guidelines may not guarantee that you'll never overlook another item as long as you're practicing, their use will hopefully encourage a more systematic and consistent approach for preparing documents, which may in turn give you more time for a better quality-control check.

What we hope to achieve through this book is a standardized, consistent method or language for communicating. Each chapter focuses on a specific area of communication. Some chapters are very, very specific in their scope and very literal in their application. Others are more broad and address matters of overall drawing organization. All chapters are relevant to the task being addressed. While assisting our fellow professionals in attaining a higher level of consistency within any given set of construction documents or within a particular firm is an initial goal, our broader goal is establishing an expanded level of consistency *among firms*. After all, we rely on the same universe of contractors to execute designs. There is simply no rational explanation for why these contractors should have to figure out each architect's unique way of communicating the same kinds of information, done under the guise of improving upon the ways of our predecessors, or (worse yet) to demonstrate the creative spirit that drives us all. Further, given the up and down nature of business and the seeming propensity for major projects to go on terminal hold or conversely spring up overnight, there is a great deal of fluidity in terms of staff. There is also no rational explanation for why each new staff member should have to learn two or ten different ways to accomplish the same things in different offices. Yes, there are many good reasons to seek standardization.

The committee that jointly authored this book, while all members of the Denver Chapter of AIA, was deliberately composed of individuals from a broad range of firms engaged in a wide diversity of work. Some are members of large firms, others are sole practitioners. All are committed to the common goal of increasing quality and simplifying communication.

As for your use of this book, while we would love to sell thousands of copies and make a pile of money for our personal use, that's not the plan. Read it. Copy it for your staff's use, edit it (if you must), add to it.

Our only request is that you use it.[1]

---

[1] Our wildest dream in preparing this manual was that it might receive widespread acceptance and use throughout the profession of architecture and the construction industry. In order to achieve that, we encourage every firm to buy at least one copy, but then to make in-house copies available to all members of the firm. Yes, we encourage copying. However, we do ask that you limit this copying to in-house use only. Thanks for your cooperation.

"Standard of Care" is now a common legal concept used to help determine the outcome of lawsuits in local jurisdictions all over the country. The practice of architecture is going to look different in Manhattan, New York than it does in Manhattan, Louisiana. That is as it should be. It is not the intent of this manual to present these ideas as representing a standard of care that should be used in all practices in every part of the country. On the contrary, our intention is, hopefully, to present ideas as a point of departure so that interested firms do not have to start at ground zero to prepare a manual that serves its particular needs. Of course, we would not be disappointed if some firms elected to use it verbatim. Can you imagine that?

The drawings and other information contained in this book were obtained from a variety of sources, including professional architects, architectural firms, construction general contractors or firms, and the like. The American Institute of Architects and the publisher have made every reasonable effort to assure that this reference work is accurate and authoritative, but do not warrant, and assume no liability for, the accuracy or completeness of the text or ideas contained herein, and cannot warrant its fitness for any particular purpose. It is the responsibility of the users to apply their professional knowledge in the use of the information contained in this book, to consult other sources for additional information when appropriate, and (if they themselves are not professional architects) to consult an architect when appropriate.

Architectural Office Standards and Practices:
A Practical Users Guide

PURPOSE

The difficulty communicating a design described in English to a Dutch general contractor and Argentine subs is obvious. No one would even attempt something so obviously doomed to failure. Yet, as a group, we do something very similar when we use different words to describe the same thing in a set of working drawings, or when we use the same words to describe different things, even if the words are all in English. As a profession, we should agree on some common definitions for commonly used terms, and then be consistent—and relentless about being consistent—in their usage.

PROPOSITION

Any effort in communication first requires that a common language be established between participants. The English language generally serves us well for this purpose, but there are some terms that have special meanings when used in a construction context. By reference or by inclusion, construction documents should begin by defining terms, standards, abbreviations, and symbols that will be necessary to clearly interpret and understand the information presented. These are most often identified on an initial drawing sheet, in the General Conditions of the contract, and in Division 1 of the specifications. Make it your mission to know the words used in the general conditions, and elsewhere in the specifications, and then to use these words, terms, or expressions to describe the same things every time they are used.

Except for simple English, only identified terms, abbreviations, and symbols should be used. These should be identified for use prior to the start of the drawing. Referenced standards often use specific words to communicate information or identify materials and methods. These same words should be used for the same intentions in the construction documents.

Creation of the project specifications should begin with this same process of defining the language to be used. Specified products should generally be identified by the same non-proprietary terms as are used by manufacturers. In the drawings, the use of the non-proprietary terms from specifications aids the reader in finding the matching specification. A proprietary name should not be used in drawings. The drawings identify where specified products are required and how they are to interface with other specified products. By not repeating information from the specifications in the drawings, small changes in the specifications can be made without affecting the drawing notation.

Words not having a consistent spelling or meaning within the industry will always be present. If a set of documents is consistent within itself and its referenced standards, there should be little chance for confusion. For words not taken from referenced standards or from manufacturers, it is recommended that one dictionary be established as the reference of choice for that project. Spellings used should generally be the first listed.

Some words in common use in the industry are not appropriate. "Lineal," for example is a poor variant of the word "linear" because its preferred use is in reference to genealogical lineage rather than measurement. Care should be exercised to avoid use of product names such as "vinyl asbestos tile" which identifies a product that is no longer manufactured. Words that do not say exactly what is meant, such as "sound proof" or "fire proof," should also be avoided. "Sound resistive" and "fire resistive" are more accurate.

Many words or word uses have been identified as poor choices by liability insurance carriers. Having been pivotal in deciding liability cases against design professionals, such words have become suspect for being interpreted in ways other than intended. The most common example is the word "approved." Without qualification of what is approved, much may be assumed. For guidelines regarding liability issues associated with the use of certain words, consult the firm's liability insurance carrier.

POSTSCRIPT

Words barely succeed in communicating ideas between people. This fact is demonstrated by the frequency of circumstances in which people find that they must restate their message with substitute words. Words and drawings combined do better than words alone, and words combined with drawings and a big stick are even more effective. In all cases, consistency in the language used is the key to clarity.

Contract Documents
The contract documents include the agreement between the owner and the contractor, the conditions of the contract, drawings, specifications, addenda, other documents listed in the agreement, and modifications (change orders, construction change directives, and written orders for minor changes in the work issued by the architect). The invitation to bid, instructions to bidders, and bid forms are not part of the contract documents.

Owner-Contractor Agreement
The owner-contractor agreement defines the terms *owner*, *contractor* and *architect*, *contract sum*, *contract completion date*, and the *contract documents*.

Conditions of the Contract
The general and supplementary conditions of the contract define the basic relationships, rights, and responsibilities of the parties, and establish broad provisions under which specifications are written.

The Work
The construction and services required by the contract documents, whether completed or partially completed, and including all other labor, material, equipment, and services provided or to be provided by the contractor to fulfill the contractor's obligations.

Project
The total construction. The work may be the whole or a part of the project. The project may include work by other contracts or by the owner.

Project Manual
A bound volume which may include bidding requirements, sample forms, conditions of the contract, specifications, schedules, or details.

Specifications
The text portion of the contract documents that explains required performance, materials, and equipment. The general requirements (Division 1) provide certain performance requirements of the contract which are applicable to all portions of the work. Product specifications (Divisions 2 through 16) provide a complete detailed description of each material or equipment item and the method of its installation.

Drawings
The graphic and pictorial portions of the contract documents showing the design, location, and dimension of the work, generally including plans, elevations, sections, details, schedules, and diagrams.

Subcontractor
A person or entity who has a direct contract with the contractor to perform a portion of the work.

Addenda
Written and graphic instructions issued during bidding and prior to execution of the agreement to clarify, revise, add to, or delete information in the original bidding documents or in previous addenda.

Alternates

Alternate products, materials, equipment, systems, methods, units of work, or major elements of the work which may, at the owner's option, be selected instead of the corresponding requirements of the contract documents.

Indicated ("as indicated")

This term is meaningless unless clarified by some measure of direction. Similarly the terms "as shown," "as noted," "as scheduled," and "as specified" require additional direction to be meaningful. If such phrases are used, it must also be clear whether or not any limitation on the location of the reference is implied.

Directed ("as directed")

Terms such as "directed," "requested," "authorized," "selected," "approved," "required," "accepted," and "permitted" must be defined to mean "directed by the architect," "required by the architect," and similar phrases.

Installer

The entity engaged by the contractor (an employee, subcontractor, sub-subcontractor or other) to install a particular portion of the work at the project site.

Approve

The use of this word should be clarified. Approval, when given in conjunction with the architect's action on the contractor's submittals and requests should be limited to the architect's responsibilities and duties as specified in the conditions of the contract. Such approval should not release the contractor from responsibility to fulfill requirements of the contract. "No Exception Taken" is preferred by liability insurance carriers, and therefore should be preferred by architects as well.

Contractor's Option

Where materials, products, systems, or methods are specified to be at the contractor's option, the choice of which will be used is solely the choice of the contractor. No change in contract time or sum will be granted because of the choice made.

Furnish

To supply and deliver to the project site, ready for unloading, unpacking, assembly, installation, and similar operations.

Install

To unload, unpack, assemble, erect, place, anchor, apply, work to dimension, finish, cure, protect, clean, and perform similar operations at the project site.

Provide

To furnish and install

Typical/Typically

Applying to all similar conditions

Any

Chosen at random, of whatever quantity. (Use "all," or specify which, when tempted to use this word).

Omit

To leave out, to neglect to provide; usually used to describe an item that was never present (omitted) in the first place.

Delete

To remove, to eliminate; usually used to describe an item that is now present, but that should be taken out (deleted).

Modifications

Change orders, instructions, field orders, directives.

Record Documents

Documents prepared at the end of a project incorporating modifications made during the construction process and incorporating contractor measured dimensions to concealed items previously shown graphically in the contract documents. (Do not use the term "as-built drawings"; without being present at the job site at all times, and bearing personal witness to the construction, you are in no position to warrant anything as being "as-built." Your involvement in "record drawings" suggests only that you are assisting in the documentation of the contractor's record of how things were built, provided you have defined the terms for everyone in advance).

References:

1. *Architectural and Building Trades Dictionary*, third edition, Putnam and Carlson. Van Nostrand Reinhold Company, New York, 1974.
2. *Construction Dictionary, Construction Terms and Tables*, fifth edition. Greater Phoenix, Arizona Chapter #98 of The National Association of Women in Construction, P.O. Box 6142, Phoenix, Arizona 85005, 1981.
3. *Means Illustrated Construction Dictionary*, first edition. R. S. Means Co., Inc. 536 Construction Plaza, Kingston, Massachusetts, 02364.
4. *Lessons in Professional Liability*, A Notebook for Design Professionals. Design Professionals Insurance Company, 2959 Monterey-Salinas Highway, Monterey, California 93940, 1988.
5. *CSI Manual of Practice* MP-1-10, "Specification Language," The Contract Specifications Institute, 601 Madison Street, Alexandria, Virginia. 22314.

PURPOSE

Abbreviations in print and speech run rampant throughout the architectural profession. They have long been considered fair game for individual expression and ingenuity in adapting drawing notations to the limited space usually available in a set of working drawings. However, it is important to be mindful that abbreviations will have to be interpreted and understood by people with a wide variety of interests and backgrounds. Since the use of abbreviations can lead to misinterpretations and confusion, they should generally be avoided. There are some good reasons to abbreviate, though. Perhaps space is limited or perhaps the abbreviated form is more common and readily understood than the long form (gyp.bd., for example, or max). Where abbreviations are desirable, only those abbreviations which are generally understood and accepted throughout the industry should be used. AIA, PA, JC, GC, CDs, CA, and the like, require no further explanation except to those outside the field.

Abbreviations should be easily recognizable to promote understanding of a specific note — not obscure it. When misused, abbreviations can frustrate and annoy, taking far more time to decipher than lettering the entire work or note.

PROPOSITION

If you encounter a special situation for which you feel it is desirable to abbreviate, there are some guidelines which should be followed. Abbreviations should conform to commonly accepted practice, and should be easily recognized in order to achieve this:

1. Be consistent. Choose one abbreviation for a specific term and use it throughout a set of drawings. Do not use STR, STRUC, STRUCT, STRUCT'L at random, depending on allowable space.

2. Limit abbreviations to four or five letters. Do not use abbreviations that are nearly as long as the original word or phrase. Some common exceptions are ea, w/, w/o, @, PR, etc.

3. Do not use apostrophes (B'L'K'G). The purpose is to limit space, not provide punctuation. Besides, the contraction is implied by the use of a period at the end of an abbreviation (BLKG).

4. If multiple definitions exist for an abbreviation (something that should be avoided), the context should provide a clear meaning. If it doesn't, do not abbreviate.

5. Coordinate abbreviations used by other disciplines and within the specifications to avoid conflict and confusion.

6. Provide an abbreviation and symbols list specific for each discipline. Do not include those abbreviations listed in the specifications. Edit the list to incorporate any job-specific abbreviation included on the drawings.

POSTSCRIPT

If in doubt, do not abbreviate. Any time spent contemplating an abbreviation is better used writing out the full word or phrase. While use of appropriate abbreviations can speed completion of a drawing and provide a cleaner, more readable drawing, misuse can render a drawing incomprehensible.

PRACTICE

A sample word and symbol list is included in the Appendix for your reference. This is intentionally a restrained list. Familiarize yourself with this list. When preparing your drawings, use only the abbreviations which appear on this list. Do not make up new variations, and **do not abbreviate anything that is not on this list.**

The list that appears in the Appendix is ready to be photocopied and applied to your drawing sheet.

PURPOSE

Symbols are an essential aid in promoting a systematic progression through a set of working drawings. Since they are the "roadsigns" which guide a document reader through a set of drawings, they are fundamental to the hierarchy of basic drawing information. Symbols are conventional signs that represent specific operations.

Materials indications are a necessary (if sometimes tedious) part of working drawings. This "poché" is used to make the extent and relationships among various materials readily discernible. Materials indications must be consistent throughout a set of drawings and, where possible, they should be consistent with what are generally considered to be industry standards.

PROPOSITION

1.1   Standard Symbols

Think of symbols in the same way you think of roadsigns. Each sign or symbol should be placed in a spot that makes it as clear and simple as possible for you to move around the neighborhood you are in, to know where you are now, where you've been, and where you're going.

When symbols are used well, they enhance the readability, clarity, and graphic quality of working drawings or they can confuse, obscure, and obfuscate. The following guidelines should help us to use symbols well.

1. Symbols should be simple to draft. Any drafter should be able to draw them with little trouble. Most CAD systems provide a library of common symbols. These symbols should conform to industry standards, and if they do not, you should seriously consider customizing them. Then, send your CAD manufacturer a copy of this book, along with an admonishment about the need to standardize throughout the industry.

2. Symbols should be standardized so that the drawing can be easily understood. Preference should be given to symbols that are commonly used throughout the industry.

3. Symbols should be unique. Anyone who reads the drawing should be able to ascertain the meaning of each symbol with no trouble. It should not be easily confused with other symbols.

4. Symbols should be readily discernible from other elements on the drawings. The reader should not confuse symbols with drawing elements or have difficulty finding symbols.

5. Symbols must not obscure the drawing. Symbols must be drawn so that they are informative, but not the predominant features of the drawing.

6. Symbols must show the importance of information. A hierarchy of symbols should be developed so that the prominence of the symbol relates in a general way to the importance of the information to which it applies.

1.2   Standard Material Poché

When material poché is used well, it enhances the readability, clarity, and graphic quality of working drawings. The following guidelines will help the architect use material poché well.

1. Material poché should be consistent throughout a set of drawings. A material should be pochéd the same way in all drawings in the set.

2. Material poché should be consistent with industry standards.

3. Material poché should be done freehand whenever possible, unless a CAD version is readily accessible.

4. Material poché should be done at the appropriate scale. Quite often, poché should have a different graphic scale on a large scale drawing than one drawn at a small scale.

5. Limit the use of materials indications to those areas where they will most effectively clarify the intent. Never was the cry so loud for "Less is More" than in the use of materials indications. Use poché at the boundaries or extremities of a material, or where it meets another material. Long brick walls rendered in their entirety are much more difficult to read than if the materials are indicated sparingly.

6. Keep in mind the reproduction techniques that may be used. Continuous tones do not generally reproduce well by photographic methods (including xerox), and should be avoided. Dot screens can be used to similar effect, but make your choices carefully. If the drawing is going to be reproduced as a half-tone, dot screens will produce an objectionable moiré pattern. Fine dot screen pat-

terns will be splotchy if a reduced size reproduction is made. CAD poché is readily available, and is generally a superior method for accomplishing this task. The same criteria should be used in making selections from the available patterns.

POSTSCRIPT

Several basic rules govern the use of symbols and materials indications:

- A symbol is generally a superior way of communicating, and is preferred over a written explanation or description whenever the symbol can do the job adequately.

- Different symbols for the same information should never be used in the same set of drawings (or other sets, either, for that matter).

- Different information should never be represented by the same symbol in a given set of drawings.

PRACTICE

There are many popular symbols which commonly appear in a set of working drawings. There are also many variations. Some selected examples appear on a sheet in the Appendix. This sheet can be copied on clear film and applied directly to your drawing sheets as your symbols legend, if you wish. Or, you can recreate it as part of the cover sheet, prepared as a standard on CAD. Then, copy it. Send it to your friends and colleagues, even competitors or enemies—anyone who might be tempted to deviate from the standard. Peruse it, use it, abuse it even. But don't lose it. And don't deviate from it. It must become the law... for all of us.

PURPOSE

You might get in your car one day, and just start driving. You might go where your fancy takes you, and you might end up in some beautiful spot where you decide to spend the rest of your life. Or, you might not. Perhaps you prefer to plan your trips, knowing where you want to go and how long you have to get there. So it is with working drawings.

Every set of working drawings must be planned to ensure that the drawings will be logically organized. Planning encourages the Project Architect to think about all the drawings that are necessary to adequately communicate the design, and gives him or her an opportunity to group or separate drawings in a way that will facilitate bidding and construction. Cartooning is a graphic way of planning and organizing the set of working drawings, and of planning the composition of each sheet within the set.

A cartoon set, or mock set, accomplishes the following:

- promotes efficient and orderly drawing layout
- allows an early determination of the number of drawings required
- assists in estimating the manpower requirements to complete the work
- aids in scheduling the work and in determining drawing assignments

PROPOSITION

Go to the Appendix, select the appropriate mock set form (for 24 x 36 or 30 x 42 sheets), and make as many copies as you need to complete the set. Use one for every sheet in the set, including the title sheet (see Section 2.2 on Drawings Identification for the proper sequence of drawings and appropriate sheet numbers).

Block out each sheet, showing the approximate size, shape, and location of each drawing on the sheet.

- Give some thought to the details that will be needed, and try to organize them in some logical order (such as from the ground up, or in a sequence corresponding to CSI divisions). Don't merely set aside three sheets of drawings for details

- Include any schedules that will be needed

- Allow yourself some flexibility in your sheet composition; leave some open areas where possible to help in accommodating those inevitable unforeseen drawings

- Remember that it is more important to maintain clarity and cogency in the organization of the set than it is to fill up each sheet; however, this idea must be balanced with the idea that we should use as few sheets as possible.

The usefulness of the cartoon sets can be doubled if they are used as part of the work plan. The work plan begins with a list of basic requirements that each drawing must comply with, and a checklist of elements that should be included on the drawing. The work plan is then copied on the back of each cartoon set sheet, and acts as a road map for the person to whom that sheet has been assigned. Sample work plans for various kinds of sheets are included in the Appendix.

POST SCRIPT

Contractors see many different drawings from many different architects, and the drawings are not all as well organized or planned as well as yours are. Contractors usually have a very short time to figure out our drawings, anticipate the things we forgot, and prepare a bid that is competitive but requires no change orders. It is our responsibility to make this process as direct and as clear as possible. A little planning at the beginning will go a long way towards accomplishing that goal.

PRACTICE

The Appendix contains some gridded cartoon sheets which you can copy and use to compose your mock sets. It also contains some example work plan sheets, which you can use "as is," or modify to suit your specific needs.

PURPOSE

What would you think if you got into a new car, a model you had never seen before, and as soon as you sat down, you discovered that the steering wheel was in the backseat? Or that the speedometer was in the trunk, and the fuel gauge was in the glove compartment? Maybe the engine was mounted to a separate trailer you were dragging behind you, and the switch for the headlights was under the hood? After your initial wonderment, you would probably start to become outraged. "What were these guys thinking about?" you ask yourself, more than a little agitated. This scenario sounds ridiculous, but it is very similar to the kind of thing we do to contractors nearly every day. We may think we are organizing our drawings logically, coherently. But the guy down the street has the same notion, and he organizes his drawings totally differently. No wonder contractors get so annoyed with us. We can do better. We need to move in the direction of a more consistent approach to presenting information from office to office. And we should have a darned good reason for departing from established standards and conventions. Keep in mind, too, that there are many other individuals who look at our drawings– owners, lenders, members of the boards of directors, materials suppliers, building officials, and more. By being more consistent in our approach to our drawings, we can all do a great service to our profession, and the construction industry.

PROPOSITION

There is a certain minimum amount of information that should appear on every drawing. It is most convenient to provide this information in a title block, which can be preprinted, prepared on sticky-back material, or created as a reusable entity in CAD. The title block should include:

- Project Name
- Project Address
- Project Number
- Architect's Name and Address
- A place to identify the consultants on their respective sheets, along with their addresses and phone numbers
- Date of Issue
- Type of Issue ("DD pricing," for example)
- Sheet Number
- A place for the architect's or engineer's stamp
- A Revisions Record
- Sheet Contents
- Sheet Number
- A place to record the initials of the individuals who participated in the drawing of the sheet, and in reviewing it.

Other information that may not be appropriate for the title block includes:

- Drawing Name
- Key Plan or Section
- North Arrow
- Scale

A strip approximately 2 1/2" wide adjacent to the right-hand margin seems to work best for the title block. Certain parts of the title block are repetitive from project to project (such as the architect's name and address, and the graphic linework used to separate different areas of the title block). Ideally, these should be preprinted on the appropriate size of drafting film or vellum, leaving a void in the middle. The void can then be filled in with project-specific information, such as, project name, address, and number. Other areas of the title block will have to be completed by hand, or by computer where appropriate. A standard CAD title block sheet can be created, also, eliminating the need to preprint mylar or vellum.

Drawings are sometimes used from phase to phase and the organization of the drawings and the numbering sequence should be consistent from phase to phase and project to project. It is helpful to include a sheet index on the general information sheet at the beginning of the set. This index should show each sheet number and sheet contents (matching the description shown in the title block), organized by discipline. Each discipline should be identified by a single letter designation, if possible, and the disciplines should always occur in the same sequence, as follows:

C   Civil
L   Landscape
A   Architectural
I   Interior design
S   Structural
M   Mechanical
P   Plumbing
F   Fire protection
E   Electrical
( ) Specialty consultants, such as Graphics (G), Kitchen or Food Service (K), Elevator (EL), Parking (PK), Asbestos Abatement (AA), Acoustical (AC), etc.

The content of the drawings should also be consistent from job to job, and the information shown on consultant drawings should parallel that on the architectural, when possible. The drawing content should be organized as follows:

0 - general information, abbreviations, symbols, index, surveys

1 - site information, including demolition and phasing

2 - plans (demolition, floor, roof, enlarged plans, other)

3 - reflected ceiling plans

4 - building elevations

5 - building sections

6 - wall sections

7 - interior elevations

8 - schedules (door, finish, accessories, hardware)

9 - wall types, details

It is highly desirable for consultants' sheets to correspond to the architectural. If the architectural drawings show level one on sheet A2.1, then mechanical sheet M2.1 should also show the level one plan. The same applies for plumbing sheet P2.1, electrical sheet E2.1, etc.

Electrical drawings commonly include a power plan, which corresponds to the architectural floor plan, and a lighting plan, which corresponds to the architectural reflected ceiling plan. Therefore, it is helpful to put each reflected ceiling plan directly following the corresponding floor plan, to allow the sheet numbering concept to carry through.

Identification of drawings issued after the selection of a contractor should also be consistent in nature. Addenda drawings can have an AD preceding the drawing number Sometimes an "X" is used to indicate a "change" drawing, but AD is a better choice since addendum drawings can be supplemental as well as change drawings. Drawings required to accompany Supplemental Instructions or Proposal Requests should share the same number as the instruction or request and can be preceded with a SI or PR. If more than one drawing is used, follow the number with a letter (PR-12A, PR-12B). The same can be said for other additional issued information from the architect and the consultants (Change Orders, Construction Change Authorizations, etc.).

POSTSCRIPT

All graphic information should be shown in the drawings. The project manual should contain written information only. This includes abbreviations, symbols, door information (except door hardware schedule), and details. It makes sense that all graphic information be grouped together and all written information be grouped, since one literally references the other. It is also difficult to keep several volumes in the same location, and not having details at hand or to have a problem locating them in a project manual, for example, could be very frustrating.

Drawing Organization
Sheet Design

PURPOSE

I'm sure you've seen this... you get a letter on a folded sheet of paper. You start reading the front page, no problem. Then you turn the page and resume reading. But you soon realize that page two is where page three should be, and page three is on the back and upside down so that when you get there and turn the page, page four is upside down where page two should have been in the first place. Well, I'm sure the author was simply trying to be clever, but in the meantime, you've torn the letter apart and reassembled it in a sequence that seemed more logical to you. While there may be a time and place for this kind of cuteness, working drawings is not it. Working drawings must be so clearly organized that anyone with the need to decipher them can do so easily. The general contractor, subcontractors, materials suppliers, manufacturers, building officials, owners, consultants, and even checkers in your own office are all seeking different information from different parts of the drawings, in different levels of detail. Your challenge is to find a way of communicating effectively with each of these groups. The whole idea is to put page two where everyone expects to find it, and the same with page three, and so forth. This is oversimplifying, obviously, but it should be your objective to SIMPLIFY. SIMPLIFY. SIMPLIFY.

Clear and organized sheet design promotes communication of construction drawings quickly and easily. When ignored, details can disappear into a maze of lines, dimensions and notations.

PROPOSITION

The following items will help keep drawings clear and organized from the very start.

1. Determine a sheet size which is appropriate to the project scale and complexity. Avoid using odd sized formats whenever practical. Using a match line and breaking a plan into two or more drawings may be preferable to the drafting and storage problems encountered if you must draw on a 48" sheet with a 42" parallel rule, or store it in a 42" flat file. In addition, using a sheet that is too large for a particular project encourages over drafting and wasted time in trying to fill the empty space.

2. Be consistent. Locate title blocks, key plans, keynotes legends, and plans in the same position on each sheet to speed orientation. It is also desirable to have the title block on the right margin so it is visible without unrolling the entire set.

3. Group similar drawings together on the same sheet. If a project requires few details and a separate sheet is not required, locate the details around the upper and left margins. With larger or more complex projects, position details in a logical sequence starting from right to left and bottom to top. Group similar details together maintaining scale and orientation where ever possible.

4. When sketching details or sections, plan for final scale and space on the construction drawings. Allow space for titles, dimensions, keynotes, and grid designations.

POSTSCRIPT

A poorly organized set of construction drawings can drive up construction costs as well as increasing the number of questions during construction. This costs you and the contractor time that you might otherwise be using to do something fun. A little attention to organization when you begin a set of drawings can benefit all concerned.

PRACTICE

Sample sheet design mock ups for 8½" x 11", 11" x 17", 24" x 36," and 30" x 42" drawings are included in the appendix section.

PRECEPTS FOR QUALITY WORKING DRAWINGS

Detail for Realistic Tolerances
Don't indicate "zero tolerance" situations that can't be met by human contractors in the field. When two trades are working towards each other, they will *never* end up in the same place Example: a lay-in ceiling meets a window head, and the drawings show them at a perfectly matching elevation and line. Show a reveal or offset.

Be Thorough with the Building Envelope
Trace with your finger such items as insulation and positive drainage to make sure that your systems are complete. Pinpoint all interfaces between materials on the exterior to make sure you have sealant and flashing to eliminate leaks. All it takes is one oversight to invalidate the system.

Accept Your Responsibility as an Architect
Don't use notes which say "as required" unless absolutely necessary. The same thing applies to notes like "coordinate" or "coordinate with Architect" or "per code." The trend today is to pawn off responsibility whenever possible; this translates into laziness. There are some things which a Contractor simply can't be held responsible for. Don't be led into dreamland by an unreasonable expectation of what the term "performance specifications" can do. We have to perform also.

Follow Through on Coordination
If you make a note that says "Re: Elec." then it is your job to make sure that the Electrical Engineer coordinates the item. The same goes for the case when the Electrical Engineer puts down "Re: Arch." If you fail to do this, your job is worse than half done; it is not done at all.

Design for Movement
Buildings, unlike jewelry, are living, breathing creatures. They expand and contract. Different materials expand at different rates and all materials will expand and contract within a greater range if exposed to the exterior and/or sunlight than if they are indoors. Plan for slip head details at the top of all partitions below roofs and floors that will deflect (that is, 99% of all floors and 100% of all roofs). Strategize expansion joint locations early in the game. Don't overlook control joints in materials that require them more frequently than overall building expansion control (such as drywall and masonry). Think through expansion details in three dimensions. Is a particular element going to move in one direction or two?

Follow Through on Rated Construction
Maintain in your detailing the integrity of all rated partitions. Don't compromise rated walls by sustaining unrated portions that invalidate the entire wall or by showing reveals that do the same. Make sure that the engineers don't violate the rules which you set up.

Design Lean and Mean
Don't take the easy way out on solving problems by designing details that rely on massive amounts of overkill to solve a problem which could be handled in a much simpler way. When we take what seems to be the easy way out by showing unheard-of thicknesses of tapered insulation, wood blocking, or mortar beds, we set ourselves up for eventual ridicule by a contractor who is justified in inquiring as to what is going on.

Accept Responsibility for Structural Requirements for Architectural Item
Make sure that handrails, guardrails, steps, and other human-body-supporting elements are designed so it can be absolutely assured that they will perform. It is not acceptable to indicate a papier maché handrail and add a note indicating that it is to support a 300 lb. lateral load per code.

Provide Adequate Documentation of Elevation Transitions
When you have steps or a ramp, don't show your elevation targets wandering off in the middle of the space. Show a target at the top, and another at the bottom, of the transition. Basic common sense (but frequently ignored).

Don't Overdraw Proprietary Sections
It makes little sense to spend an entire day drawing the ins and outs of a specific manufacturer's window sill detail, when there are 6:1 odds that you will end up with a different product. A good detailer determines what the essence is of a particular product section, and does no more. There are no awards for showing the most curlicues on an aluminum extrusion.

Make Detail Alignment Consistent with the Plans
If your plans are organized with north on the top of the sheet, then your details (and your blow-up plans) *must* be done with the same orientation. The argument that "it fit better on the sheet that way" won't hold water if your drawings leave the contractor scratching his head.

Use the Office Standards
All it takes is a minimum of effort and caring. What you did at another office doesn't mean diddly here.

Know How Details Are Going to Be Built
If you show an unusual wood profile or metal shape, you had better know how it is going to be made (or at least one viable option). Sooner or later–probably sooner–the contractor will throw this one back at you. Solve the problem today rather than letting it come back tomorrow. Generally this is an area where interior designers and specialists like graphic designers are better than architects. Let's learn to do better.

Pay Attention to Consistency
Be consistent in the use of architectural nomenclature or terminology. Don't refer to the "First Floor" in one place and "Level One" in another.

Plan Your Documentation Strategy for Simplicity, Clarity, and Economy

Decide whether partition types and ceiling heights should be indicated on the 1/8" plans, the 1/4" plans, or the reflected ceiling plans. Don't show this kind of information more than once.

Question standard or traditional approaches. Ask yourself whether you really need a door schedule or a finish schedule before you jump in and make one. Ask yourself whether one of the alternative scheduling methods will suffice for this particular project. Think about whether building sections are really necessary, or the finishes plans. Don't do it simply because it was done that way on your last project or in your last office. Choose the most economical method that gets the job done.

Don't layer several kinds of information on top of each other. For example, don't put reference bubbles on top of dimensions, or room names on top of sprinkler heads, etc. Be especially attentive to this when creating CAD drawings, if some layers are turned off.

PURPOSE

Time is money. Repetition of information on multiple drawings and the subsequent multiple corrections that inevitably result cost both time and money. Similarly, duplication of information may add to the cost of construction. Most simply stated, do not repeat the same information on different drawings. When preparing the cartoon set, determine which information or level of detail should appear on which drawing. Strive for clarity, simplicity, and consistency.

PROPOSITION

- Design your working drawings as hierarchical shopping lists, moving from broadscope drawings to larger scale drawings and then to specific details.

- Show room, door, and window identifications on floor plans. Do not repeat on building sections, wall sections, exterior and interior elevations.

- Avoid repeating similar details. Mark them as similar and note variations from the standard.

- Avoid drawing interior room elevations unless wall pattern, details, or ornamentation require graphic depiction. Most room elevations, including many classrooms, offices, toilets, and the like can be described using the floor plan in conjunction with a casework schedule, standard mounting height notes, or details.

- Look for methods of simplification in room finish, door and window schedules, and other similar schedules (e.g. casework, louvers, toilet accessories, etc.). If there are 100 rooms in a project, there are probably no more than 10 standard room finishes (and perhaps some minor variations to those). Create a room finish legend of the 10 types and subtypes and show a symbol on the floor plans with the legend adjacent. Avoid sheets of duplicative schedules.

- Avoid repeating notes from wall section to wall section or detail to detail. On a given drawing, completely note the most typical section or detail and simply reference other sections or details to the one noted. Note any variations to the typical on the affected section or detail. Locate the "noted" section or detail on the right hand side of the drawing.

- Avoid showing room elevations in the backgrounds of building or wall sections.

- Avoid describing material characteristics, product names, or assembly instructions on drawings. This information more appropriately belongs in the technical specifications of the project manual. Drawings should show how different materials come together.

- Avoid showing the same information on both small- and large-scale drawings. If there is room to provide sufficient detail at small scale, omit the large scale. If not, draw it in detail at large scale and show only a schematic representation at small scale.

- Avoid plan details in general. If a small-scale plan shows a door jamb tight to an adjacent wall, there is no reason to draw an enlarged plan detail. If it is remote from a wall juncture, dimension it.

- Consider drawing wall sections or building sections, not both. Wall sections should be of sufficient scale to include critical vertical detailing. Building sections will typically be of sufficiently small scale to require detail enlargements (adjacent if possible) of key junctures. As a minimum, limit the number of building sections to those necessary to generally describe building cross sectional characteristics.

- Locate door and window frame detail references consistently, typically on door and window frame elevations, not on floor plans or building/room elevations. Move from plan to schedule to details.

- Avoid unnecessary information such as "to or from" swing information on a door schedule. The plan clearly shows this information and the shop drawings will confirm it.

- Avoid repeating site drawing information on floor plans.

- Reflected ceiling plans–consider calling for coordination drawings by contractor. Every symbol shown on Architectural RCP is a duplication of engineering drawings and consequently a potential source of conflict.

PRACTICE

Every office should have a Department of Redundancy Department to help eliminate our natural tendency to be redundant, to repeat ourselves, to say the same things over and over. Invariably, as a design evolves, certain earlier decisions must change. If that decision was documented in many different locations throughout a set of drawings, it will have to be changed at each location. If one spot is missed, there is an inconsistency in the drawings that jumps off the page to owners and contractors as a throbbing "change order...change order...change order." Reducing the number of opportunities for this kind of oversight should result in drawings with fewer conflicts, requiring less time for corrections.

POSTSCRIPT

Making the determination about the proper location for showing certain kinds of information can be subjective. In our zeal to create drawings that are easily understood, we find ourselves tempted to make the contractor's job easier by providing the information right here and now, on the same page, saving him or her of having to go to other drawings to find certain information. We must resist this temptation. While we must strive to make travel through our drawings as convenient as possible, it is still more important for the information we provide to be correct than it is for it to be convenient. The rule should be to show information once, in the appropriate location–then consider each exception carefully before allowing it to happen.

Standard Practices
Lettering

PURPOSE

In the first grade, you learned how to "print" the alphabet, and you were graded on penmanship. In those days, you simply wanted to make an impression on your teacher, and be recognized for having a skill that none of the other kids had. But the innocence of youth is fleeting. Now you find yourself having to "letter" the alphabet, and the reasons why this is important may not be all that much clearer than they were in the first grade.

Believe it or not, there are many good reasons why uniform and consistent lettering on drawings is important and desirable. Among them are the following:

- One objective in preparing a set of working drawings is to make the drawings as clear and as easily understood as possible, in order to communicate our ideas effectively to the builder.

- Furthermore, drawings are frequently reduced to sets one-half the size of the originals; clear lettering is essential in order to preserve the legibility once the drawings are reduced.

PROPOSITION

All lettering, including lettering on consultant's drawings, should be plain, block vertical lettering, all capitals.

Spacing between letters and between lines of lettering should be adequate to result in clear, legible, half- sized reduced drawings.

- Use the accompanying underlay for guideline spacing; since each individual tends to fill the space between guidelines in a different way, consider enlarging or reducing the space between the guidelines on the copy machine; regardless of the spacing, the objective is still to produce clear lettering that is legible when reduced.

- The size of the letters should be approximately twice as high as the space between the lines of lettering; this 2:1 ratio should be preserved for all sizes of lettering.

Fancy lettering and lowercase lettering should not be used on working drawings. Office policy may permit these styles of lettering on schematic design or other preliminary types of drawings, but they should not be used on technical drawings.

SLANTED LETTERING should not be used.

Consistency in forming individual letters is the single most important aspect of creating good lettering. The shape and proportion of each letter are also important, but are secondary to consistency.

There is no shortcut to acquiring skill in lettering; it takes practice, practice, practice. However, there are some aids or techniques that may make your practice more productive.

- Always use guidelines; or, as described above, use a guidelines underlay

- Freehand lettering is encouraged because of speed, but triangles may be used. If you do use a triangle, a small 4"/45° triangle works best because it can be moved easily from letter to letter. Another advantage of using a triangle is that you can scribe lines parallel to the edges at convenient intervals. You can then use those scribed lines to facilitate making lettering guidelines (mark a line and then move the triangle so the scribed line falls on top of it, mark another line, etc.) and hatch patterns, such as brick poché.

- Find an example of some good lettering, and then try to copy it; try all the letters of the alphabet, and work harder on those letters which are most difficult for you (especially R and S); after you have tried copying some good lettering, then try tracing over it; you will learn instantly how the spacing, proportion, and formation of each letter differs from your own.

- Make the letters wider than you think you should; most letters should occupy a space that is approximately square.

- Make horizontals slope up slightly from left to right (but all at a consistent angle).

- Once you have learned what your letters should look like, and you have practiced, practiced, practiced, then work on your speed; your speed will increase as you try to loosen up your style somewhat; try doing verticals without a triangle; try to go faster (about twice as fast) as you think you can. But don't sacrifice consistency.

- Try different kinds of pencils, especially if you are using plastic lead. Try a woodclinched pencil in the softest plastic lead grade available that allows you to produce dark letters without having to press too hard. Try a .3mm, .5mm, .7mm, or a .9mm mechanical pushbutton pencil with plastic leads (soft) to see what works best for you.

- Experiment with fountain pens (not technical pens) that are designed for lettering or freehand drawing. Use waterproof ink. See if this helps loosen you up.

- Try a chisel point, especially on letters 1/4" high or larger.

- Experiment with a fine point soft tip pen (.2–.4mm) with permanent ink.

- Practice with different pencils, pens, leads, etc., on different media (film, vellum, trace) and get familiar with the characteristics of each combination.

- Once you feel comfortable and confident with your lettering, go practice some more... you still have a long way to go.

If you follow the recommendations in this manual, most of the notation required on the drawings will be accomplished using keynotes, but keynotes will not eliminate the need for all notation. When you find that additional notation is necessary, create it in compact paragraphs rather than in long lines;

- Connect notation to an item with a simple, curved line ending in a plain, hand-drawn arrow or dot.

- Use arrows when pointing to lines, and dots when pointing to the space between lines; use arrows whenever possible

- Make curved lines with a french curve in drafted drawings, and freehand in freehand drawings; curved lines are easily distinguished from the straight lines that typify most of our drawings

- Begin the curved line from the right end of the last line of notation when pointing to the right, and from the left end of the first line when pointing to the left.

- You may decide to use diagonal, straight lines instead of curved; this is acceptable, as long as you are consistent.

- Draw a box around notes requiring special emphasis, but use this technique sparingly.

- Avoid *UNDERLINING* and exclamation points!

- Keep lettering distinctly separate from drawing elements.

- Separate notations from dimensioning to improve graphic clarity.

- Use typical notes on the first drawing, but do not repeat on later drawings.

Unless you are working on CAD, you should do as much lettering and notation by hand as possible. The drawing title is one important exception. In order to create a hierarchy of emphasis, drawing titles should be larger and bolder than other lettering. You may also want to consider using stencils, or Kroy/Merlin tape lettering systems.

PRACTICE

This manual includes two pull-outs in the Appendix that may help you in your never-ending efforts to improve your lettering skills:

- guidelines underlay
- sample lettering

POSTSCRIPT

In order to become a well-rounded architect, you must be able to communicate your ideas effectively to those who will be transforming them into a built reality.

Lettering is a small but important ingredient that can help you achieve this goal. Work on a rhythmic fluidity rather than a deliberate and painstaking style. Don't give up. You can do it.

If you are fortunate enough to be able to do your lettering on CAD, you will have to make some decisions regarding size and style. Slightly smaller sizes are acceptable for CAD lettering (approximately 3/32" high for typical notation). Choose a simple (single stroke/sans serif) style, to reduce byte consumption and to improve clarity. Use upper- and lowercase letters, since it is more familiar and comfortable for the eye when the lettering resembles typesetting.

PURPOSE

Hands and feet. I suppose there was a time when these seemed like wonderful measuring devices. After all, you always had them with you. Obviously, things were simpler then. In the intervening years, those of us still using this English system of measurement have made countless improvements to make the system more workable. First, we standardized the length of a foot. Good move. Then we divided it into twelve equal parts. How convenient. Then we divided these parts into halves and into halves again and again and again–just to make certain that our base-10 calculators could never be used to add up the parts. But we are not trying to change that here. We are simply trying to work with the system we have. There are many, many spectacular buildings built using this system, and these buildings are uncompromised by dimensional "busts," redesign costs, or change order increases. This chapter is for the rest of us.

Dimensioning is necessary to define the size and location of various building materials and components. When well done, dimensioning can simplify and clarify the construction of the most complex building. However, even the simplest building can be rendered indecipherable if dimensioning is not adequately considered.

PROPOSITION

If, as architects, there were to be only one thing we do right on a set of drawings, that one thing should be to make the dimensions add up correctly. Dimensioning is a comparatively simple arithmetic exercise, and it is so important that there is no excuse for not taking the time to do it right. However, there are ways to make this process simpler and easier to manage and these techniques should be used on every job.

1. Try to make the floor plan work out on a grid or module.

   • Start with a 5' or 4' grid, to see how much of the plan will work out.

   • Then go to a 2' grid and a 1' grid to pick up any uncooperative stragglers.

   • There may still be a few renegades that simply will not conform to these grids, but they should be very few; try to get them on 6", 4", or 1" even-inch increments; avoid fractions wherever you can.

2. Arrange dimensions in a hierarchy that corresponds to the building hierarchy.

- Work from the broad and general to the narrow and specific

- Generally, for exterior dimensioning, there should be four dimension lines:

  - The line furthest from the building should be an overall dimension from the outside face to the outside face of the building; when the dimension lines cross over the grid lines or extension lines, break the line so that there will be no confusion about whether a dimension dot was forgotten.

  - The next line, moving toward the building, should dimension the column grid.

  - The third line should dimension building offsets.

  - The fourth line should locate the small elements, such as openings.

- Locate the closest dimension line no closer than 1½" from the building linework; this allows space for cross-reference symbols that read more clearly when placed close to the building lines.

3. Dimension all items from an established reference point, such as a grid, and do not necessarily close the string of dimensions to the next grid.

4. The nature and complexity of each building will dictate whether to dimension to finish faces, or to the faces or centerlines of building elements. For most projects, the default should be to dimension to the face of concrete, masonry, or studs.

   - Dimension to one face of manufactured materials, such as metal studs, and to both faces of site constructed materials.

   - Dimensioning to the centerlines of partitions is common, and may be acceptable if the thickness of the partition is described in a legend of partition types; however, dimensioning to the face of one side of the stud is more consistent with the manner in which partitions are actually laid out during construction.

5. Dimension to the centerlines of columns, grid lines, or modular partitions.

6. Dimensions under 1'-0" should be noted in inches only (not 0'-6," but 6"); dimensions over 1'-0" should be expressed in feet and inches.

   • For dimensions expressed in feet and inches, the inch symbol (") should be omitted, because the "inches" part is understood.

7. Limit the smallest fractional increment to 1/8".

8. Do not dimension items such as partitions or doors that are centered or otherwise located by being on a grid, mullion, or by typical detail condition.

9. Fractions should be shown with a diagonal slash: ½

   $\frac{1}{2}$ unacceptable

   1_2 (no slash) unacceptable

10. Dimension as much as possible from structural elements rather than from items that may not be installed when the layout takes place.

11. Do not dimension openings that are dimensioned in a schedule.

12. Dimension to the centerlines of windows when the dimension of the actual unit installed (as determined by competitive bidding) may vary from the size of the unit you have shown on the drawings (except where window units are within masonry walls, in which case masonry openings should be used).

13. Use actual (as opposed to nominal) dimensions for all construction except masonry. Use nominal dimensions for unit masonry, and make sure that masonry openings are indicated as such.

14. Make liberal but studied and judicious use of terms such as ALIGN, CENTER, MINIMUM, MAXIMUM, and CLEAR to show intent; in many cases, a dimension may not be necessary when the intent is indicated.

15. Do not dimension to the centerlines of doors. Doors should be located by dimensioning to one jamb (at the edge of the opening) only when the location is not clear (as it would be when centered in a corridor), or when it is not shown in a detail.

16. When dimensioning unit masonry, always use coursing dimensions, both horizontally and vertically. Never dimension any part of a masonry wall on the assumption that the difference can be made up by stretching or shrinking the mortar joints. Always keep in mind the exact coursing intervals for the particular block or brick you are using.

17. Give consideration to the overall dimensioning strategy in dimensioning large and small scale drawings.
    • Don't be redundant by repeating dimensions on the small plan that are more appropriately indicated on the large scale plan.
    • Use the small plan for dimensioning areas that don't appear in plan enlargements.
    • Use the small-scale plan for locating the perimeter points of areas shown at larger scale..

18. When dimensioning common features in different parts of the plan, make sure the different ways of dimensioning them result in the same location for those items (the same dimension).

19. Make sure long strings of dimensions are tied to gridlines.

20. For doors in typical partitions, don't dimension the door or the opening size on the plans-- let the door schedule handle this.

21. When the location of a door jamb is clearly indicated on a detail, don't dimension it on a plan.

POSTSCRIPT

Dimensions should be checked, then double-checked, and then checked again. Use an *Add-Feet, Jr.* or a feet-and-inches calculator; do not try to do it in your head, or even on a scratch pad. Don't even try to convert to decimals to use a regular calculator.

Look for alternative ways to arrive at the dimensions for a cross-check, and then scale the dimension to make sure you are in the ballpark.

Use common sense in determining a dimensioning strategy, and make it clear when you are deviating from the norms you have established for your project.

• For example, if you have decided generally to dimension to the face of rough framing members, but you discover a condition where you feel it would be clearer to dimension to the face of a finish material, make sure you are clear in indicating that deviation to the contractor.

- Dimension for the installer; use reference points that will be clear to the installer and that will be in place at the time new pieces of the construction are being installed.

- Dimension for the desired effect; if you want a masonry scoring line to align with the edge of a window, make it clear that that is the desired effect.

- Don't dimension to a gridline if there will be a concrete wall between the installer and the gridline at the time of construction. Dimension to the face of the concrete wall, and then tie that face back to the gridline.

- If the plan features a series of rooms defined by partitions 10 feet apart (for example), establish a dimensioning strategy that allows a dimension of 10'-0 to be shown; dimension to the centerlines consistently, or better yet, dimension to one face (the same face) of each partition. Don't dimension to the left face in one instance and the right face the next time. And don't dimension the thickness of the partition– that is the job of the partition types.

- Make any special requirements clear; if a window must meet the brick on both sides of it the same way, make sure you indicate that.

A final reminder: Keep it simple, and make sure it's right.

PRACTICE

Our bias is toward dimensioning to the rough face of framing materials; to one face of manufactured products, such as metal studs, and then to identify the exceptions and handle them in the most appropriate way. A sample drawing included at the end of this chapter shows these biases, along with many of the other principles described above.

Some firms are adamant about dimensioning to the face of a finish material to ensure a particular "desired effect." Others are equally adamant about dimensioning to the rough face of structural or framing members to simplify the layout. Others may favor dimensioning to the centerlines of partitions, or creating nominal dimensions for partitions and dimensioning that way. There is no right way or wrong way of doing it– only the way preferred by the office you are in. Each method has its advantages and its disadvantages, and certain projects may present very compelling arguments in favor of one method or another. These arguments should be considered, even if the most favored method is not the current office standard. If you are not absolutely clear on what the preferred method is, go find out. It is imperative that the dimensioning methodology be consistent throughout the entire set of documents.

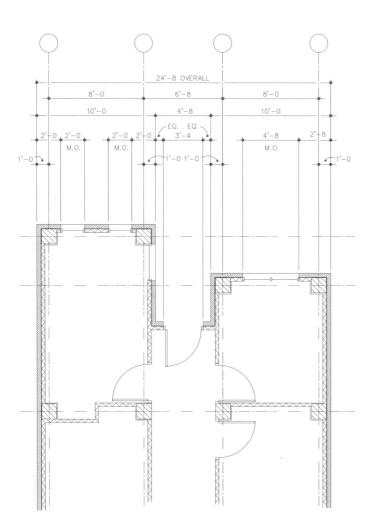

Sample plan drawing showing dimensioning hierarchy.

Let's say you want to bake a layer cake. You could mix up the batter for the first layer, and then bake it, and then frost it. And then start over for layer two. You could, but since you don't want to devote the entire day to baking the cake, you probably opt in favor of mixing the batter for both layers at the same time, baking both layers at the same time, and then frosting them at the same time. You would follow a logical sequence of events that allowed each activity to happen at the appropriate time, resulting in the most efficient process for doing the work.

As architects, our reputations depend on our ability to conceive creative ideas. But our livelihoods depend on our abilities to communicate these ideas effectively to the people who will be translating our ideas into built reality. A systematic, hierarchical approach to communicating our ideas is important for the following reasons:

- to allow the most important information on a drawing sheet to occupy its rightful place on the drawing

- to avoid overlapping and conflicting drawing elements

- to allow the drawing to become meaningful and useful at the earliest possible point in its development

Drawing components can be divided into the following broad categories:
- initial drawing linework
- dimensions
- cross-referencing
- poché
- notations
- titles

The information contained within each of these basic drawing elements can be prioritized in order to achieve the proper organization of the drawing elements, to avoid overlapping information, and to deliver information to our consultants and in-house team members according to a sequence which allows them to be most productive.

Structural engineers need the following information at the start of working drawings:

- floor plans for all levels, but especially at foundation or below grade levels (the grid has been determined during an earlier phase, in concert with the engineer); include column grid lines with dimensions between grid lines

- show wall and partition locations (including opening sizes and locations) and construction materials
- roof plan
- building sections
- wall sections

Mechanical engineers need the following information at the start of working drawings:

- site plan
- floor plans (similar to the requirements for structural drawings, but include plumbing fixture types and locations)
- reflected ceiling plans
- building sections
- mechanical equipment room plan
- building elevations
- roof plan

Electrical engineers need the following information at the start of working drawings:

- site plan
- floor plans
- reflected ceiling plans
- furniture layouts
- telephone and electrical room locations

Hierarchical Organization

In preparing each of the following types of working drawings, keep in mind the information that each discipline needs to know, and develop the drawings accordingly. Don't clutter the drawings with a lot of architectural information until the engineers have what they need. Remember that our mechanical and electrical engineers may want to use sepias, CAD plots, or magnetic versions of our drawings as backgrounds for their work.

FLOOR PLANS (generally follow this sequence)
- title block showing project name
- drawing identification and scale
- north arrow
- column/grid lines with bubbles and alpha-numeric designations and dimensions
- walls and partitions (clearly identify concrete and masonry walls)
- openings in floors and walls
- issue drawings to structural engineer
- add doors, door swings, and windows
- add stairs, elevators
- add plumbing fixtures (toilets, lavatories, sinks)

- issue backgrounds to mechanical and electrical consultants
- issue prints to structural consultant for coordination
- add balance of exterior dimensions (leave space between dimension lines and building lines for cross-referencing symbols)
- add remaining plan features such as vanity tops, toilet partitions, railings, changes in floor materials
- add interior dimensions
- add cross-referenced symbols such as building section marks, wall section marks, detail marks, interior elevation marks
- add room names, room numbers, room finish codes
- place room names in rooms as possible, but not in conflict with dimensions or cross-referencing
- place outside but near rooms where necessary, with leader lines
- add door symbols and marks
- add notation
- issue coordination sets to consultants
- add poché (materials indications)
- make necessary revisions
- prepare final redlines

The above sequence applies to the development of the floor plans. Similarly, certain drawings in the set should be started before others. The same criteria apply.

Drawings that should be started first, all at about the same time, are:

> Site improvements plan
> Below-grade floor plans
> Above-grade floor plans
> Wall sections

Then, in descending order of importance:

> Reflected ceiling plans
> Floor plan enlargements
> Building elevations
> Building sections
> Details
> Partition types
> Interior elevations
> Schedules

Obviously, the preferred operating procedure will vary among consultants. Talk to them; find out what they want. If their particular needs vary from this sequence, that's OK. It is better to deviate from this sequence than it is to make assumptions that impede the productivity of our consultants.

Hierarchical organization is similarly important on other kinds of drawings as well. For building and wall sections, it helps to keep the construction sequence in mind as you develop the drawing. For example:

Start at the footing and work your way up the building.

Put the structural elements in your drawing first; show the foundation wall, floor joists, beams, etc., as you develop the drawing.

Develop the drawing from the outside in; make sure you have established the proper relationships between the structure and the skin materials.

Determine the parts of the construction that will drive decisions about the rest of the building; for example, determine vertical masonry coursing early, and work the rest of the construction around it.

POSTSCRIPT

The drawings you create will be the products of the thought process that you put into them. If your thought process is clear, logical, and coherent, then your drawings will communicate clearly. If your process is haphazard, then that is what will be communicated to the contractor. Take care with your work, and let it say good things about you.

PURPOSE

Unfortunately, it is not uncommon to find handwritten (or CAD written) notes such as these: gyp bd., drywall, sheetrock, gyp rock, wallboard, etc,. on the same set of drawings. A contractor may ask himself, or even you, whether you wanted a specific manufacturer of gypsum board (sheetrock) at certain locations but not at others. Or he may ponder the difference you had in mind between gyp. bd. and drywall, when the truthful explanation is that Dick used the term "drywall" to describe gypsum board, while Jane used the term "gyp. bd." Multiply this by, oh, maybe 500 opportunities, and it is easy to understand why consistency in the use of architectural nomenclature is so essential in creating drawings that communicate effectively. A master notation system including keyed notation can eliminate this problem. But that is not the only advantage a notation system has to offer.

We have three goals in the use of keynotes:

- to save time
- to make our notation consistent, from sheet to sheet, from drafter to drafter, and from project to project
- to tie the drawings to the specifications

As the production of working drawings becomes more computerized, the use of CAD will automate some of the above objectives. Our notation will come from a library of notation, based on the master list of notation you see here. Notation will be inserted into our drawings as blocks, with attributes. This will accomplish our objectives of saving time and making our notation consistent. We can then add a 5-digit number to tie the material to its proper address in the specifications.

Even if you choose not to access notes from a computer library of notation, or even if you choose not to use keyed notation at all, use the master list anyway. It will help keep your notation consistent, a noble achievement in itself.

Some drawings will probably benefit from keyed notation, simply because there is not sufficient space on the drawing to write notes out longhand. In this category are 1/8" scale plans, and there may be others. In these instances, use the numeric portion only from the notes shown on the master list; a keynotes legend will also have to be included in the drawing. The numeric designation for the note will use the 5-digit CSI designation indicating the specific section in which the material is specified. However, the use of a keynote means that the actual notation does not accompany the key, or the broadscope CSI section number. That means that you could have any number of notes with the same number. Not a good idea. Add a letter suffix to each number to distinguish each note, such as "04200.A." Since only the broadscope level of CSI section numbers is used, an additional time-saver is worth considering, especially if you are noting manually. Omit the zero at the beginning of the number, and the two zeroes at the end, and state the key simply as "4.2A."

In addition to producing drawings that are more graphically legible, the proper use of keynotes automatically establishes a direct and deliberate relationship between the drawings and the specifications. Conversely, if improperly used, they can result in anything from simple confusion to potentially costly legal action.

PROPOSITION

In the early days of architectural practice, a system of drawing keynotes was about as essential as high tensile strength steel, bulletproof glass, or a good trial lawyer. But with the death of the last mastodon, we graduated from caves to stacked adobe to four story walk-up to high-rise structures as containers for our work and play. As our system of construction became more complex, so did the documents needed to describe them to others. Today, with the extensive use of computers in practice for everything from word processing to CAD to computer modeling of potential design solutions, we cannot help but have a "systems orientation" to the production of our construction contract documents. Ease, clarity, and preciseness of communication have (with good reason) replaced the notion of construction drawings as art form. It is both what we say and how we say it that counts.

Some other considerations in using a master notation system:

1. Notes as they appear on the drawings will consist of numerals and the actual notation. Go through this list and choose whatever notes you think you will need and highlight them for editing and sorting by support staff. Add the necessary letters if you will be using a keyed notation system. If you discover later that you need some that you haven't previously identified, you can select additional ones at any time.

2. References to Civil, Landscape, Structural, Mechanical, Electrical, and other disciplines must be carefully coordinated with those disciplines. It is extremely problematic to refer to consultant drawings if the information isn't there. If you use this reference, make certain that someone following your instructions will find the information you say they will. Otherwise, it would be better to leave out this instruction altogether, since some requirement for a reference to consultant drawings is implied by language in the General Conditions.

3. With few exceptions (such as demolition notes), notes should refer only to materials. Imperative notes or clarifying notes should be written in full directly on the drawing.

4. Remember that the drawings quantify and the specifications qualify. Try not to include information in the keynotes that rightfully belongs in the specifications, and vice versa. Use of the attached master list should help accomplish this.

5. The use of a tag can be very helpful in reducing the number of keynotes needed. For example, a single project may require several different sizes or types of gypsum board. One method of keynoting might be to create a separate keynote for each size or type. A simpler and more effective method would be to create a single keynote, such as 09270, to cover all sizes and types of gypsum board with a tag to differentiate them. The size or type which is most prevalent on the job should be identified and the basic note in the legend would read "09270; 5/8" unless otherwise noted." Any variations would be tagged when the keynote symbol is applied to the drawing. The tag would indicate a different thickness (such as 09270; 1/2") or type (such as 09270; Type "X" or 09270; M.R.) The tagging system is particularly useful in differentiating different colors of the same material, such as paint, plastic laminate, carpet, etc. Once the limits of various sizes, finishes, or colors are indicated in the drawings, the specifications take over to spell out the required finish in detail.

6. This master list of keynotes should be used as the basis for all keynote lists created by our office. Where there is some question as to the appropriate section or location for a material not already in the master list, refer to the Sweets Desk Top Index of Key Words or/and the CSI Masterformat book from the Manual of Practice. Either will serve as a guide for making this determination. Remember that just because an item is metal does not necessarily mean that it belongs in the metals section– it may be an accessory that should be specified in an entirely separate section.

7. It is possible for the same note to appear in more than one section. This usually occurs with certain accessories. For instance, *weeps* may be under stone and under brick. Be careful to use the proper note for the condition in question.

8. Demolition keynotes must be carefully coordinated with specific project conditions. It is very easy to get overly detailed with these notes. More generic notes, used with a qualifier, or "tail," may be more useful and effective than a separate note for every instance.

9. The wording of notes on documents that are not keynoted should also be based on this list.

PRACTICE

While there are a variety of what might be considered "keynotes" in a full set of construction documents (including work notes, demolition notes, "flag" notes, toilet accessories notes, etc.) this discussion will focus on the use of material keynotes. As stated earlier, one of the most important aspects of the use of a keynote system is the link it establishes between drawings and specifications. To facilitate this, each keynote is assigned a number which correlates exactly with one of the sixteen divisions outlined in the CSI Manual of Practice.

As with any type of lexicon, it is important to develop a standard list of items which is as comprehensive as possible. This "Master Menu" of potential keynotes should include not only the most commonly used materials, but also some that you don't use that often. Yet it is also important to keep the list as brief as possible, to streamline its use. At some point, usually not too far into its development, a long list becomes unwieldy and detrimental to the process. If that happens, the list will fall quickly into disuse. The Master Menu should be consulted as early as practical in the course of the work so that a preliminary working list of keynotes can be generated and the project team can get accustomed to its use on the particular project. In using the Master Menu, make a copy of the entire menu of keynotes. Highlight the notes you know you will need. If other members of the team need to have input, have them use the same list. Once the preliminary selections are made, have the list edited on the word processor and reprinted. As the project evolves, more notes will be necessary. The project architect should keep one project list which can be edited as the need for additional notes is discovered. All other members of the team must clear new notations with the project architect to ensure that the same designation is not used for more than one note, or vice versa.

Use of the keynote system requires discipline and self-control. The fewer keynotes required to communicate the basic systems and assemblies the better.

Editing the Master Menu not only makes for a much more manageable keynote list, it provides only that information which is relevant to the project and also helps to define the elements of a particular assembly at a glance for bidders and contractors. This is where it becomes critical for the content of each detail to be checked and rechecked for completeness. Having a "shorthand" method for identifying components in an assembly should not open the door to inaccuracy, and quite objectively, it may be easier to overlook the absence of "07160A" in a wall section than it might be to miss "BITUMINOUS VAPOR BARRIER" glaring at you. Regardless of how you choose to communicate construction information, "if it ain't there, it ain't there" is hard to argue with.

The size and complexity of the project will probably dictate how and where your Keynote List is communicated in the drawing set. If the project is small, you may be able to establish one comprehensive list of keynotes that applies to all drawings. Larger projects will likely require that you prepare a separate list for each drawing or group of drawings with those keynotes which are most relevant to that group (for example, one set of keynotes should be prepared for the 1/8" plans, another for the exterior elevations, etc.). Regardless of the number of separate keynote lists required within a set of construction documents, ALWAYS publish a comprehensive list of keynotes within the Project Manual.

Last, in terms of coordination among disciplines, make certain that all project consultants are aware of, and actively use, your keynote system. It was designed to cover all 16 specification divisions and that covers concrete, floor drains, and electrical raceways as well as bricks.

Where overlap occurs between disciplines (e.g,. on site development, landscape, civil engineering, and plumbing or electrical site plans) make certain that common elements utilize a common designation.

POSTSCRIPT

Use of the computer to produce our drawings creates an important opportunity for us to depart from the idea of keyed notation. The "Master Menu" of keynotes can be stored in the CAD database as a library of notes. Just as toilets or doors can be inserted as "entities," so can notes. Depending upon the system you use, you may need some consulting help to set up a system that allows pull-down menu trees or tablet icon selections. Since hand speed would no longer be a significant factor in creating computerized notation (assuming computer operators have some facility for keyboard entry), keynotes would no longer be as desirable as they once were. Each note can be inserted into the drawing in its entirety, each composed in the same way described above (complete with its CSI designation), something every contractor will be ecstatic about. When assigning CSI numbers for this method, group materials into sections of 5 digits, where the last two digits remain "0," as described earlier. The other three digits will direct a contractor to the appropriate CSI division and broadscope category of the specifications, and the CSI numbering system will take over from there. Construction pricing could be reduced by 5%, if you would believe many contractors, who despise keynotes. And the two other objectives— consistency of terminology and nomenclature, and a tie to the specifications— are still intact. Think about it. The dividends could be enormous.

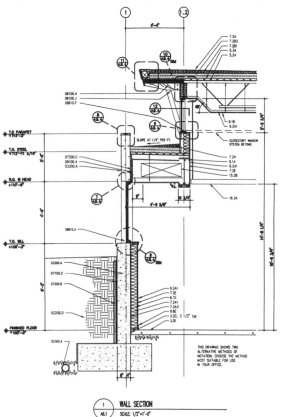

Sample of keyed notation strategy

KEY NOTES SYSTEM
Master List

DIVISION 1 - GENERAL REQUIREMENTS

SECTION 01010 - SUMMARY OF WORK

01010	WORK BY OTHERS; not in contract
01010	WORK BY OWNER; not in contract
01010	FIXTURE/FURNISHING/EQUIPMENT; provided by Owner; installed by General Contractor
01010	FIXTURE/FURNISHING/EQUIPMENT; provided by General Contractor; installed by Owner
01010	EXISTING CONSTRUCTION
01010	FUTURE WORK; not in contract
01010	ALLOWANCE
01030	ALTERNATE

SECTION 01500 - TEMPORARY FACILITIES

01500	TEMPORARY UTILITY; see Civil, Mechanical, Electrical
01500	TEMPORARY CONSTRUCTION HOIST; see Structural
01500	TEMPORARY BARRICADE
01500	TEMPORARY ENCLOSURE
01500	TEMPORARY COVERED WALKWAY
01500	TEMPORARY FENCING
01500	TEMPORARY GATE
01500	TEMPORARY ACCESS ROAD
01500	TEMPORARY PARKING AREA
01500	TEMPORARY SIGNAGE; see Civil
01500	TEMPORARY TRAFFIC SIGNAL; see Civil
01500	TEMPORARY PROJECT IDENTIFICATION SIGN
01500	CONSTRUCTION FIELD OFFICE
01500	CONSTRUCTION SHED

DIVISION 2 - SITEWORK

SECTION 02060 - DEMOLITION

02060	REMOVE CONSTRUCTION; see Structural
02060	REMOVE BUILDING; see Structural
02060	REMOVE BUILDING FOUNDATION SYSTEM; see Structural
02070	SELECTIVE DEMOLITION
02060	REMOVE ASPHALTIC CONCRETE PAVING; see Civil
02060	REMOVE CONCRETE PAVING; see Civil
02060	REMOVE ROOFING SYSTEM
02060	REMOVE UTILITIES; see Civil, Mechanical, Electrical
02060	RELOCATE UTILITIES; see Civil, Mechanical, Electrical

SECTION 02110 - SITE CLEARING

02110	REMOVE LANDSCAPING; trees, sod, etc.
02110	REMOVE AND STOCKPILE TOPSOIL
02110	RELOCATE LANDSCAPING; trees, sod, etc.

SECTION 02200 - EARTHWORK

02200	COMPACTED BACKFILL
02200	COMPACTED FILL
02200	GRANULAR SUB-BASE
02200	SAND SUB-BASE
02200	EROSION CONTROL; MEMBRANE SYSTEM, FILTER FABRIC, ETC.; see Civil

SECTION 2360 - DRIVEN PILES

02360	PIER AND PIER CAP; see Structural
02370	CAISSON; see Structural
02360	DRIVEN PILE; PRECAST CONCRETE, STEEL, ETC.
02370	BORED/AUGERED CAISSON; see Structural

SECTION 02500 - PAVING AND SURFACING

02511	ASPHALTIC CONCRETE PAVING; see Civil
02520	CONCRETE PAVING; exposed aggregate finish; smooth finish; integral color
02515	BRICK PAVERS
02515	CONCRETE PAVERS
02515	STONE PAVERS
02515	ASPHALTIC BLOCK PAVERS
02515	ASPHALTIC CONCRETE CURB
02520	CONCRETE CURB; see Civil
02520	CONCRETE CURB & PAN; see Civil
02520	CONCRETE PAN; see Civil
02511	ATHLETIC PAVING; ASPHALTIC CONCRETE, CONCRETE, ETC.
02511	ASPHALTIC CONCRETE; PATCHING; RESURFACING
02511	PAVEMENT MARKING; paint
02511	ATHLETIC COURT MARKING; paint

SECTION 02600 - PIPED UTILITY MATERIALS

02600	MANHOLE; see Civil
02600	CLEANOUT; see Civil
02600	METER OR VALVE PIT; see Civil
02600	HYDRANT; see Civil
02600	FIRE WATER PIPING; see Civil
02600	WATER WELL; see Civil
02600	GAS PIPING; see Civil
02600	OIL PIPING; see Civil
02600	STEAM PIPING; see Civil

SECTION 02700 - SEWERAGE AND DRAINAGE

02700	FOUNDATION DRAIN; see Mechanical
02700	UNDERSLAB DRAIN; see Mechanical
02700	CATCH BASIN; see Civil
02700	CURB INLET; see Civil
02700	STORM SEWER; see Civil
02700	FRENCH DRAIN; see Civil
02700	STORM WATER DETENTION AREA; see Civil
02700	STORM WATER RETENTION AREA; see Civil
02700	SANITARY SEWER; see Civil
02700	SAND/OIL INTERCEPTOR; see Civil
02700	SEPTIC TANK; see Civil
02700	GREASE INTERCEPTOR; see Civil and Mechanical
02700	CULVERT; see Civil
02700	MANHOLE COVER AND FRAME

SECTION 02800 - SITE IMPROVEMENTS

02800	IRRIGATION SYSTEM; see Landscape
02800	FOUNTAIN; see Landscape
02800	CHAIN LINK FENCE & GATE
02800	ORNAMENTAL METAL FENCE & GATE
02800	WIRE FENCE & GATE
02800	WOOD FENCE & GATE
02800	TRAFFIC SIGNAGE; see Civil
02800	SITE SEATING
02800	PRE-FABRICATED PLANTER
02800	PRE-FABRICATED SHELTER
02800	TRASH RECEPTACLE
02800	TREE GRATE
02800	PLAYGROUND EQUIPMENT
02800	BICYCLE RACK
02800	GUARDRAIL
02800	PARKING BARRIER
02800	PARKING BUMPER

SECTION 02900 - LANDSCAPE WORK

02900	TOPSOIL
02900	SOD
02900	SHRUBBERY
02900	GROUND COVER
02900	TREE(S)

DIVISION 3 - CONCRETE

SECTION 03100 - CONCRETE FORMWORK

03100	FORM TIE HOLES
03100	FORM JOINT LINE
03100	VOID FORM

SECTION 03200 - CONCRETE REINFORCEMENT & ACCESSORIES

03200	STEEL REINFORCING
03200	STEEL DOWELS
03200	THREADED ROD & INSERT
03200	STEEL STRESSING TENDON
03200	WELDED WIRE FABRIC REINFORCING
03200	WATERSTOP

SECTION 03300 CAST-IN-PLACE CONCRETE

03300	CAST-IN-PLACE CONCRETE; form finish with tie holes; steel trowel finish
03300	CONCRETE TOPPING; lightweight
03300	VAPOR RETARDER
03300	GRANULAR SUB-BASE
03300	CONCRETE SLAB ON GRADE; see Structural
03300	CONCRETE HOUSEKEEPING PAD
03300	CONTROL JOINT; tooled, sawcut, etc.
03300	CONCRETE CONSTRUCTION JOINT
03300	CONCRETE EXPANSION JOINT

SECTION 03400 PRECAST CONCRETE

03400	PRECAST CONCRETE; SAND-BLASTED; acid-etched, exposed aggregate
03400	GLASS FIBER REINFORCED PRECAST CONCRETE
03400	PRECAST CONCRETE SCUPPER
03400	PRECAST CONCRETE SPLASHBLOCK
03400	PRECAST CONCRETE LINTEL
03400	PRECAST CONCRETE PAVER
03400	PRECAST CONCRETE STORAGE TANK
03400	PRECAST CONCRETE VAULT

SECTION 03500 CEMENTITIOUS DECKS

03500	GYPSUM CONCRETE FLOOR UNDERLAYMENT
03500	GYPSUM CONCRETE ROOF DECK
03500	LIGHTWEIGHT INSULATING CONCRETE DECK
03500	COMPOSITE CONCRETE AND INSULATION DECK

DIVISION 4 - MASONRY

SECTION 04200 UNIT MASONRY

04200	BRICK MASONRY
04200	BRICK SOLDIER COURSE
04200	BRICK ROWLOCK
04200	BRICK SAILOR
04200	BRICK STRETCHER
04200	BRICK HEADER
04200	FLUE LINER
04200	FIRE BRICK
04200	MASONRY TIES
04200	STANDARD LADDER TYPE REINFORCING
04200	CONCRETE UNIT MASONRY;exposed aggregate, fluted pre-insulate
04200	EXPOSED AGGREGATE CONCRETE UNIT MASONRY
04200	FLUTED CONCRETE UNIT MASONRY
04200	INTERLOCKING CONCRETE UNIT MASONRY
04200	MOLDED FACE CONCRETE UNIT MASONRY
04200	MORTARLESS CONCRETE UNIT MASONRY
04200	PREFACED CONCRETE UNIT MASONRY
04200	PRE-INSULATED CONCRETE UNIT MASONRY
04200	SOUND ABSORBING CONCRETE UNIT MASONRY
04200	SPLIT-FACE CONCRETE UNIT MASONRY
04200	REINFORCED GROUTED BRICK MASONRY
04200	REINFORCED GROUTED CONCRETE UNIT MASONRY
04200	PREASSEMBLED MASONRY PANEL
04200	CLAY TILE UNIT MASONRY
04200	STRUCTURAL FACING TILE
04200	SOUND-ABSORBING STRUCTURAL FACING TILE
04200	CERAMIC VENEER
04200	TERRA COTTA VENEER
04200	ADHERED MASONRY VENEER
04200	MECHANICALLY SUPPORTED MASONRY VENEER
04270	GLASS UNIT MASONRY; vision unit, PATTERN UNIT
04200	ADOBE MASONRY
04200	WEEP HOLES; PVC, rope wick
04200	FLEXIBLE FLASHING; continuous
04200	1" AIR SPACE
04200	FILL INSULATION; granular; loose
04200	RIGID BOARD INSULATION
04200	BATT INSULATION
04200	CONCRETE MASONRY UNIT BOND BEAM; unit lintel
04200	CONCRETE MASONRY UNIT CORNER FILLER

SECTION 04400 DIMENSIONED STONE

04400	SANDSTONE
04400	ROUGH STONE
04400	GRANITE
04400	CUT STONE
04400	SLATE
04400	SIMULATED STONE
04400	LIMESTONE
04400	MARBLE
04400	FLAGSTONE
04400	SHIM(S)
04400	STAINLESS STEEL CLIPS
04400	STAINLESS STEEL ANCHOR
04400	STAINLESS STEEL SUPPORT ANGLE
04400	WEEPS; PVC, Rope Wick
04400	SETTING PLASTER

DIVISION 5 - METALS

SECTION 05100 - STRUCTURAL STEEL

05100	STEEL STRUCTURE
05100	STEEL TUBE
05100	STEEL CHANNEL
05100	STEEL ANGLE
05100	STEEL EMBED PLATE
05100	STEEL CABLE
05100	STEEL PIPE
05100	STRUCTURAL ALUMINUM
05100	SPACE FRAME

SECTION 05200 - STEEL JOISTS AND JOIST GIRDERS

05200	STEEL JOIST

SECTION 05300 - STEEL DECKING

05300	STEEL DECK; see Structural
05300	ALUMINUM DECK; see Structural
05300	COMPOSITE METAL DECK; see Structural
05300	CELLULAR METAL DECK; see Structural
05300	CLOSURE ANGLE; see Structural

SECTION 05400 - COLD-FORMED METAL FRAMING

05400	LOAD BEARING METAL FRAMING SYSTEM
05400	COLD-FORMED METAL JOIST SYSTEM
05400	SLOTTED CHANNEL FRAMING SYSTEM

SECTION 05500 - METAL FABRICATIONS; SHEET METAL FABRICATIONS

05500	METAL STAIR; prefabricated
05500	METAL LADDER
05500	METAL RAILING; pipe, tube
05500	METAL GRATING
05500	METAL CATWALK
05500	HANDRAIL SUPPORTS; metal, steel pipe
05500	SHEET METAL ENCLOSURE
05500	HEATING-COOLING UNIT ENCLOSURES
05500	GRATING
05500	FLOOR PLATE

SECTION 05700 - ORNAMENTAL METAL

05700	PREFABRICATED SPIRAL STAIR
05700	ORNAMENTAL HANDRAIL
05700	ORNAMENTAL RAILING

SECTION 05800 - EXPANSION JOINT COVER ASSEMBLIES

05800	EXPANSION CONTROL ASSEMBLY; metal, neoprene
05800	EXPANSION JOINT COVER; metal, neoprene, etc.
05800	STRIP SEAL FLOOR JOINT COVER
05800	ELASTOMERIC JOINT COVER ASSEMBLY

DIVISION 6 - WOOD AND PLASTICS

SECTION 06100 - ROUGH CARPENTRY

06100	WOOD BLOCKING; fire-retardant treated, preservative treated, etc.
06100	WOOD PLATE
06100	WOOD STUD
06100	WOOD JOIST
06100	WOOD BEAM
06100	WOOD POST
06100	WOOD FURRING
06100	EXTERIOR PLYWOOD SHEATHING
06100	PLYWOOD
06100	PLYWOOD BLOCKING
06100	PARTICLE BOARD; sub-flooring
06100	FIBERBOARD SHEATHING
06100	WOOD TRIM
06100	WOOD DECKING
06100	WOOD RAIL
06100	WOOD SIDING; CLAPBOARD, REDWOOD LAP, SHIPLAP, ETC.
06100	THRU BOLT
06100	METAL POST BASE
06100	JOIST HANGER
06100	BEAM HANGER
06100	HURRICANE CLIP
06100	STEEL ANCHOR BOLT
06100	TIMBER TRUSS
06100	TIMBER DECKING
06100	WOOD CHORD METAL JOIST
06100	GLUED-LAMINATED DECKING
06100	GLUED-LAMINATED BEAM
06100	GLUED-LAMINATED PURLIN
06100	PREFABRICATED WOOD TRUSS
06100	PLYWOOD WEB JOIST
06100	PLYWOOD BOX BEAM
06100	MINERAL FIBER REINFORCED CEMENT PANEL

SECTION 06200 - FINISH CARPENTRY

06200	HARDWOOD TRIM
06200	WOOD TRIM
06200	HARDWOOD SILL
06200	HARDWOOD BASE
06200	HARDWOOD RAIL
06200	VENEER PLYWOOD; OAK, MAPLE, BIRCH, ETC.
06200	HARDWOOD EDGING
06200	WOOD SHELF
06200	PARTICLE BOARD SHELF

06200	METAL SHELF STANDARDS AND BRACKETS
06200	PLASTIC LAMINATE
06200	PRE-FINISHED WOOD PANELING; OAK, MAPLE, BIRCH, ETC.

SECTION 06400 - ARCHITECTURAL WOODWORK

06400	WOOD CABINET; plastic laminate faced, shop finished, etc.
06400	FLUSH PANELING; plastic laminate, wood veneer, etc.
06400	STILE AND RAIL PANELING
06400	WOOD STAIR
06400	WOOD HANDRAIL
06400	STANDING WOOD TRIM
06400	RUNNING WOOD TRIM
06400	WOOD SCREEN
06400	WOOD BLIND
06400	WOOD SHUTTER
06400	PARTICLE BOARD
06400	PLYWOOD
06400	CHEMICAL RESISTANT PLASTIC LAMINATE
06400	TEMPERED HARDBOARD; 1/4"
06400	PERFORATED TEMPERED HARDBOARD; 1/8"
06400	PLEXIGLAS; 1/4"
06400	DRAWER GLIDES
06400	CONCEALED HINGE
06400	PUSH RELEASE HARDWARE
06400	MAGNETIC CATCH
06400	DRAWER/CABINET PULL

SECTION 06600 - PLASTIC FABRICATIONS

06600	GLASS RESIN FABRICATION
06600	GLASS FIBER FABRICATION
06600	CAST PLASTIC FABRICATION

DIVISION 7 - THERMAL AND MOISTURE PROTECTION

SECTION 07100 - SHEET MEMBRANE WATERPROOFING

07100	NEOPRENE SHEET WATERPROOFING
07100	BITUMINOUS SHEET MEMBRANE WATERPROOFING
07100	ELASTOMERIC SHEET MEMBRANE WATERPROOFING
07100	FLUID-APPLIED WATERPROOFING
07100	BENTONITE WATERPROOFING
07100	METAL OXIDE WATERPROOFING
07100	CEMENTITIOUS WATERPROOFING

SECTION 07150 - DAMPPROOFING, VAPOR BARRIERS

07150	BITUMINOUS DAMPPROOFING
07150	WATER REPELLENT COATING
07150	CEMENTITIOUS DAMPPROOFING
07150	BITUMINOUS VAPOR BARRIER
07150	PLASTIC VAPOR BARRIER

SECTION 07200 - BUILDING INSULATION AND FIREPROOFING

07200	BATT INSULATION
07200	RIGID BOARD INSULATION
07200	TAPERED RIGID BOARD INSULATION
07200	LOOSE-FILL INSULATION

07200	FOAMED-IN-PLACE INSULATION
07250	SPRAYED MINERAL FIBER INSULATION
07250	SPRAYED-ON MINERAL FIBER FIREPROOFING
07250	SPRAYED-ON CEMENTITIOUS FIREPROOFING
07270	FIRE STOPPING
07275	INTUMESCENT MASTIC FIREPROOFING
07240	EXTERIOR INSULATION AND FINISH SYSTEM

SECTION 07300- ASPHALT SHINGLES

07300	ASPHALT SHINGLES
07300	FIBERGLASS SHINGLES
07300	SLATE SHINGLES
07300	WOOD SHINGLES
07300	WOOD SHAKES
07300	METAL SHINGLE
07300	PORCELAIN ENAMEL SHINGLE
07300	MINERAL FIBER-CEMENT SHINGLE
07300	CLAY ROOFING TILES
07300	CONCRETE ROOFING TILES
07300	METAL ROOFING TILES
07300	PLASTIC ROOFING TILES
07300	ROOFING FELT
07300	MINERAL FIBER-CEMENT ROOFING TILE

SECTION 07400 - SIDING

07400	PREFORMED WALL PANEL
07400	COMPOSITE ALUMINUM BUILDING PANEL
07400	AGGREGATE COATED COMPOSITE BUILDING PANEL
07400	GLASS FIBER REINFORCED CONCRETE BUILDING PANEL
07400	PORCELAIN ENAMELED BUILDING PANEL
07400	TILE FACED BUILDING PANEL
07400	ALUMINUM CLADDING/SIDING
07400	COMPOSITION CLADDING/SIDING
07400	MINERAL FIBER-CEMENT CLADDING/SIDING
07400	CLADDING/SIDING; plastic, wood, plywood

SECTION 07500 - MEMBRANE ROOFING

07500	BUILT-UP ASPHALT ROOFING
07500	BUILT-UP COAL TAR ROOFING
07500	COLD-APPLIED MASTIC ROOF MEMBRANE
07500	GLASS FIBER REINFORCED ASPHALT EMULSION
07500	PREPARED ROLL ROOFING
07500	FULLY ADHERED ELASTOMERIC/PLASTOMERIC SHEET ROOFING
07500	LOOSE LAID/BALLASTED ELASTOMERIC/PLASTOMERIC SHEET ROOFING
07500	MECHANICALLY ATTACHED ELASTOMERIC/PLASTOMERIC SHEET ROOFING
07500	MODIFIED BITUMEN COMPOSITE SELF-ADHERING SHEET ROOF-ING
07500	MODIFIED BITUMEN REINFORCED COMPOSITE SHEET ROOFING
07500	FLUID APPLIED ROOFING
07500	PROTECTED MEMBRANE ROOFING
07500	COMPOSITE WALK PAD
07500	PRECAST CONCRETE WALK PAD
07500	SURFACE-APPLIED ELASTOMERIC TRAFFIC TOPPING
07500	SURFACE-APPLIED COMPOSITION TYPE TRAFFIC TOPPING

SECTION 07600 - FLASHING AND SHEET METAL

07600	BATTEN SEAM SHEET METAL ROOFING; standing seam, flat seam, batten seam, etc.
07600	SHEET METAL FLASHING
07600	SHEET METAL REGLET
07600	SHEET METAL COUNTER FLASHING
07600	SHEET METAL CAP FLASHING
07600	SHEET METAL DRIP FLASHING
07600	SHEET METAL TRIM
07600	SHEET METAL GUTTER
07600	SHEET METAL DOWNSPOUT
07600	SHEET METAL SPLASH BOX
07600	SHEET METAL STRAPS
07600	SHEET METAL SCUPPER
07600	SHEET METAL GRAVEL STOP
07600	SHEET METAL COPING
07600	SHEET METAL EXPANSION JOINT COVER
07600	SHEET METAL PITCH PAN
07600	SHEET METAL DIVERTER
07600	SHEET METAL CONDENSATE GUTTER
07600	ANODIZED ALUMINUM FLASHING
07600	LAMINATED SHEET FLEXIBLE FLASHING
07600	PLASTIC SHEET FLEXIBLE FLASHING

SECTION 07700 - ROOF SPECIALTIES AND ACCESSORIES

07700	PREFABRICATED ROOF COPING
07700	PREFABRICATED ROOF EXPANSION JOINT
07700	PREFABRICATED ROOF GRAVEL STOP
07700	PREFABRICATED ROOF FASCIA
07600	PREFABRICATED ROOF RELIEF VENT
07600	PREFABRICATED ROOF CURB
07600	PREFABRICATED ROOF HATCH
07600	PREFABRICATED ROOF GRAVITY VENTILATOR
07600	PREFABRICATED PENTHOUSE VENTILATOR
07600	PREFABRICATED RIDGE VENT
07600	PREFABRICATED SMOKE VENT
07600	PREFABRICATED ROOF DECK VENT

SECTION 07800 - SKYLIGHTS

07800	DOMED PLASTIC SKYLIGHT
07800	PYRAMID PLASTIC SKYLIGHT
07800	VAULTED PLASTIC SKYLIGHT
07800	LEAN-TO METAL-FRAMED SKYLIGHT
07800	RIDGE METAL-FRAMED SKYLIGHT
07800	VAULTED METAL-FRAMED SKYLIGHT

SECTION 07900 - JOINT SEALERS

07900	COMPRESSION SEAL
07900	SEALANT
07900	BACKER ROD
07900	COMPRESSIBLE FOAM FILLER
07900	CLEAR SILICONE JOINT
07900	NEOPRENE GASKET
07900	CAULKING
07900	JOINT FILLER
07900	JOINT GASKET

DIVISION 8 - DOORS AND WINDOWS

SECTION 08100 - STEEL DOORS AND FRAMES

08100	HOLLOW METAL DOOR
08100	HOLLOW METAL FRAME
08100	STAINLESS STEEL DOOR
08100	STAINLESS STEEL FRAME
08100	BRONZE DOOR
08100	BRONZE FRAME
08100	ALUMINUM DOOR
08100	ALUMINUM FRAME
08100	DOOR FRAME ANCHOR
08100	GLAZING STOP
08100	METAL DOOR LOUVER

SECTION 08200 - WOOD DOORS

08200	FLUSH WOOD DOOR; solid core, hollow core
08200	PLASTIC FACED FLUSH WOOD DOOR; solid core, hollow core
08200	METAL FACED WOOD DOOR; solid core, hollow core
08200	TEMPERED HARDBOARD FACED WOOD DOOR; solid core, hollow core
08200	PANEL WOOD DOOR
08200	STILE AND RAIL PANEL WOOD DOOR

SECTION 08340 - OVERHEAD COILING GRILLES

08340	METAL ACCESS DOOR
08340	METAL ACCESS PANEL
08340	SLIDING GLASS DOOR
08340	SLIDING METAL FIRE DOOR
08340	SLIDING GRILLE
08340	OVERHEAD COILING DOOR
08340	COILING COUNTER DOOR
08340	SIDE COILING DOOR
08340	OVERHEAD COILING GRILLE
08340	SIDE COILING GRILLE
08340	OVERHEAD COILING DOOR HOUSING
08340	OVERHEAD COILING DOOR TRACK
08340	OVERHEAD COILING DOOR MOTOR OPERATOR
08340	OVERHEAD COILING DOOR CONTROLS
08340	ACCORDION FOLDING DOOR
08340	PANEL FOLDING DOOR
08340	ACCORDION FOLDING GRILLE
08340	FOLDING DOOR TRACK
08340	SECTIONAL OVERHEAD DOOR
08340	SCREEN DOOR
08340	STORM DOOR

SECTION 08400 -- ALUMINUM ENTRANCES AND STOREFRONT

08400	STOREFRONT FRAMING; aluminum, steel, stainless steel, bronze
08400	ENTRANCE FRAMING; aluminum, steel, stainless steel, bronze
08400	ALL GLASS ENTRANCE SYSTEM
08400	AUTOMATIC ENTRANCE DOOR
08400	REVOLVING ENTRANCE DOOR

SECTION 08500 - STEEL WINDOWS

08500	STEEL WINDOW
08500	ALUMINUM WINDOW
08500	STAINLESS STEEL WINDOW
08500	BRONZE WINDOW
08500	METAL JALOUSIE WINDOW
08500	METAL STORM WINDOW
08500	METAL WINDOW OPERATING HARDWARE
08500	METAL WINDOW MULLION
08500	METAL STORM SASH
08500	METAL WINDOW SCREEN

SECTION 08610 - WOOD WINDOWS

08610	WOOD FRAME WINDOW
08610	WOOD WINDOW; metal clad, plastic clad
08610	STORM WINDOW; wood, plastic
08610	REINFORCED PLASTIC WINDOW
08610	SCREEN
08610	WOOD WINDOW OPERATING HARDWARE
08610	WOOD WINDOW MULLION
08610	WOOD WINDOW STORM SASH

SECTION 08700 - FINISH HARDWARE

08700	DOOR CLOSER; concealed
08700	PIVOT
08700	THRESHOLD
08700	ELECTROMAGNETIC HOLD-OPEN DEVICE; see Electrical
08700	WEATHERSTRIP; wool pile insert, vinyl insert, magnetic insert
08700	DOOR HINGE
08700	AUTOMATIC DOOR OPERATOR
08700	PANIC HARDWARE
08700	ELECTRICAL LOCKING SYSTEM
08700	FLUSH BOLT
08700	LATCH SET
08700	LOCK SET

SECTION 08800 - GLASS AND GLAZING

08800	CLEAR GLASS; tempered, wire, laminated, 1/4"
08800	MIRROR GLASS; 1/4"
08800	TINTED GLASS; tempered, wire, laminated, 1/4"
08800	CLEAR INSULATING GLAZING; tempered, 1"
08800	TINTED INSULATING GLAZING; tempered, reflective, 1"
08800	TINTED SKYLIGHT GLAZING; reflective, 1"
08800	ACOUSTICAL GLAZING
08800	INSULATING PLASTIC GLAZING
08800	HIGH IMPACT RESISTANT GLAZING
08800	GLAZING COMPOUND
08800	GLAZING GASKET
08800	GLARE REDUCING GLASS
08800	GLAZING ACCESSORIES

SECTION 08900 - GLAZED CURTAIN WALLS

08900	GLAZED CURTAIN WALL SYSTEM; STEEL, ALUMINUM, STAINLESS STEEL, BRONZE
08900	WEEP HOLE
08900	NEOPRENE GASKET
08900	TRANSLUCENT WALL SYSTEM
08900	TRANSLUCENT SKYLIGHT SYSTEM
08900	SLOPED GLAZING SYSTEM
08900	STRUCTURAL GLASS CURTAIN WALL SYSTEM

SECTION 09200 - LATH AND PLASTER

09200	GYPSUM LATH
09200	METAL LATH
09200	GYPSUM PLASTER
09200	VENEER PLASTER
09200	PORTLAND CEMENT PLASTER
09200	ADOBE FINISH
09200	METAL CONTROL JOINT
09200	METAL EXPANSION JOINT
09200	METAL DRIP REVEAL
09200	ACOUSTICAL PLASTER
09200	PLASTER ACCESSORY
09200	PLASTER MOLDING
09200	PLASTER BOARD

SECTION 09250 - GYPSUM DRYWALL SYSTEMS AND ACCESSORIES

09250	EXTERIOR GYPSUM BOARD SHEATHING; 1/2' u.n.o.
09250	GYPSUM BOARD; 5/8" type "x" water resistant
09250	GYPSUM BOARD; 1"
09250	GYPSUM BOARD; 2 layers 1/2"
09250	GYPSUM BOARD; 2 layers 5/8" type "x"
09250	GYPSUM BOARD SHAFTWALL SYSTEM
09250	METAL FURRING; 7/8" @ 24" o.c., u.n.o.
09250	METAL FURRING; 1-1/2" @ 24" o.c., u.n.o.
09250	METAL "Z" FURRING; 1-1/2" @ 24" o.c., u.n.o.
09250	METAL STUDS; 2-1/2" @ 24" o.c., u.n.o.
09250	METAL STUDS; 3-5/8" @ 24" o.c., u.n.o.
09250	METAL STUDS; 6" @ 24" O.C., U.N.O.
09250	3-5/8" METAL STUD CHANNEL TRACK
09250	METAL STUD CHANNEL TRACK; 6"
09250	METAL SHAFTWALL J-CHANNEL
09250	METAL SHAFTWALL C-H STUD
09280	METAL EDGE BEAD
09280	METAL CORNER BEAD
09280	ACOUSTICAL INSULATION BLANKET
09280	GYPSUM BOARD EXPANSION JOINT
09280	ACOUSTICAL CAULKING
09280	ACOUSTICAL SEALANT
09280	GYPSUM BACKERBOARD
09280	CONCRETE BACKING BOARD
09280	LAMINATED SOLID GYPSUM PARTITION SYSTEM

SECTION 09300 - TILE

09300	CERAMIC TILE; 1" X 1"
09300	CERAMIC TILE; 2" X 2"
09300	CERAMIC TILE; 1" X 2"
09300	CERAMIC TILE; 4" X 4"
09300	CERAMIC TILE; 4-1/4" X 4-1/4"
09300	CERAMIC TILE; bullnosed edge
09300	CERAMIC TILE; cove base
09300	QUARRY TILE; 6" X 6"
09300	CHEMICAL RESISTANT QUARRY TILE
09300	PAVER TILE
09300	GLASS MOSAIC TILE
09300	PLASTIC TILE
09300	METAL TILE
09300	CONDUCTIVE TILE

09300	PRECAST TILE
09300	WATERPROOF MEMBRANE
09300	CLEAVAGE MEMBRANE
09300	MORTAR BED

SECTION 09400 - TERRAZZO

09400	PORTLAND CEMENT TERRAZZO
09400	PORTLAND CEMENT TERRAZZO BASE
09400	PRECAST TERRAZZO UNITS
09400	CONDUCTIVE TERRAZZO
09400	PLASTIC MATRIX TERRAZZO
09400	ZINC DIVIDER STRIP
09400	NEOPRENE DIVIDER STRIP
09400	PRECAST TERRAZZO SILL
09400	METAL CONTROL STRIP
09400	TERRAZZO UNDERBED
09400	SAND BASE
09400	CLEAVAGE MEMBRANE

SECTION 09500 - ACOUSTICAL TREATMENT; SPECIAL SURFACES

09500	SUSPENDED ACOUSTICAL CEILING TILE; 2' X 2'
09500	SUSPENDED ACOUSTICAL CEILING TILE; 2' X 4'
09500	SUSPENDED ACOUSTICAL CEILING TILE; 20" X 60"
09500	VINYL FACED ACOUSTICAL CEILING TILE; 2' X 4'
09500	PERFORATED METAL ACOUSTICAL CEILING TILE; 2' X 4'
09500	SUSPENDED METAL CEILING GRID; 2' X 4'
09500	FABRIC-FACED ACOUSTICAL WALL PANEL
09500	PERFORATED VINYL-FACED ACOUSTICAL PANEL
09500	PERFORATED METAL ACOUSTICAL WALL PANEL
09500	SOUND BARRIER BLANKET
09500	SOUND BARRIER BOARD
09500	ACOUSTICAL INSULATION
09500	LINEAR METAL CEILING SYSTEM
09500	ACOUSTICAL CEILING SUSPENSION SYSTEM
09500	LEAF METAL CEILING SYSTEM
09500	METAL PAN CEILING SYSTEM
09500	ACOUSTICAL WALL TREATMENT
09500	ACOUSTICAL SPACE UNIT
09540	REINFORCED GYPSUM UNIT
09540	REINFORCED PLASTIC COATED PANEL

SECTION 09550 - WOOD FLOORING

09550	WOOD STRIP FLOORING
09550	WOOD BLOCK FLOORING
09550	WOOD PARQUET FLOORING
09550	WOOD COMPOSITION FLOORING
09550	RESILIENT WOOD FLOORING SYSTEM

SECTION 09600- STONE, UNIT MASONRY, CARPET, AND RESILIENT FLOORING

09600	FLAGSTONE FLOORING
09600	MARBLE FLOORING
09600	GRANITE FLOORING
09600	SLATE FLOORING
09600	BRICK FLOORING
09600	PRESSED CONCRETE UNIT FLOORING
09600	RESILIENT TILE FLOORING
09600	RESILIENT SHEET FLOORING
09600	CONDUCTIVE RESILIENT FLOORING
09600	FLUID-APPLIED RESILIENT FLOORING

09600	RESILIENT BASE
09600	CARPET PAD/CUSHION
09600	SHEET CARPET
09600	CARPET TILE
09600	WALL CARPET
09600	INDOOR-OUTDOOR CARPET
09600	CARPET EDGE STRIP

SECTION 09700 - SPECIAL FLOORING

09700	RESINOUS FLOORING
09700	EPOXY-MARBLE FLOORING
09700	SEAMLESS QUARTZ FLOORING
09700	ELASTOMERIC LIQUID FLOORING
09700	MASTIC FILL

SECTION 09800 - SPECIAL COATINGS

09800	ABRASION RESISTANT COATING
09800	HIGH-BUILD GLAZED COATING
09800	CEMENTITIOUS COATING
09800	TEXTURED PLASTIC COATING
09800	POLYURETHANE COATING
09800	FIRE RESISTANT PAINT
09800	CHEMICAL RESISTANT COATING
09800	ANTI-GRAFFITI COATING
09800	INTUMESCENT PAINT

SECTION 09900 - PAINTING

09900	PAINT
09900	TRANSPARENT FINISH
09900	CLEAR SEALANT
09950	VINYL COATED FABRIC WALL COVERING
09950	VINYL WALL COVERING
09950	CORK WALL COVERING
09950	WALLPAPER
09950	WALL FABRIC
09950	PRE-FINISHED PANEL

DIVISION 10 - SPECIALTIES

SECTION 10100 - VISUAL DISPLAY BOARDS

10100	CHALKBOARD
10100	TACKBOARD
10100	ERASABLE MARKER WRITING BOARD
10150	METAL TOILET COMPARTMENT
10150	PLASTIC LAMINATE TOILET COMPARTMENT
10150	SHOWER COMPARTMENT
10150	DRESSING COMPARTMENT

SECTION 10200 - LOUVERS AND VENTS

10200	METAL WALL LOUVER; operable
10200	METAL SOFFIT VENT
10200	METAL WALL VENT
10200	METAL BRICK VENT
10200	METAL CRAWLSPACE VENT
10200	INSECT SCREEN
10200	METAL DOOR LOUVER
10200	METAL EQUIPMENT ENCLOSURE

10240	METAL GRILLE
10240	METAL SCREEN
10260	METAL CORNER GUARD
10260	PLASTIC CORNER GUARD
10270	ACCESS FLOORING SYSTEM; rigid grid, snap-on stringer, stringerless

SECTION 10300 - FIREPLACES

10350	PREFABRICATED FIREPLACE
10350	PREFABRICATED FIREPLACE CHIMNEY
10350	FIREPLACE DAMPER
10350	FIREPLACE WATER HEATER
10350	FIREPLACE SCREEN
10350	FIREPLACE DOOR

SECTION 103500 - FLAGPOLES

10350	GROUND SET FLAGPOLE
10350	WALL-MOUNTED FLAGPOLE
10350	AUTOMATIC FLAGPOLE

SECTION 10400 - IDENTIFYING DEVICES, SIGNS

10400	DIRECTORY
10400	DIRECTORY INSERT
10400	BULLETIN BOARD
10400	DIMENSIONAL LETTERS; exterior
10400	DIMENSIONAL LETTERS; interior
10400	ILLUMINATED SIGN; exterior; see Electrical
10400	ILLUMINATED SIGN; interior; see Electrical
10400	NON-ILLUMINATED SIGN; exterior
10400	NON-ILLUMINATED SIGN; interior
10400	POST AND PYLON SIGN
10400	POST AND PANEL SIGN
10400	DOOR SIGN
10400	ENGRAVED SIGN
10400	ROTARY GATE
10400	PORTABLE STANCHION
10450	PORTABLE POSTS
10450	PORTABLE RAILING
10450	TURNSTILE
10450	DETECTION DEVICE

**SECTION 10500 -METAL LOCKERS, FIRE PROTECTION SPECIALTIES, PROTEC-
TIVE COVERS, POSTAL SPECIALTIES**

10500	METAL LOCKERS
10500	WOOD LOCKERS
10500	LOCKER ROOM BENCH
10520	FIRE EXTINGUISHER
10520	FIRE EXTINGUISHER CABINET
10520	FIRE VALVE CABINET
10520	FIRE VALVE AND HOSE CABINET
10530	FABRIC AWNING
10530	METAL AWNING
10530	FABRIC CANOPY
10530	METAL CANOPY
10550	MAIL CHUTE
10550	MAIL BOX

SECTION 10652 - PARTITIONS

10600	WIRE MESH PARTITION
10600	FOLDING GATE
10600	GYPSUM BOARD DEMOUNTABLE PARTITION
10600	METAL DEMOUNTABLE PARTITION
10600	WOOD DEMOUNTABLE PARTITION
10600	FOLDING PANEL PARTITION
10600	ACCORDION FOLDING PARTITION
10600	SLIDING PARTITION
10600	COILING PARTITION
10600	FOLDING PARTITION HEAD TRACK
10600	FOLDING PARTITION FLOOR TRACK
10600	FOLDING PARTITION MOTOR OPERATOR
10600	PORTABLE PARTITION
10600	PORTABLE SCREEN
10600	PORTABLE PANEL
10600	METAL STORAGE SHELVING
10600	AUTOMATED SHELVING SYSTEM
10600	WIRE SHELVING
10600	PREFABRICATED WOOD STORAGE SHELVING

SECTION 10700 -EXTERIOR SUN CONTROL DEVICES, TELEPHONE SPECIALTIES

10700	PREFABRICATED METAL LOUVER FOR SUN CONTROL
10700	PREFABRICATED METAL FIN FOR SUN CONTROL
10700	PREFABRICATED METAL SUNSCREEN
10700	PREFABRICATED METAL CEILING SUNSCREEN
10700	PREFABRICATED SHUTTER PANEL FOR SUN CONTROL
10700	PREFABRICATED TELEPHONE ENCLOSURE
10700	PREFABRICATED TELEPHONE STALL
10700	PREFABRICATED TELEPHONE DIRECTORY UNIT
10700	PREFABRICATED TELEPHONE SHELF

SECTION 10800 - TOILET AND BATH ACCESSORIES

10800	PAPER TOWEL DISPENSERS
10800	PAPER TOWEL DISPENSER/WASTE RECEPTACLE
10800	WASTE RECEPTACLE
10800	TOILET PAPER DISPENSER
10800	SANITARY NAPKIN DISPENSER
10800	SANITARY NAPKIN DISPOSAL
10800	LIQUID SOAP DISPENSER
10800	CONTRACEPTIVE DEVICE DISPENSER
10800	STAINLESS STEEL GRAB BARS
10800	WALL MOUNTED ASH TRAY
10800	SOAP DISH
10800	WARDROBE HOOKS
10800	TOWEL BAR
10800	TOWEL BAR WITH SHELF
10800	STAINLESS STEEL CURTAIN ROD; 1"
10800	FACIAL TISSUE DISPENSER
10800	METAL FRAMED MIRROR
10800	METAL SHELF

SECTION 10900 - MISCELLANEOUS SPECIALTIES

10900	PREFABRICATED HAT RACK
10900	PREFABRICATED COAT RACK

DIVISION 11 - EQUIPMENT

SECTION 11000 - MAINTENANCE, SECURITY, TELLER, AND LIBRARY EQUIPMENT

11000	WINDOW WASHING SYSTEMS
11000	VAULT DOOR
11000	SAFE DEPOSIT BOXES
11000	SAFE
11000	BOOK THEFT PROTECTION EQUIPMENT
11000	LIBRARY STACK SYSTEM
11000	STUDY CARRELS
11000	BOOK DEPOSITORY
11000	NIGHT DEPOSITORY

SECTION 11150 - PARKING CONTROL EQUIPMENT

11150	PARKING GATE
11150	TICKET DISPENSER; see Electrical
11150	CARD CONTROL UNIT; see Electrical
11150	PARKING CONTROL EQUIPMENT; see Electrical
11150	DOCK LEVELLER
11150	DOCK LEVELLER FRAME
11150	DOCK SEAL
11150	DOCK BUMPERS
11150	DOCK LIFT
11150	COMMERCIAL WASHER
11150	COMMERCIAL EXTRACTOR
11150	COMMERCIAL DRY CLEANING EQUIPMENT
11150	COMMERCIAL DRYER
11150	MONEY CHANGING MACHINE
11150	BEVERAGE VENDING MACHINE
11150	CANDY VENDING MACHINE
11150	CIGARETTE VENDING MACHINE
11150	FOOD VENDING MACHINE
11150	SUNDRY VENDING MACHINE
11150	STAMP VENDING MACHINE
11150	MOTORIZED PROJECTION SCREEN
11150	WASTE COMPACTOR
11150	WASTE BIN
11150	PACKAGED INCINERATOR

SECTION 11400 - FOOD SERVICE EQUIPMENT

11400	FOOD STORAGE EQUIPMENT; see Kitchen
11400	REFRIGERATOR; see Kitchen
11400	FREEZER; see Kitchen
11400	FOOD PREPARATION EQUIPMENT; see Kitchen
11400	FOOD COOKING EQUIPMENT; see Kitchen
11400	BAR; see Kitchen
11400	BACK BAR; see Kitchen
11400	DISH WASHING EQUIPMENT; see Kitchen
11400	GARBAGE DISPOSER; see Kitchen
11400	REFRIGERATED CASE; see Kitchen
11400	SERVING LINE EQUIPMENT; see Kitchen
11400	COOKING HOOD AND VENTILATION SYSTEM; see Kitchen and Mechanical
11400	TRANSFER CABINET
11400	DARKROOM PROCESSING EQUIPMENT
11400	REVOLVING DARKROOM DOOR
11400	SCOREBOARD
11400	BACKSTOP

11400	GYM DIVIDER
11400	GYMNASIUM EQUIPMENT
11400	EXERCISE EQUIPMENT

SECTION 11700 - MEDICAL EQUIPMENT

11700	MEDICAL STERILIZING EQUIPMENT
11700	MEDICAL EXAMINATION EQUIPMENT
11700	MEDICAL TREATMENT EQUIPMENT
11700	PATIENT CARE EQUIPMENT
11700	DENTAL EQUIPMENT
11700	OPTICAL EQUIPMENT

DIVISION 12 - FURNISHINGS

SECTION 12100 - ART WORK

12100	PAINTING
12100	MURAL
12100	SCULPTURE
12100	STAINED GLASS

SECTION 12300 - MANUFACTURED CASEWORK

12300	METAL CASEWORK
12300	WOOD CASEWORK
12300	PLASTIC LAMINATE-FACED CASEWORK
12300	BANK FIXTURES AND CASEWORK
12300	LIBRARY CASEWORK
12300	RESTAURANT AND CAFETERIA CASEWORK
12300	EDUCATIONAL CASEWORK
12300	DORMITORY CASEWORK
12300	MEDICAL CASEWORK
12300	NURSE SERVER CABINETS
12300	PHARMACY CASEWORK
12300	METAL LABORATORY CASEWORK
12300	WOOD LABORATORY CASEWORK
12300	LABORATORY TOPS, SINKS AND ACCESSORIES
12300	HOSPITAL CASEWORK
12300	DENTAL CASEWORK
12300	OPTICAL CASEWORK
12300	VETERINARY CASEWORK
12300	HOTEL AND MOTEL CASEWORK
12300	ECCLESIASTICAL CASEWORK
12300	DISPLAY CASEWORK
12300	RESIDENTIAL CASEWORK

SECTIONAL 12500 - WINDOW TREATMENT

12500	HORIZONTAL LOUVER BLINDS
12500	VERTICAL LOUVER BLINDS
12500	INSULATING SHADES
12500	LIGHT PROOF SHADES
12500	SOLAR CONTROL FILM
12500	CURTAIN
12500	FABRIC DRAPERIES
12500	LIGHTPROOF DRAPERIES
12500	VERTICAL LOUVER DRAPERIES
12500	DRAPERY HARDWARE
12500	CURTAIN HARDWARE

SECTION 12600 - FURNITURE AND ACCESSORIES; RUGS AND MATS

12600	LANDSCAPE PARTITIONS AND COMPONENTS
12600	FURNITURE
12600	FURNITURE SYSTEMS
12600	FURNITURE ACCESSORIES
12600	RUGS
12600	FOOT GRILLE
12600	ENTRANCE MAT
12600	ENTRANCE MAT FRAME

SECTION 12710 - AUDITORIUM SEATING

12700	INTERLOCKING CHAIRS
12700	PORTABLE FOLDING CHAIRS
12700	STACKING CHAIRS
12700	AUDITORIUM SEATING
12700	TELESCOPING STAND
12700	TELESCOPING BLEACHERS
12700	TELESCOPING CHAIR PLATFORMS
12700	MULTIPLE-USE FIXED SEATING

SECTION 12800 - INTERIOR PLANTS AND PLANTERS

12800	INTERIOR PLANTS
12800	PLANTERS

DIVISION 13 - SPECIAL CONSTRUCTION

SECTION 13030 - SPECIAL PURPOSE ROOMS

13030	PREFABRICATED RACQUETBALL PANEL CONSTRUCTION SYSTEM
13030	PREFABRICATED RACQUETBALL GLAZING SYSTEM
13030	PREFABRICATED RACQUETBALL PANEL CEILING SYSTEM
13030	PREFABRICATED SAUNA
13030	PREFABRICATED STEAM ROOM CONSTRUCTION SYSTEM
13030	PREFABRICATED VAULT

SECTION 13120 - PRE-ENGINEERED STRUCTURES, POOLS

13120	PRE-ENGINEERED METAL BUILDING SYSTEM
13120	PRE-ENGINEERED GREENHOUSE
13120	PRE-ENGINEERED GRANDSTAND
13120	PRE-ENGINEERED BLEACHERS
13150	POOL CONSTRUCTION
13150	PRECAST CONCRETE POOL COPING
13150	POOL EQUIPMENT; see Mechanical and Electrical for connections
13150	HOT TUB
13150	SPA POOL

DIVISION 14 - CONVEYING SYSTEMS

SECTION 14100 - DUMBWAITERS

14100	MANUALLY OPERATED DUMBWAITER
14100	ELECTRIC DUMBWAITER
14100	HYDRAULIC DUMBWAITER

SECTION 14200 - ELEVATORS

14200	PASSENGER ELEVATOR; hydraulic
14200	PASSENGER ELEVATOR; traction
14200	SERVICE ELEVATOR
14200	FREIGHT ELEVATOR
14200	SILL BY ELEVATOR MANUFACTURER
14200	HOLLOW METAL DOOR BY ELEVATOR MANUFACTURER
14200	HOLLOW METAL FRAME BY ELEVATOR MANUFACTURER
14200	ELEVATOR CALL BUTTON
14200	ELEVATOR INDICATOR PANEL
14200	ELEVATOR BEAM BY ELEVATOR MANUFACTURER
14200	ELEVATOR RAIL BY ELEVATOR MANUFACTURER
14200	ELEVATOR EQUIPMENT

SECTION 14300 - MOVING STAIRS AND WALKS

14300	ESCALATOR
14300	MOVING WALK

SECTION 14400 - LIFTS

14400	WHEELCHAIR LIFT
14400	PLATFORM LIFT
14400	LIFT CONTROLS

SECTION 14500 - MATERIAL HANDLING SYSTEMS

14500	BAGGAGE CONVEYOR
14500	LAUNDRY CHUTE
14500	PNEUMATIC TUBE SYSTEM

SECTION 14600 - HOISTS AND CRANES

14600	CRANE RAIL
14600	FIXED HOIST
14600	TROLLEY HOIST

DIVISION 15 - MECHANICAL

SECTION 15050 - BASIC MECHANICAL MATERIALS AND METHODS

15050	WATER METER; see Mechanical
15050	GAS METER; see Mechanical
15050	PUMP; see Mechanical
15050	MOTOR; see Mechanical

SECTION 15300 - FIRE PROTECTION

15300	WATER METER; see mechanical
15300	SPRINKLER HEAD; see Mechanical
15300	STANDPIPE AND HOSE SYSTEMS; see Mechanical
15300	FIRE DEPARTMENT TEST HEADER
15300	FIRE DEPARTMENT SIAMESE CONNECTION

SECTION 15400 - PLUMBING

15400	WATER HEATER; see Mechanical
15400	FLOOR DRAIN; see Mechanical
15400	DECK DRAIN; see Mechanical
15400	ROOF DRAIN; see Mechanical
15400	OVERFLOW DRAIN; see Mechanical
15400	FLOOR SINK; see Mechanical
15400	TRENCH DRAIN; see Mechanical
15400	WATER FOUNDATION; see Mechanical
15400	WATER CLOSET; see Mechanical
15400	URINAL; see Mechanical
15400	LAVATORY; see Mechanical
15400	POOL EQUIPMENT; see Mechanical
15400	FOUNTAIN EQUIPMENT; see Mechanical

SECTION 15500 - HVAC

15500	ROOFTOP HVAC EQUIPMENT; see Mechanical
15500	FAN; see Mechanical
15500	DUCT; see Mechanical
15500	DIFFUSER; see Mechanical
15500	MECHANICAL EQUIPMENT; see Mechanical
15500	COOLING TOWER; see Mechanical
15500	LINEAR DIFFUSERS; see Mechanical
15500	RETURN AIR GRILLE; see Mechanical

SECTION 15750 - HEAT TRANSFER

15750	RADIANT HEATING PANELS; see Mechanical
15750	FIN TUBE RADIATOR; see Mechanical
15750	HYDRONIC BASEBOARDS; see Mechanical

DIVISION 16 - ELECTRICAL

SECTION 16050 - BASIC ELECTRICAL MATERIALS AND METHODS

16050	RACEWAY; see Electrical
16050	UNDERFLOOR DUCT; see Electrical
16050	UNDERFLOOR DUCT ACCESS PANEL; see Electrical
16050	PLUGMOLD; see Electrical
16050	ELECTRIC BASEBOARD; see Electrical
16050	EMERGENCY GENERATOR SET; see Electrical
16050	TRANSFORMER; see Electrical
16050	ELECTRICAL EQUIPMENT; see Electrical
16050	ELECTRIC MOTOR; see Electrical
16050	ELECTRICAL CONDUIT; see Electrical
16050	ELECTRICAL PANEL; see Electrical
16050	ELECTRICAL CABINET; see Electrical

SECTION 16500 - LIGHTING

16500	2' X 4' LAY-IN-FIXTURE; see Electrical
16500	20" X 48" LAY-IN-FIXTURE with extensions to fill 60" grid; see Electrical
16500	20" X 60" LAY-IN-FIXTURE; see Electrical
16500	2' X 2' LAY-IN-FIXTURE; see Electrical
16500	2' X 4' SURFACE MOUNTED FIXTURE; see Electrical
16500	RECESSED CAN FIXTURE; see Electrical
16500	WALL MOUNTED LIGHT FIXTURE; see Electrical
16500	POLE LIGHT; see Electrical
16500	LIGHT BOLLARD; see Electrical
16500	STEP LIGHT; see Electrical

PURPOSE

Each door on a project requires many decisions to be made and documented for the contractor. The size, material, hardware, frame and finish, among other things, must be communicated. On a large project you may have to communicate this information for scores, even hundreds, of doors. It is essential that this information be organized in a logical, coherent manner. A door schedule seems to be the best way to accomplish this kind of organization.

The purpose of door schedules is to convey detailed information that can be copious, repetitious, tedious, and arduous. The schedule organizes salient information about a door and frame for easy and accurate reference. The information provided should be adequate to describe all the necessary requirements to enable the contractor to supply the correct door and frame.

PROPOSITION

Scheduling is a matter of setting up tables or matrices and filling in the proper data. Each door is given a reference number. These numbers are aligned in a column and a row is allocated for each door. Additional columns provide a place to indicate other kinds of information about each door.

Door schedules need to fit the complexity of the project. As a minimum requirement, door schedules should describe size, material, finish, and physical properties of both door and frame. The following schedule has a column for each of the features matched to a row for each door. The schedule may be expanded to include a column for veneers, gage, etc. for items which differ from door to door. Hardware and frame suppliers seem to prefer a separate row for each door, rather than generic door types which repeat (such as door "A" for all offices). This allows the suppliers to indicate the hand of the door as well as provide an accurate quantitative takeoff. The schedule should be accompanied by drawings which graphically depict the variety of door and frame types included in the project, usually drawn at 1/4" scale. A sample is contained in the appendix. The doors shown are standard choices with the appropriate symbols used by the Steel Door Institute. Add necessary door and frame types to fit the particular project.

A complete schedule will be generated by the door and or hardware supplier. This schedule may show location of door ("from and to"), clearances required, hinge location, opening sizes and locations. The more complete and accurate the initial door schedule, the easier it should be to check the shop drawing versions. Our research on door scheduling and door numbering revealed several time-tested and proven techniques for numbering doors. For a smaller residential project, it may be adequate to indicate "3068H6" along the face of the door, and eliminate the need for a door schedule. For larger projects, you may find it more desirable to number each door consecutively, starting with 100 for level 1 doors, 200 for level 2 doors, and so forth. But the system we have come to favor begins with the room number, such as 315. Then, every door which

Door Schedules

swings from that room into an adjacent room is designated with a letter (315A). This number is then indicated along the face of the door. This system makes it much easier to find specific doors because they are always associated with room numbers.

POSTSCRIPT

Make sure you are familiar with the fire-resistive requirements of various walls, and be certain that the door types and hardware match the fire rating required. For example, don't schedule a full glass door with a B label or use untested hardware in a fire door. Be aware of maximum glass sizes, where mullions are required, and stop sizes.

Also be aware that many standard sizes, styles, and types of construction have been developed by the door industry and they should be used wherever possible. Deviation from these standards should be well defined and as precise as possible.

PRACTICE

A sample door schedule, door types drawing, and hardware schedule are included in the Appendix for your use. These samples should be suitable for most projects. You may want to consider various ways of actually recording the necessary information. The samples can be copied directly onto sticky-back material (in reverse), so it can be applied to the back of the sheet), and the information can be entered manually. Or, a copy can be made on paper, and the information can be typed on. Or, you may want to make a computer version of the form that can be edited electronically as a word processing, spreadsheet, or CAD document.

DOOR SCHEDULE

Door #	DOORS						FRAMES						Fire Rating	Hdw. Group	REMARKS
	TYPE	MAT.	FIN.	SIZE			TYPE	MAT.	FIN.	DETAILS					
				WIDTH	HEIGHT	THICK				JAMB	HEAD	SILL			
101A	A	WOOD	PT	3'-0	7'-0	1-3/4	A	HM	PT	1/A17	3/A17	3/A17	1 HR	3	SMOKE SEALS
101B	B	HM	PT	3'-0	7'-0	1-3/4	A	HM	PT	4/A17	5/A17	6/A17	1 HR	3	SMOKE SEALS
101C	A	WOOD	PT	3'-0	7'-0	1-3/4	B	HM	PT	13/A17	2/A17	-	-	1	
102A	A	WOOD	PT	3'-0	7'-0	1-3/4	B	HM	PT	1/A10	2/A10	-	-	2	
103A	A	WOOD	PT	3'-0	7'-0	1-3/4	B	HM	PT	1/A17	2/A17	-	-	4	
104A	C	HM	PT	3'-0	7'-0	1-3/4	A	HM	PT	11/A17	10/A17	12/A17	1 HR	3	SMOKE SEALS
105A	A	WOOD	PT	3'-0	7'-0	1-3/4	B	HM	PT	1/A17	2/A17	-	-	5	
105B	A	WOOD	PT	3'-0	7'-0	1-3/4	B	HM	PT	1/A10	2/A10	-	-	6	
106A	A	WOOD	PT	3'-0	7'-0	1-3/4	C	HM	PT	1/A17	2/A17	-	-	7	WIRE GLASS
106B	A	WOOD	PT	3'-0	7'-0	1-3/4	B	HM	PT	1/A10	2/A10	-	-	1	
107A	B	HM	PT	3'-0	7'-0	1-3/4	A	HM	PT	8/A17	9/A17	10/A17	1 HR	3	SMOKE SEALS
108A	A	WOOD	PT	3'-0	7'-0	1-3/4	B	HM	PT	1/A17	2/A17	-	-	2	
109A	A	WOOD	PT	3'-0	7'-0	1-3/4	B	HM	PT	1/A17	2/A17	-	-	4	
110A	B	HM	PT	3'-0	7'-0	1-3/4	A	HM	PT	7/A17	8/A17	9/A17	1 HR	3	SMOKE SEALS
111A	A	WOOD	PT	3'-0	7'-0	1-3/4	B	HM	PT	1/A17	3/A17	-	-	6	
112A	C	HM	PT	3'-0	7'-0	1-3/4	A	HM	PT	13/A17	13/A17	W/A17	1 HR	3	SMOKE SEALS

Example of a typical door schedule.

Schedules
Finish Schedules

PURPOSE

The finishes selected for a given project are likely to be fairly limited–a few kinds of carpet, several paint colors, some plastic laminates. Communicating the locations of each of these finishes is when it gets complicated. Just as for door schedules, this information must be organized and presented in a logical, coherent manner.

PROPOSITION

Finish Schedules must identify the finish materials applied to each surface in a given room (the walls, the floor, the ceiling) and, in some cases, the substrate to which these finishes are applied as well. The complexity of the finish scheduling method should match the complexity of finishing requirements. Three types of schedules are most commonly used:
- Written
- Written with symbols
- Keyed to the plan

The written schedule provides probably the most effective method of managing large amounts of information when many different finishes are required, or when the locations where these finishes are required are highly variable. It is arguably the most direct and clear method of organizing the information which can be read directly with little chance of error. It consists of rows for rooms and columns for each finished surface. Abbreviations are commonly used to indicate different selections (such as CPT1 for one carpet selection, CPT2 for another, etc.) Each abbreviation and material selection should be identified in the appropriate section in the specifications.

A variation of the written schedule can be created which lists all of the finishes along the top row. The matrix is then completed by marking the appropriate finish and room intersection. This can lead to long schedules since they may contain many finishes, but it requires less time to complete than the more conventional type of written schedule. A further variation of this type of schedule is to indicate specifically which walls of a given room are to receive specific finishes.

The symbol method is probably the simplest, because it avoids "schedules" and provides symbols on the plan of each room to denote finishes. This is useful for simple projects where each wall, floor, and ceiling in a given space is finished using a single material, and where there is extra room on the plan. This method is not recommended where walls may have some paint and some wall fabric, or where floors may have some carpet and some tile. The symbol method can be achieved using a box divided into two parts. The room number occupies the left part, with an alphanumeric symbol for floor and base, wall, and ceiling finishes in the right part. This method also requires a legend to identify the room finish codes being used.

Schedules
Finish Schedules

ROOM NAME

Room #	2 A 4

- Ceiling finishes code
- Floor and Base finishes code
- Wall finishes code

POSTSCRIPT

Remodeling and renovation adds an additional layer of complexity to the task of communicating finishes. This can be addressed by giving each room two lines of the written form of the schedule. The first line may be used to show new finishes intended for existing surfaces, while the second line may be used in the typical manner to show new finishes for new surfaces.

PRACTICE

The Appendix includes sample versions of the schedules discussed above. Once you have selected the desired scheduling method, you may copy the appropriate schedule (in reverse) on sticky back material, and apply it to the back of your drawing sheet to complete by hand. You may also want to consider typing it, or creating word processing or CAD versions of it instead.

FINISH SCHEDULE

ROOM #	NAME	FLOOR	BASE FINISH	BASE MAT.	North Wall FINISH	North Wall MAT.	East Wall FINISH	East Wall MAT.	South Wall FINISH	South Wall MAT.	West Wall FINISH	West Wall MAT.	Ceiling	Ceiling Height	REMARKS
101	CORRIDOR	CPT1	PT1	WD	PT1	GB	PT1	GB	PT1	GB	PT1	GB	SAC	8'-0	
102	CLOSET	VCT	-	RB	PT1	GB	PT1	GB	PT1	GB	PT1	GB	PT1	8'-0	
103	TOILET	CT	-	CT	-	CT	PT2	GB	PT2	GB	PT2	GB	PT1	7'-8	
104	WORKROOM	CONCRETE	-	-	PT5	GB	PT1	GB	PT1	GB	PT1	GB	-	-	
105	MAIL	VCT	-	RB	PT4	GB	PT1	GB	PT1	GB	PT1	GB	SAC	8'-0	
106	STORAGE	VCT	-	RB	PT1	GB	PT1	GB	PT1	GB	PT1	GB	-	-	
107	COATS	CPT1	-	RB	PT1	GB	PT1	GB	PT1	GB	PT1	GB	PT1	8'-0	
108	MEN	CT	-	CT	-	CT	-	CT	PT2	GB	PT2	GB	PT1	8'-0	
109	ELECTRICAL	CONCRETE	-	-	PT5	GB	PT5	GB	PT5	GB	PT5	GB	-	-	
110	WOMEN	CT	-	CT	-	CT	-	CT	PT2	GB	PT2	GB	PT1	8'-0	
111	HALL	VCT	-	RB	PT1	GB	PT1	GB	PT1	GB	PT1	GB	SAC	8'-0	
112	CONFER.	CPT2	-	RB	PT5	GB	PT5	GB	PT5	GB	PT5	GB	PT1	VARIES	
113	OFFICE	CPT3	-	RB	PT5	GB	PT5	GB	PT5	GB	PT5	GB	SAC	8'-0	
114	OFFICE	CPT3	-	RB	PT5	GB	PT5	GB	PT5	GB	PT5	GB	SAC	8'-0	
115	TRAINING	CPT2	-	RB	PT5	GB	PT5	GB	PT5	GB	PT5	GB	SAC	8'-0	
116	CORRIDOR	CPT1	-	RB	PT1	GB	PT1	GB	PT1	GB	PT5	GB	SAC	8'-0	

Example of a typical finish schedule.

PURPOSE

Casework on a project must be located for the contractor to show its type and to identify the number of pieces required. It can be located in plan or elevation, as well as on a casework schedule to help communicate the appropriate information. Casework can be either manufactured or custom-made, and the information required for the contractor is dependent upon which type it is. As a minimum, dimensions for casework should be shown, as well as its arrangement of doors, drawers, and shelves. A numeric identifier used to reference the piece of casework may be a model number, a reference indicating its dimensions, or it may be another generic reference.

PROPOSITION

The identification of casework should be appropriate to the type and amount used for a project. The approach for a smaller job can be simple, while a larger job requires an approach that clearly organizes additional information. Smaller jobs can use an identifier to call out casework in plan or section. Other jobs can use an identifier that refers to a schedule where additional information is provided.

An approach to identifying casework for a simple job should be brief and straightforward. For example, when the owner is already familiar with the elevations of the casework, it may not be necessary to draw the elevations of the casework in order to communicate the intent to the owner. In this case, if the floor plans allow for it, an identifier can be placed adjacent to each piece of casework in plan. The identifier should note either base or upper cabinets when both are being used. If space is not provided in plan, a larger-scale plan may be desirable, or casework can be shown in elevation.

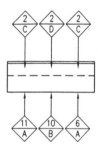

Casework can be shown in elevation by itself or within other interior elevations already required for the job. Elevations are used if the casework must relate to something else vertically or the owner would like to see how multiple pieces of casework relate to each other. If a casework schedule is not necessary, an identifier can give the contractor the information he needs to determine the piece to be used. For larger or more complicated jobs, additional casework information may be

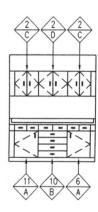

Sample approach to scheduling casework.

necessary.

When the depth of the casework or the manufacturer varies, it may be difficult to communicate this information so it is easily understood. In this case, a casework schedule can be used. The schedule may consist of one or more sheets indicating a graphic representation of each piece of casework, with a matrix or table adjacent to each piece. The table combines spaces for dimensions and the manufacturer's information. The casework schedule might work like this: Casework is elevated within interior elevations. For each piece, a diamond, divided into a top and bottom half, references the casework schedule. The top half contains a number which refers to a casework model. The bottom half of the diamond contains a letter for a casework style within its model. Tables adjacent to each piece of casework list the styles used for each model within the project. Each style then is given dimensions for length, depth, and height, as well as a manufacturer. When all pieces are available from a single manufacturer, a general note can indicate this. When graphics are used for models that come from a single manufacturer, it should be verified that competitors have acceptable units available.

POSTSCRIPT

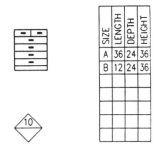

SIZE	LENGTH	DEPTH	HEIGHT
A	36	24	36
B	12	24	36

Sample approach to scheduling casework.

So far, it has been assumed that the casework is manufactured. When casework is custom-built for a particular job, much more information is required. Custom casework should be identified sufficiently in plan, elevation, and section so that the builder has enough information to build it. Details are also necessary, even at full scale. Their extent is determined by the type and complexity of the casework desired. Use the Architectural Woodwork Institute (AWI) standards to control the quality of workmanship.

Specifications should be used to note materials and finishes for casework. If several types of casework are used, drawings can clarify where they occur. Countertop materials can also be covered in the specifications, but the dimensions of splashes should be noted on the drawings. Rather than dimensioning filler pieces, note that they're equal to each other (when they are).

Schedules
Toilet and Bath Accessories

PURPOSE

Toilet and bath accessories compose one of many systems that are critical to a building's performance and, if improperly referenced and organized via drawings and/or schedules, can mean confusion and lost time for the architect and contractor.

PROPOSITION

The complexity of the project will dictate how the accessories are described. For those projects that do not demand a set of technical specifications, the information will necessarily be limited to the drawing set.

There are four common ways to communicate the necessary information about accessories:

- Typical elevations of the accessories showing appearance and typical locations and mounting heights
- A code system on the drawing plans (floor plans or enlarged scale plans) referring to information in the specifications;
- Accessories schedule
- Interior elevations as part of the drawing set

Accessory schedules may be categorized as either "Quantitative" or "Non-quantitative"[1] types. For complex or smaller customized projects the "quantitative" system uses room names and numbers for accessory locations, indications of quantities of each accessory (in the respective column of each item or group of items); and specifications to identify various accessory types.

The "non-quantitative" schedule system locates each accessory via the typical plumbing fixture location. This system seems particularly applicable for large repetitive projects with little or no variation in accessory type.

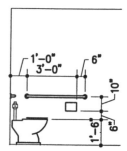

TYPICAL HANDICAP TOILET STALL

Sample toilet room elevation showing typical mounting heights to be incorporated in library of toilet room accessory elevations.

Finally, accessory schedules should be used in conjunction with specific information in the drawings, the specifications, or the "remarks" column, which designates locations and mounting heights.

POSTSCRIPT

Accessories are usually finite on any project, but the methods to describe them are many, only a few of which occur in this chapter. Whatever system or combination of systems you might choose, be consistent and avoid redundancy. As always, keep it as simple as possible.

PRACTICE

Examples of schedules and typical elevations with accessory mounting heights are included in the Appendix for your reference and use.

[1] Committee on Production Office Procedures, Northern California Chapter, American Institute of Architects, July, 1980

COMPUTERS ARE CHANGING THE WAY ARCHITECTURE IS PRACTICED

Years ago, the first primitive architects swung from tree to tree carrying their business tools with them in their belts. In those days, the tools of design consisted primarily of a stone axe, which was used as much for its powers of persuasion as it was for its ability to make changes in designs that were etched in stone. For centuries the stone axe had been used in housing development, civic improvement, and interior design. It was the accepted way of doing things, a time tested and proven technology. To possess a stone axe was a symbol of success, a sign of having "made it" in the business jungle.

One day a trader swung into town selling new-fangled metal axes. Shoot, 'twas nothin' like we ever saw before. Few axes were sold, amongst much ridicule. Soon, though, the advantages of the metal axe became clear. The metal axe did the same jobs better, faster, and with less maintenance.

Not since we first started using the telephone in the practice of architecture, have we seen a machine that could "create" time for us by speeding up the communication process involved in conveying design ideas to others. Bell's invention was considered a novelty, because after all, who could you talk to? Nobody had one. Communication had been done by letter or by travel. The telephone, in allowing information to be transferred faster, created more time for us to spend in the office, in the design process, and less time traveling or waiting for the mail.

The computer, when first introduced into the architects' office, was treated as little more than a complicated typewriter. Computer drafting, well, that was just a novelty, a kind of video game similar to an etch-a-sketch. Critics were quick to buy discount computers with engineering software, hire an untrained operator, and proudly proclaim CAD a boondoggle, a waste of good money.

If you've read this far you probably realize that the computer, along with the fax & cellular phone, is here to stay. Architecture will influence the computer and the computer will influence architecture. The time is now to start thinking about what roles the computer will play in your office and how it can be used to "create" time for you.

There are many jobs a computer can do to speed your arrival into a world of unprecedented complexity (on the theory that you will be able to do the same things you do now, only faster). All of these functions require some education and decision making on your part. To start by defining the task you want accomplished, or creating a computer job description, you've taken a realistic first step in making a computer pay for itself.

Word Processing

Create letters and other forms of correspondence in a uniform type style and format for use throughout the office. Company letterhead can be printed as needed, as part of the correspondence, for various types of projects. Editing and corrections to rough drafts can be made quickly and easily.

Create standard forms, such as a transmittal, which can be called on screen at the touch of a key and automatically dated. Type in the name of the person you are sending it to and have the computer automatically add the firm's name and address. Type your message and you're finished. All types of construction correspondence and forms can be accomplished in this manner.

Use a modem with a dedicated phone line to send correspondence directly to a consultant's or contractor's computer. Meeting minutes can be created in a standard format and sent to all concerned parties by computer instead of by regular overland mail.

Specifications can be edited directly on screen by the architect and sent out for publishing on a floppy disk or by modem. This may eliminate the need to copy a master section, redline the master, have it modified, print it out, proofread it, send it back for corrections, print it out, proofread it again, and then send it out for publishing.

Data Base

Replace the Rolodex with a computerized list of names and addresses that can be used to address envelopes, or inserted on standard forms, record telephone conversations, record marketing possibilities, and keep other personal notes.

Keep inventories of equipment, furniture, personnel, dead storage inventories, and so on, for facility management projects.

Develop listings for in-house record keeping, sources of information, etc.

Projects under construction can be photographed using cameras which record digital images. These photos can be sent from the job site via modem to your computer and organized according to date and project. This streamlines record keeping and reduces photography costs.

Develop door and finish schedules in conjunction with CAD software.

Desk Top Publishing

Do the marketing for your firm in 4-color graphics in your choice of type style and format. Include photographs of projects that you can print out as you need them.

Include CAD drawings directly into marketing presentations.

Create marketing slide show presentations from a lap top computer directly connected to an overhead projector or VCR.

Create "publication ready" documents for submission to magazines and journals.

Create large "poster-type" charts and displays quickly that can be easily and inexpensively modified prior to printing into hard copy.

Spreadsheets

Spreadsheet programs can be used for project scheduling and formulating multi-task time lines. The relationships between activities can be readily understood when shown graphically in simple bar chart fashion. Schedules can be expanded upon and updated quickly and easily.

Fee proposals can be presented so they are easily understood when organized in categories on a spreadsheet. Many phases and disciplines can be shown side by side and rapidly compared.

If your CAD software does not feature an automated door schedule creation capability, spreadsheets are an excellent second choice. The editing capability of current spreadsheet software streamlines the schedule-making process dramatically. Schedules can then be imported into CAD drawings, or included in the Project Manual.

Accounting

Time sheet information entered by each employee can be linked through an accounting program to produce job cost reports, invoicing for services performed, and cost estimating data for future proposals.

General accounting, investment tracking, equipment payback periods, projected expenses, projected income, office expenditures, and profit sharing can be done quickly and inexpensively.

Automatic check printing systems are available that will calculate the deductions required for each employee and print out payroll checks for the proper amounts based upon recently entered time sheet data.

Project Tracking

This software will let you establish a production schedule and then track a project financially and hourly at various intervals. This tracking can be based on time sheet entries with input for items such as supplies and reprographic costs. Potential problems can be spotted and actions taken to head off small problems before they become big ones.

Computerization

Personal Organizers

These electronic calendars record appointments for you and help to organize your time.

Many feature "To Do List" capabilities for creating lists of items to accomplish on a personal or per project basis. They replace the multitude of scrap paper reminders that you have scattered around your desk.

Small, hand-held "notebooks," are widely used as scratchpads when attending meetings or touring the job site. These notebooks will recognize your handwriting and turn your written notes into a type-faced report. This information can then be downloaded into a computer to print or modem to others.

Calculators are easily accessed by "shelling out" or calling it on screen without leaving your original program. Quick figuring can be done without saving and exiting your present program.

Computer Aided Design

Computers will draw as accurately or as inaccurately as you desire, just like sketching on bumwad; you decide.

Computers can duplicate images, stretch/modify images, and mirror images, just like you can do on bumwad.

Computers can sketch, in isometric, in axonometric, or in perspective, just like on bumwad; you decide.

Computers can sketch over an established background, they can copy this background again and again to develop more schemes, just like sketching on bumwad over xerox copies.

Unlike bumwad sketching however, computers are fast. The fact that CAD is faster is seldom perceived. If you've commonly allocated a month for the design process in the past, you'll probably find designing with a computer will take a month also. The difference is that you will have had time to pursue dozens more design ideas and directions than you previously would have had time for.

Computer Aided Drafting

By using a modem we can send sets of drawings to engineering consultants for use as plan backgrounds. We no longer have to wait for them to pick them up, or send them using a messenger service. Drawings can be sent to contractors, clients, plan rooms, sales reps, and so on, reducing the cost of blueprinting them ourselves.

Details can be taken from past projects, modified, and inserted into a drawing in less time than it would have taken to stickyback it. No more blueprints that look like a cu-and-paste job with varying shades of blue background. No more splotchy, eradicated sepias. The result is always a clean, crisp-looking drawing.

Lettering can be standardized to your liking, not too small, not too large, not too weird. No more teaching people how to print legibly (provided you never need them to do hand sketching or manual drafting).

Programs are available which link drawing entities to construction cost estimation and facilities management programs. Lists of equipment and quantities of materials can be added and subtracted graphically, automatically updating the data base each time.

With CAD programs becoming increasingly more complicated, an inexperienced or unenthused drafter can really torpedo a team production effort. That is where you have to know enough about the software to be able to spot trouble and take steps to correct the situation.

CAD is similar to the obsolete pin register overlay system in the sense that it requires forethought and organization at the start of working drawing production. Once the project production techniques have been established, changes can be made very easily. If each drafter is free to do his or her own thing, chaos will reign and changing things becomes a long, worrisome chore.

Modem communication with the contractor during construction administration will enable you to answer questions quickly and easily through clarification correspondence, CAD drawings, and even the exchange of digital photography.

Many manufacturers are putting their product catalogs on compact disks. Details and specifications can be retrieved from these CD's, modified, and included in the construction documents.

The computer can and will "create " time for you. As the pace of doing business increases, you may not notice this extra time; after all it's still a 10 hour day! By making the investment in learning to use the equipment however, you will be doing more of what's enjoyable to you and leaving the mundane for the computer to perform.

How are Architecture Schools Preparing Students for Today's World?

Architectural firms are facing a difficult dilemma: they need staff trained in the use of CAD, but architectural schools are not producing CAD users proficient at a level high enough to be useful to most firms. Firms are then faced with having to train new employees (an extremely expensive proposition), and then face the probability of replacing that employee as soon as (s)he feels more marketable and able to command a higher wage. Therefore, why should the firm be interested in hiring a recent graduate? Why shouldn't the firm hire a person from someone else's office who has already been trained?

Schools have traditionally emphasized architecture as an art form, stressing design, with a secondary acknowledgement of engineering and graphic arts. Knowledge of the technical aspects of construction and working drawings production does not generally receive the appropriate level of emphasis required to prepare graduates to compete for the few entry-level positions available upon graduation. Few architecture students would choose extended study in computer applications over designing the city beautiful.

CAD drafting is not commonly stressed in school but then neither is Small Business Administration, Finance, Marketing, or Law. Typing (keyboarding) classes would be extremely useful in preparing someone for today's job market. Architecture schools are adapting slowly to the changing world as the cost of hardware and software become more affordable. They will eventually catch up with the real world, although CAD skills, like hand-drafting skills in the past, will most likely be mastered at the personal initiative of the individual.

The computer did not create this debate of architectural design study versus marketable job skills, and it will certainly not be the final answer. Money will be spent either by the school or by the student to imbue students with the necessary skills, and to purchase the necessary drafting equipment for college study.

Interns Must Now Spend the First Years of Their Internship Learning CAD, Often at the Expense of Learning Architecture

There is no way around it—in this profession you have to know how to draw. Whether it is ink on linen, plastic lead on mylar, or pixels on a CRT, the drafter will have to master the prevailing technology of the age in order to communicate his or her ideas.

In the past, this process began for most of us at an early age, doodling during English class. Paper and pencil were readily available and ever-present. Art classes and drafting classes followed, enhancing whatever abilities we had acquired on our own with specialties such as pastels, paints, T-squares, and technical pens.

Computer-aided drafting however, involves a significant investment in hardware and software. CAD classes seldom have enough equipment for each student, and the time a student actually spends on the computer is therefore limited and rationed.

Drawings produced on computer require more planning and foresight than was required of manual drafters just a short time ago. A CAD drawing requires an organized system of layering information based upon requirements for repetitive use. This organizational system must be adhered to relentlessly for easy and predictable retrieval and reuse of information. It requires an interest by the drafter in understanding how the software works and in finding the fastest and most efficient ways of doing things.

Becoming a competent, responsible designer requires, among other things, a well-founded knowledge of materials and of joining materials, a knowledge not commonly conveyed adequately in college. Time spent learning CAD often defers learning architecture–the acquired knowledge of how to put buildings together. Moreover, they must also master the subtleties of communicating their ideas graphically to people untrained in graphic communication, such as contractors and clients.

Learning CAD requires an investment in time by the individual and by the firm. Technology is advancing so rapidly that it is in the firm's best interest to hold lunchtime seminars in order to keep CAD users, and yourself, up to speed. It is also in the drafter's best interest to be knowledgeable in the use of the software and to share information so as to be able to meet deadlines. A continuing education effort from both parties is mutually beneficial.

By acknowledging the need for a training process and actively pursuing one, CAD can be mastered sooner, employees become productive sooner, and the learning of architecture and building construction can continue sooner.

Computers are Necessary to Remain Competitive in a Competitive World

Like it or not, computers are here to stay. Are you still typing letters and using carbon paper to make copies? The days of calling an engineering consultant to come and pick up information are over. Now, the modem accomplishes the task much more quickly. Computers and the associated software have progressed to the point where they will perform most aspects of the business of architecture better than the old methodology, provided of course, that the operator knows what (s)he is doing.

Despite prevailing opinions to the contrary, there is nothing to be gained by procrastinating. No matter what you buy, or when you buy it, it will be obsolete soon. Plan for it. Develop a stairstep progression for the computer's path out the office door. Remove the computer from its role as the 3D rendering workstation and make it the CAD workstation. From the CAD workstation transfer it to accounting and from accounting to word processing, then to personal organizer. Then sell or donate it out of your life.

This may not exactly be "planned obsolescence," but it is a fact of life. As hardware speed and power increase, software can become more powerful, and more powerful software requires more powerful hardware. Think about whether you need the capability that is offered in the upgrades for the software you have. Yet keep in mind that it may sometimes be desirable to upgrade your software even if you don't need the specific new capabilities because someday there will be a capability you do need. It may be easier to upgrade incrementally than in large chunks.

Invest in your own future now by learning how to use the computer.

- Keyboarding
- Macros
- Composing Correspondence
- Detail Libraries
- Computer Design

Decide What It Is You Do in Practicing Architecture that Could Be Improved, or Made Easier, or Done Faster if It were Done on a Computer

You must be comfortable with the notion that time you spend today learning how to use hardware and software will be repaid manyfold once you have become a moderately skilled user.

- Eventually, your ability to take *full advantage* of the potential a computer offers will save you a great deal of time, but this savings comes only after a substantial investment in training.
- If you commit to using a computer, you must also commit to learning the software well enough to know how it can be used to the benefit of an architectural practice; you must also develop the insight to see how the software can be customized (by using macros, script files, etc.) for your specific office.

You must have realistic expectations about using computers.

- The computer might not actually be the fastest way to accomplish a menial task when compared with traditional manual ways of accomplishing the same thing, but an appreciation for how computer use fits into the big picture may make it desirable to do this work on the computer anyway.

You must also be knowledgeable enough about the use of CAD to know how to short-circuit some of those things that seem to take longer. It may be productive for a project architect to make some redline corrections directly on the computer, or to create a special redline layer for the reviewer's notes.

- You should prepare yourself for great disappointment if you simply buy the hardware, buy the software, and then turn it over to a staff member with the admonition to "produce."

You may have to develop an appreciation for a new aesthetic, and let go of some of the things architects have traditionally valued over the years:
- The aesthetic appeal of a floor plan drawn freehand on a sheet of bumwad
- The appearance of a hand-crafted pen and ink drawing, or one done in colored pencil, or marker
- Being mindful of the things your client values, as opposed to your personal attraction to certain drawing media–things like better ways of visualizing the building; better because (s)he can see it from a wider variety of views, or see it depicted in a photo-realistic manner

PROPOSITION

Once you have bought into the value of using computers in your practice, how do you prepare yourself for success? Some decisions that should be made early:

Office layout
- space requirements— does CAD use require less space, or more?
- do you want to have a computer at every drafting station (on the assumption that eventually, all of your drawing will be accomplished on computer)?
- do you want to isolate computers in an environmentally controlled room (on the assumption that you will have CAD drafters working on CAD, and designers in another room not working on CAD, or designers sharing CAD stations)
- lighting
- ergonomic workstation design (computer-induced physical ailments are very real)

Who will be using computers, and for what purposes?
- Principals or partners, for access to accounting and personnel records, or for marketing and project correspondence
- Designers, for creating, developing, and communicating design concepts
- CAD drafters (for drafting working drawings?)
- Job Captains (perhaps for the same thing, or for designing and drafting details?)
- Project Architects (perhaps for writing owner correspondence, or meeting minutes, or scheduling tasks on a project?)
- Support staff (for word processing?)
- Marketers (for preparing proposals, brochures, and other promotional handouts?)
- Accounting and bookkeeping staff (for accounting and bookkeeping, and tracking job costs?)

How much of your work do you want to do on computer, and how much will be done the traditional ways?
- What do your current or future clients want to have done on computer?

How much responsibility are you willing to accept for your consultants in coordinating with your system, and your CAD standards? How much information are you going to provide for them, and how much will they be expected to generate from files you provide for them?
- Make your intentions clear up front

Will you be content with a micro-station (PC) system, or do you want something more powerful (and more expensive)?

What platform suits you– DOS, Windows, Sigma, Macintosh?

What software suits you– AutoCAD, CADvance, etc.?

What software are your consultants using, and is it a consideration for choosing your software?
- Do you want to choose the software that best accommodates the way you practice, even if it is obscure? Or, might you want to choose software that is very popular, knowing that it will be easier to find new staff already familiar with it?

Will you buy, lease, or rent equipment?

What can you do with obsolete equipment?
- You may find that the hardware required for CAD use is much more powerful than you need for other applications. You might plan a phased implementation program to use equipment that is obsolete for CAD for less intensive uses, such as word processing, spreadsheets, etc.

What forms of output will you need to accomplish the above tasks, and how will you communicate with other members of the team, both in-house and out-of-house?
- The "paperless" or virtual office is a virtual fantasy for architects; rather than diazo printing updated versions of each drawing, the drawings must first be replotted every time an update is required, and then it probably needs to be diazo printed for distribution to team members
- You may want to consider having yourself and your staff call up drawings directly on the computer for review
- Do you want to do your own in-house plotting, or rely on a service bureau?

- Laser printers for letter or legal size
- Color printers for marketing pieces
- Do you want to be able to transmit electronic versions of files via phone lines using a modem?
- Be sure you understand the implications of plotting, printing, and transmitting files as you begin to plan the work and organize the drawings; each project should be planned, both internally and with out-of-house consultants, to coordinate file naming, title blocks, layering, entity combinations (blocks), plotting, file transfer, etc. CAD has changed the approach to creating a drawing; no longer is a drawing made up of solely lines; while drawings are still built of gridlines, columns, perimeter walls, interior walls, etc., drawings are also made up of "entities," or "assemblies of lines," or duplicated elements, modified elements, etc.; this offers great flexibility in manipulating drawing elements, and the potential for greater accuracy (while making unnecessary accuracy necessary).

How do you want to store files and retrieve them?
- Do you want all members of the office to have ready access to files via a network?
- Do you want each workstation to function as a stand alone station?
- What kind of archival storage and retrieval systems do you feel comfortable with, and what systems might be required by your clients?
- What can you do to anticipate the future? What software will you be using in 15–20 years? What hardware? Will current storage media survive the legal records retention period stated in the statute of limitations, uncorrupted and undamaged?

What level of qualifications and expertise do you need to keep a system like the one you need functioning?
- Do you need staff trained to manage the system, or will you hire this work done when you need it done (or within 24–48 hours of when you need it done)
- Do you need a full or part-time computer manager to handle all of these issues?
- The communications environment will be much more technological and more complicated that before–the firm's owners must get involved and be somewhat knowledgeable about how to use the computer and the software; a hands-off approach will lead to disaster and possible financial ruin

Will you do training in-house, hire a trainer, send employees to technical training classes, or require that they find their own ways to get themselves trained?
- Will you pay for employee training?
- How will you evaluate the computer skills of prospective employees?

Standardizing the office use of CAD
- File naming

- layering
- line colors and pen weights
- degree of accuracy to be used
- using the same drawing to show large and small scale versions
- using attributes to create a database
- text styles
- symbols libraries
- materials indications— should some traditional poché be changed to allow it to be done by CAD?

Should packaged software be customized or should office standards be changed?

Use of CAD with others outside the office
- compatibility with other CAD software used by clients or consultants
- compatibility with other CAD hardware used by clients or consultants
- compatibility with service bureaus for plotting services
- compatibility for use by contractors and subcontractors for bidding or estimating purposes

POSTSCRIPT

Determine what the firm's policy is going to be on requiring (or not) employees to invest in their own futures to get themselves trained in the use of the computer and various software capabilities. It's not unusual for an applicant to be hired on the condition that they come into the office on their own time to learn CAD or word processing. Once proficient, they are then allowed to use CAD during office hours. Lunchtime seminars can also help not only to train new people but keep current users up to speed as well.

Determine what the firm's policy is going to be regarding compensation for CAD trained employees. An office may decide to develop a separate classification for CAD operators, somewhere between a drafter and a senior drafter, with its own job description and pay scale. New employees may start out in a drafting position until such time as they are able to prove themselves proficient at CAD operations.

Be sure you understand the implications of an agreement with a client to translate your CAD files into another software format. Communication between different softwares is possible but not always easy. Many of the time-saving techniques you had used in creating the drawing, such as layering, blocks, cross referencing, attributes, etc., are not directly translatable.

Take the time to generate macros to relabel or regroup information after it has been translated. Redoing layering and line weights to match a certain standard can be accomplished faster through using a macro, instead of changing each individual bit of information separately.

Clients who have a facilities management program and a computer format of their own can be accommodated quite easily if the requirements are known in advance. Translation can be planned for, macros developed, and work accomplished quickly. Not planning ahead will be an unorganized headache and can cost time and money.

Architects should support copyright laws. Most software enables the program to be run on one computer only. Additional computers will require additional licenses. All of your employees know this! Laying people off, or even outright firings are very unpleasant experiences, which could be made even more so by a visit from the software police. Some companies sell licenses for 1–5 computers, 10–15, 15–30, and so on. Check with each software company as to their policy. As creative professionals, we should be especially sensitive to software piracy, analogous to our clients' using our working drawings to build the same building all over the country. Usually, the cost of software is recovered many times over by time saved, but even if it isn't, even if you think the software is overpriced (as much CAD software seems to be), if you want to use it, bite the bullet and pay the money

Keep in mind that every computer in the office does not need every possible type of software. A CAD workstation will work just fine with word processing, CAD, and modem software only. Utilities programs are useful for data recovery and troubleshooting, some of the most recent disk operating systems have included these as part of their package.

Every drafter has, at one time or another, kept a file of common details they had drawn that they felt might be used again someday. How many times have you drawn a roof drain detail? How many times have you stickybacked a roof drain detail? These files usually move with the drafter from office to office, providing a quick reference in getting a job out on time.

What is your firm's policy regarding employee use of your standard details? Do you feel that this violates your copyright? Some things to consider in formulating a policy may include:

Who actually drew the detail? Did you or was it copied from someone else's work?

Is this detail an industry standard or is it a product of extensive research, a very specialized and unique design?

Who financed the creation of this detail? Was it drawn on company time? On company equipment?

Was this detail part of a commercially marketed package? Who purchased it and do they have permission to use it?

The same policy should be considered regarding specifications, who authored them and who typed them?

How will your office manage standard detail libraries? Leaving it up to the individual drafter or even project architect does not seem to generate much use. Management specifically requesting to be shown exactly which details will be utilized in a project will create usage. Management requesting to be shown which details will be added to the library after the completion of a project will keep the detail library updated.

Determine the firm's policy on billing (or not) for use of the computer. Somehow the overhead expense of acquiring computer hardware and software must be recovered. Sometimes it may be factored into billable rates for users and tracked as a cost of the job, or sometimes computer time is billed separately. If you are renting computer equipment, are you going to invoice for it, and are you going to apply a mark-up?

You should be familiar with how other architects in your area are doing it so that you can remain competitive with them.

Develop a policy on whether to bill for CAD plots. CAD plots are going to be a cost of doing business; the more equipment you have and the more knowledge-able your staff is, the fewer plots you will have to run. Are you going to bill the plots individually as a reimbursable, in the same fashion as blueprinting?

Determine how much freedom you will allow to individual drafters to customize their individual computers? Don't shut yourself out from new ideas or quicker ways of getting things done. You will probably want them to know and use your office software, not what they had been using, so as to maintain a continuity in production documents. Will every drafter have their own workstation or will workstations be used by all?

Project managers and project architects have as much need to view drawings and make comments or minor corrections as drafters do. They also use the computer for product research, developing details, sketching, correspondence, scheduling, and estimating.

PRACTICE

Develop a written policy statement on the use of electronic data by clients, contractors, and subcontractors.

Policies protecting your work or stipulating certain uses and restrictions should be spelled out in the Owner/Architect agreement. Article 6 of the A.I.A. Document B141 states specifically what the use of the Architect's Drawings, Specifications, and other Documents shall be. Nevertheless, the typical owner is more interested in deriving the greatest benefit from services that have already been paid for, and is vulnerable to contractor claims that there is money to be saved by preparing shop drawings from the architect's CAD drawings. And, let's face it: When push comes to shove, it is the rare architect who will risk a commission over this issue. So it would be prudent if you prepared yourself for this eventuality. You should consult an attorney to identify specific legal concepts that must be addressed in a cover letter you prepare to accompany the diskettes you give to an owner or a contractor. Some issues to consider and include in such a letter follow:

- Include a statement that the information is being provided at the request of the owner
- Identify the specific drawings which are being included
- Explain your understanding of how the drawings are to be used
- Include an admonishment that the computer files included are instruments of the architect's service, and that the information contained on them is subject to change, particularly when the project is not yet built
- Include a statement that it is expressly understood by the recipient that the owner/contractor/subcontractors use the information at their own risk, and that you are offering no guarantee that the information provided represents the final coordinated design solution
- Include a statement acknowledging your trust that the recipient recognizes the potential difficulties, problems, and opportunity for error inherent in the use of computer generated and stored data
- Indicate your understanding that the recipient accepts full responsibility for the use, application, and handling of all computer data provided to him or her
- Express a requirement that the recipient conduct his or her own confirmation of any field conditions which may be reflected in the data provided, and that (s)he assumes all responsibility for any deviations between the data provided, the final design, and the existing field conditions
- Indicate that the drawings were not prepared in anticipation of using them for preparing shop drawings, and therefore you cannot warrant that they are suitable for that use
- Indicate that traditionally, shop drawings are drawings, diagrams, schedules, or other data prepared by the contractor, a subcontractor, a manufacturer, a supplier, or a distributor to illustrate some portion of the work relating specifically to this particular project
- Indicate that the information required in shop drawings may be based on construction tolerances and coordination requirements that will remain within the domain of the contractor
- Indicate that the organization and arrangement of the drawings, including electronic layering methodology shall have no bearing on how the work may be divided among subcontractors, or in establishing the extent of the work to be performed by any trade
- Indicate that the contractor shall remain responsible for any acts and omissions of the contractor's employees, subcontractors, or other persons performing work under contract to the contractor
- Indicate that the contractor is responsible for carrying out the work in accordance with the contract documents
- Indicate that, by submitting shop drawings, the contractor has determined and verified materials, field measurements, and field construction criteria, and has checked and coordinated the information contained within such submittals with the requirements of the work and the contract documents

- Indicate that the contractor is not relieved of responsibility for deviations from the contract documents, or for errors or omissions in the shop drawings or other submittals as a result of having prepared the submittals using the architect's electronic data
- Indicate the purposes for which the electronic data may be used, and limit permission for its use to those uses specifically stated
- Indicate that the use and application of this data requires special training, knowledge, and experience, and that the architect has no control over the manner in which the recipient may use the data

Develop a written policy statement on in-house backing up of electronic files.

At the end of each day, each drawing file should be backed up onto disk or tape, depending on the system being used in your office. If you are using a network and backing up onto tape, you can set the system parameters to do this automatically. If you are backing up onto tape or disk without a network, choose a consistent time frame each day to do this. Once a day is not too frequent, and would mean that a maximum of one day's effort is all that would be lost in the event of the original file being lost or destroyed. If you are using the floppy diskette method, be sure the entire file fits on the disk. Use one disk per file. If the file is too large for a single disk, compress the file using appropriate software.

The project architect or CAD manager should organize subdirectories for the project on the computer to make locating files easy. Files should be backed up to directories on a tape with the same directory name, or one file per disk. A box of active backup files should be created for each job.

If you are working in an office without a network, more than one "original" can exist. Therefore, work on any one file only after you have determined that you have the current version of the file. This may mean that you have to update the box of backup disks for a particular job each time a drawing file is edited.

The project architect or CAD manager should create two backup copies of all drawings, specifications, and project correspondence at least once each week. One copy should be kept off site. Backup copies could be overwritten at the end of each month; keep one copy for archival purposes off site. This backup procedure should be used for all non-project files also.

Develop a written policy statement on screening foreign diskettes for viruses.

A virus check should be run on all diskettes received from consultants and other outside sources prior to copying any information to the hard drive of any local computer. Special software is available for this purpose.

No games of any kind are to be played on or loaded onto company computer equipment. Diskettes being used to transfer information from home computers or computers containing video games shall be checked for viruses prior to transferring information to company computers.

Develop a written policy statement on records retention.

Refer to the Records Retention Schedule in Part Two of this manual for specific information about storage of computer files.

A copy of the CAD software, the DOS software, and word processing software should be archived as well.

A mylar hard copy of all drawings and a bound hard copy of the specifications should be archived.

Drawings, Specs, and Files should be archived using the "copy" command and not the "backup" command.

Develop a written policy statement about what consultants can expect in the way of electronic media for their use as backgrounds.

- What platform will the media be created in?
  - DOS, Windows, Macintosh, Sigma, or something else?

- What software will be used to generate the media?
  - AutoCAD, CADvance, or something else?

- What size and density of diskettes will you be using to transfer your files?

Develop a prospective employee evaluation questionnaire.

- What CAD software are you proficient in?
  (not, how many programs have you dabbled in)

- What word processing software are you proficient in?

- What type of hardware are you familiar with?
  (Macintosh, IBM, UNIX, OS2, MSDOS, etc.)

- How did you learn CAD? School? Self- taught? On the job?
  (How motivated is this candidate? Does this candidate know the quickest way to do things on CAD? How much hand-holding and spoon-feeding will this candidate require?)

- Have you ever trained others in CAD? who, where, when?
  (Can this candidate teach others? Will this candidate contribute to office knowledge?)

- What macros have you written?
  (Can this candidate help customize the software to the way I want things done?)

- Can you load software?
  (Could this candidate troubleshoot a faulty computer? or faulty software?)

- Describe an ideal workstation.
  (Does this candidate work with all the lights off while the rest of your staff wants the lights on? Will this candidate be comfortable with less than custom designed surroundings?)

- What office CAD Standards have you seen work? not work?
  (What are other offices doing to solve the same problems I'm having? Are my standards any good?)

- If you have questions, what do you do?

Develop an Employee CAD Exam, to help impart an understanding of the need for continued training.

- What Macros do you use most often? What do they do?

- How do you find a file when you know its name but not its directory?

- Explain how to globally change all the text in a drawing to the same style and size.

- Explain how to insert a drawing of a different scale. How to cross reference.

- Explain how to add command options to the mouse buttons with Shift, Alternate, and Control keys.

- Which method of entry is quickest, keyboard or pull-down menu selection? Explain.

- How do you reduce image regeneration time?

- How do you create a new layer? Choose its name, color, and linetype.

- Why use layering?

- Why use Blocks (defined groups of information)?

Computerization

- How do you insert text from a word processor into your drawing?

- When did you last use an attribute and why?

- What do you do if your drawing file is too large to fit onto a diskette?

- How was your last project organized on CAD? In the course of the project were changes easy to make? Made quickly?

- How does producing a drawing in CAD differ from producing a drawing in pen and pencil?

JOB DESCRIPTIONS

We have prepared these Job Descriptions to provide staff members with a general understanding of some of the basic activities they will be engaged in on a day-to-day basis in performing their work. These descriptions are general by intent, and there will be many activities more minor or specific in nature that each staff member will be asked or expected to do during the course of an average work day. While it would be counterproductive to list them here, they are summarized by the basic statement that we want to encourage everyone to contribute in whatever capacity and at whatever level is required to help finish our work and meet out schedules. We hope to achieve a spirit of cooperation among all our staff members who then feel directed toward improving the ultimate service we provide to our clients without imposing on staff members the limitations of specified tasks. With that in mind, the general functions of each job in this section are as follows:

PRINCIPAL-IN-CHARGE

The Principal-in-Charge is responsible for overseeing of the administrative and technical functions of a variety of projects.

- *Project Management:* prepares proposals, negotiates fees, writes agreements, and follows through with execution of agreements; establishes initial guidelines for monitoring project status with Controller, and oversees scheduling and staffing; monitors project status weekly with Project Architect and Controller; monitor payments from monthly Accounts Receivable, and follow-up with clients at 30-, 45-, and 60-day intervals; helps Bookkeeper in preparation of monthly billings.

- *Project Design and Production:* responsible for Owner rapport and satisfaction; responsible for initiation and creation of planning and design concepts for selected projects and for formulation of design team; provides input and decisions for design team on a daily basis or as required; reviews construction documents for general compliance with design concept, good building practice, and government regulations; signs construction documents after review is complete.

- *Bidding/Negotiations:* oversees the work of the Project Architect.

- *Contract Administration:* reviews and approves architectural and consultants field reports; makes final walk-through with Project Architect; does follow-up with clients to evaluate design team performance.

PROJECT ARCHITECT

The Project Architect is responsible for the overall coordination and direction of one or more architectural projects to which he/she has been assigned by the Principals, and is responsible for the day-to-day success of the project. In some cases, the Principal-in-Charge may also serve as the Project Architect.

- *Project Management:* Responsible for overall administrative execution for all phases of assigned projects.

- *Project Profitability:* primary responsibility for budgeting, scheduling, and project implementation planning; makes adjustment in scheduling and/or scope (detail) of work as Principal deems necessary to respond to deficiencies.

- *Scheduling and Staffing:* responsible for directing the activities of the project personnel, scheduling, and office labor budget; works with Controller to monitor project status, and conveys problems to Principal.

- *Communications:* responsible for day-to-day communications with the Owner, the Consultants, and Government Agencies; involves the Principal-in-Charge when necessary.

- *Project Design and Production:* assists Principal with development of design concept and synthesis; initiates and directs basic building systems and design details; directs preparation of presentation materials; coordinates outline specifications; approves selections of materials, colors, and finishes. Monitors, controls, and directs all project activities, including those of the Project Designer and Job Captain; responsible for completeness and accuracy of construction documents and coordination with other disciplines; responsible for maintaining team harmony; directs technical level design staff. Makes detailed review of final drawings and specifications; obtains Principal's review and signature on drawings.

- *Bidding/Negotiation:* assists Principal; answers inquiries from bidders and coordinates issuance of Addenda.

- *Contract Administration:* administers or supervises the administration of construction contracts; performs or assigns site observations, prepares observation reports, and maintains communications with Project Manager and Superintendent; coordinates checking of shop drawings and other submittals; coordinates the predation of Proposal Requests, Change Orders, Certificates of Payment, Construction Change Authorizations, and Supplemental Instructions; provides feedback to design team on problems encountered in the field.

The Job Captain is responsible for the day-to-day non-administrative success of the project.

- *Scheduling and Staffing*: assists the Project Architect to monitor project status, scheduling, and the activities of the project personnel.

- *Communications*: assists Project Architect in communications and documentation of meetings with the Owner, the Consultants, and Government Agencies.

- *Project Design and Production*: responsible for the development and preparation of Design Development and Construction Documents for assigned projects; researches new materials, colors, finishes; acquires catalogs, and indexes technical documents and materials samples specific to project; prepares code check and secures interpretations and documentation from Government Agencies. Initiates and develops technical level design concepts and details, and is responsible for directing the technical level design team; shares responsibility with Project Architect for construction document completeness and accuracy; reviews and coordinates specifications with construction drawings; makes detailed review of final drawings and specifications; coordinates in-house and out-of-house reprographic services, and advises technical staff on reprographic techniques suitable for specific applications.

- *Bidding/Negotiation*: assists Project Architect in answering inquiries from bidders and prepares addenda.

- *Contract Administration*: checks shop drawings and other submittals and maintains submittal records; makes site observation visits with Project Architect and assists in preparation of documentation.

Roster

The following roster is a listing of the names and addresses for all of the members of the firm. This information has been provided for your convenience, in the event that you find it necessary to conduct project-related business with other members of your team who may be out of the office and at home, due to illness or other reason.

This information is confidential. Please respect this confidentiality and the right to privacy of your fellow employees.

(Insert your office standard roster here)

Distribution List

The following list can be used as a reference to keep track of the members of the firm at any given time, and the page can be copied and names highlighted in order to use the list as a distribution list. Firm members are grouped according to whether the individual is a partner, an associate, a technical staff member, or a support staff member.

(Insert your office standard list of staff members for use
as a distribution list)

Task Assignments

We have discovered many technical and operational tasks which must be attended to in order for the office to function smoothly. These tasks are divided among all members of the staff, and those assignments are recorded here for your reference. This list will remind you of your personal assignment and will provide a reference for you to go to when you need assistance in a particular area of our operations.

For certain tasks, such as the flat files and dead storage, the intention is for the assigned individuals to serve as facilitators. They will help familiarize you with the procedures, but you should not expect them to be your servants and do the work for you.

Task Assignments
Continued

(Insert your office standard list of tasks
and assignments here)

JOB NUMBER REQUEST FORM

The job number request form is to be completed by the Project Architect, if it has not already been done by the Principal in Charge, or the Marketing Department. The job number request form provides essential information to the accounting department, which they need in order to log in time sheet data, and to produce billing and job tracking data. Even if you do not know all of the information requested on the form, complete as much of it as you can.

Blank copies of this form may be found in the bins in the support staff area.

JOB NUMBER REQUEST FORM

New Project   Yes   No

Proposal   Yes   No

Project Name: _____   Date Started: _____

Client Name: _____

Address: _____   Project Number: _____

_____

_____   Partner Responsible for Billing: _____

_____   Project Architect: _____

Contact Name: _____

Phone Number: _____   Project Kick-off Meeting Scheduled for: _____

_____

Project Description: _____

_____   Other Pertinent Information: _____

_____   _____

_____   _____

_____   _____

_____   _____

Type of Fee: _____   _____

_____

_____

_____

Consultants: _____

_____

_____

_____

_____

_____

_____

_____

_____

_____

_____

_____

_____

_____

Job Numbers List

Use this list to make sure you know the correct number (including any applicable decimals) for recording time on your time sheet.

This list is updated periodically, so make sure you have a current list here in this book.

Job Numbers List
Continued

(Insert your office standard list of job numbers here)

Standard Letter Format

More and more of you will be creating letters on the computer using word processing software. As you begin to learn the capability of the software, you may find it desirable to simply enter your text, save it according to the standard naming conventions, and then have a member of the support staff apply standard formatting conventions.

However, as your skill on the computers increases, you will find that most formatting conventions can be handled automatically, and that you will want to enter your text according to those conventions. When you do, you should comply with the following letter format to make sure that all of our correspondence conforms to the same standards and conventions.

(Insert your office standard letter format here)

Standard Naming Conventions

STANDARD NAMING CONVENTIONS FOR DOS FILES

We have learned that we need to conform with certain naming conventions for the documents we create on computers. As more and more of us begin to create our own documents, the need becomes increasingly more important.

In order to properly name your documents, you will need to be familiar with some DOS conventions, and the directories and paths that DOS uses for storing and retrieving files. Each project has a word processing directory set up in the file server, using the project number. *All word processing document names begin with that number,* regardless of the type of document it may be. All document types are identified by a three-character suffix, as well. The document types we use commonly, and the appropriate suffixes, are shown below.

DOS allows four additional characters in the name, which follow the job number, and precede the suffix. For items such as letters, memos, and tables, for which long-term, sequential numbering over the course of the job is not necessary, the suffix designates the document type and the daily sequence number; for example:

A letter created for the Trump Tower, job number 9400, would begin with the job number: 9400. The suffix for a letter is LTR, so the suffix, which is separated from the first eight characters of the name by a period, is .LTR. The four remaining characters in the name are used to indicate the date. Use two numerals for the month, and two for the day. Do not be concerned about indicating the year, which is done automatically by the computer, and does not need to be part of the naming convention. Therefore, the name for a letter created on September 18 for the Trump Tower would be:

94000918.LTR

The second letter created that day would be named 94000918.LT2, and the third would be 94000918.LT3.

Other document types that can be numbered using a numerical sequence which can be renewed daily are:

Letter   94000918.**LTR** (LT2, LT3, etc.)
Memo   94000918.**MEM** (MM1, MM2, MM3, etc.)
Report   94000918.**RPT** (RP2, etc.)

Table	94000918.**TBL** (TB2, etc.)
Table of Contents	**TOC**
Action Items	94000918.**AI**
Chart	94000918.**CHT** (CT2, etc.)
Agenda	94000918.**AGD** (AG2, etc.)
Transmittal	94000918.**TRN** (TR2, etc.)

When naming project-related documents, do not use your initials as the suffix; this will defeat the sorting capability of the computer and make it very difficult to retrieve documents of a similar type. Similarly, don't make up your own suffixes for document types that do not appear here. Go to someone on the support staff and help determine what the new suffix needs to be so that it can be added to this list.

Other types of documents recur throughout the course of a project, and should be named and numbered so that the document type and its place in a long-term sequence can be readily determined. For example, meeting minutes, supplemental instructions, addenda, proposal requests, and the like should be part of a numerical sequence that continues for the duration of the job.

Some document types and the accompanying suffixes are as follows:

Meeting Minutes	9400**01.MIN**
Architectural Supplemental Instructions	9400**01.ASI**
Addendum	9400**01.ADD**
Field Report	9400**01.FR**
Proposal Request	9400**01.PR**
Construction Change Authorization	9400**01.CCA**
Change Order	9400**01.CO**

STANDARD BOOKLET COVERS

The following cover design and format should be used for all documents in booklet form. This applies to specifications booklets for all phases of the project, detail booklets, programming booklets, reports, and the like.

Use the square for a client logo, or a sketch of the project, or some other graphic device to help personalize the booklet.

If a more customized piece is desired, use the first inside page for this purpose.

Name of Client, Company, or Institution

Use a Company logo or an image of the project here

Allow slightly more margin along the left edge for binding

Title of the Submittal

NAME OF PROJECT

Date

Submitted by:
Name of Firm

Memorandum Format

Please use the attached Memo form for all in-house memos. Memos should not be used to communicate with firms or individuals outside the firm.

MEMORANDUM

To:

From:

Date:

Re:

Time Sheets

Time sheets are due on the first and sixteenth of every month. If those dates fall in the middle of the week, end your records on those dates and begin a new sheet for the balance of the week.

(Insert your office standard time sheet here)

PROJECT KICK-OFF MEETING AGENDA

The attached Project Kick-Off Meeting Agenda should be used at the kick-off meeting at the beginning of every project. It would be most useful and time-conserving to preview the items on this agenda, and come to the meeting with answers or proposals which can be discussed at the meeting.

The kick-off meeting should be conducted by the Project Architect.

The purpose of the kick-off meeting is to make specific administrative and management decisions at the beginning of the project, for the benefit of all the members of the team. There are certain issues which are of primary importance:

- *Getting the necessary input at the appropriate times from the design principals.*

- *Planning the interior design effort.* The Interior Design Manager should also be informed of the meeting, and the strategy for incorporating interior design input should be discussed and decided at the meeting. The Project Architect should have an idea in mind for making this work for the needs of the project.

- *Planning the team structure.* The Project Architect should organize the team in the most efficient and productive manner possible. This should be considered in advance of the meeting, and presented at the meeting for discussion. Every member of the team must know exactly what is expected of him or her, and it should be spelled out at this meeting.

- *Planning the use of CAD.* Each team must have a CAD Captain. The CAD strategy and goals should be discussed in advance of the meeting, and presented for discussion.

- *Understanding the project schedule, including milestone dates.* Make sure this is discussed and clearly understood.

- *Attending to the administrative matters required for the project.*

Project Data

Project Name:

Job Numbers and phases:

Owner:

Owner's Address:

Project Location:

Type of Fee:

Project Goals

What are our objectives for the project?

How does the project fit into the big picture (What are our primary motives for doing the work... to get a design award, to learn a new project type, to make a good profit)?

Administrative Issues

Responsibility for overall records management:

Time records and amount of detail:

File coding and File Codes list:

Support staff assignment:

General Issues

Directing Principal:

Principal-in-Charge/Managing Principal:

Project Architect:

Job Captain:

Other members of the team:

Grouping of the team and seating assignments:

Roles and Responsibilities:

Owner/architect agreement:

Owner/client contact:

Owner/client correspondence:

Consultant agreements:

Consultant coordination:

Billing:

Staffing projections:

Cash flow projections:

Budget and schedule monitoring:

Meeting agendas and minutes:

Telephone log:

Progress reports:

Specifications:

Documents checking:

Code research:

Consultants:

Civil:

Structural:

Mechanical:

Electrical:

Cost estimating:

Specifications:

Lighting:

Acoustical:

Food service:

Elevator:

Landscape:

Other:

Other:

Other:

Scope of Work:

Schedule:

Delivery Method: (bid—negotiated—design/build—CM/GC)

Deliverables (model, rendering, CDs, etc.):

Budget:

Anticipated schedule for team meetings:
- Internal team meetings:
- External team meetings:

Design Process

Conceptual design review with Design Principals:

Interface with Director of Design:

Approach to interior design:

How will input from the Partner-in-Charge be handled:

Owner Review Process

Documentation Process

Owner approvals and sign-offs:

Interface with Director of Quality Control:

Use of office standards:

Consultant conformance with office graphic standards:

Approach to specifications:

Use of CAD:

Standard location of subject matter:

Anticipated future use of the drawings for use as presentation drawings, awards submittals, brochure, etc.?

Standard List of File Codes

The following list of file codes has been developed and refined over many years of use. Please conform to the codes used on this list, but keep in mind some considerations that will guide its use:

This list of file codes should be used as a master list. That is, not every project will require the use of every file code number.

The size and complexity of the project will dictate the complexity of the file codes needed. You will see that the file codes are hierarchical. A small project may use only the first level in the hierarchy of codes. Some file categories may require additional detail, and additional levels may be added for these categories without using this level of detail throughout.

Remember that needless files simply take up space and make retrieval much more difficult. When in doubt, choose the least complex approach. Additional levels can always be added later if the files are becoming too large, or more detail is desired.

The Project Architect should oversee the file coding process for all project files. Each item to be filed should be stamped "FILE COPY". The job name and the file code should appear next to this stamp. Once the code has been added, the item should be placed in the "TO BE FILED" bin, in the appropriate slot for the job. Support staff will take it from there and make sure it gets into the proper file. If you want extra copies of any documents at your desk, please be sure to stamp them "DUPLICATE", so there will be no confusion about whether a document should be in the central files or not.

If additional files are needed, make sure you let the support staff member who has been assigned to your team know.

Job Name:
Job Number:

Master File Code Categories

PHASE: SCHEMATIC DESIGN, DESIGN DEVELOPMENT, DOCUMENTATION

DD.AA	**TRANSMITTALS**
DD.A1	Outgoing Transmittals
DD.A2	Incoming Transmittals
DD.B	**CORRESPONDENCE AND DATA**
DD.B11	OWNER
DD.B22	CONSULTANTS
DD.B2a	Structural
DD.B2b	Mechanical
DD.B2c	Electrical
DD.B2d	Civil
DD.B2e	Landscape
DD.B2f	Soils
DD.B2g	Elevator
DD.B2h	Lighting
DD.B2i	Acoustical
DD.B2j	Interior Design
DD.B2k	Cost Control
DD.B2l	Other (Provide name as applicable)
DD.B3	**GOVERNING AGENCIES/SUBMITTALS (miscellaneous)**
DD.B3a	Planning
DD.B3b	Zoning
DD.B3c	Building
DD.B3d	Engineering
DD.B3e	Fire Department
DD.B3f	Other (Provide name as applicable)
DD.B4	**CONTRACTOR (miscellaneous)**
DD.B4a	Contractor Correspondence and Communications
DD.B5	**AFFECTED THIRD PARTIES**
DD.B6	**OWNERS CONSULTANTS**
DD.B6a	Project Manager
DD.B6b	Architectural
	Other (Provide name as applicable)

DD.C	**PROJECT DATA (miscellaneous)**
DD.C1	Production Organization—General Administrative
DD.C1a	Mock sets
DD.C1b	Schedules, Work Assignments, Budgets
DD.C1c	CAD
DD.C1d	Notation Lists
DD.C1e	Submittal Requirements, Applications
DD.C1f	Other (memos to staff)
DD.C1g	Progress Reports
DD.C2	**MEETINGS, AGENDAS, MINUTES—GENERAL**
DD.C2a	Owner
DD.C2b	Consultants (Project Team)
DD.C2c	Governing Agencies
DD.C2d	Contractor
DD.C33.	**BUILDING AND ARCHITECTURAL DATA (miscellaneous)**
DD.C3a	Code Review
DD.C3b	Program
DD.C3c	Site Data
DD.C3d	Parking
DD.C3e	Elevators
DD.C3f	Photographs
DD.C3g	Area Calculations
DD.C4	**ESTIMATES, QUOTATIONS, COST CONTROL**
DD.C5	**SPECIFICATION DATA (miscellaneous)**
DD.C5a	Specifications Sections
DD.C5b	Product Literature and Data
DD.C5c	Manufacturer's Correspondence
DD.C6	**TELEPHONE RECORD/JOB LOG**
DD.C7	**LEGAL DOCUMENTS**
DD.C8	**HEARINGS**
DD.C9	**SUBMITTALS**
DD.C10	**SUBMITTAL REQUIREMENTS, APPLICATIONS, SCHEDULES**
DD.C11	**PLANNING DATA (CODE REVIEW AND BACK-UP)**
DD.C12	**BOOKLETS**

PHASE: BIDDING NEGOTIATION

BN.C   **PROJECT DATA**

BN.C12   **REGISTER OF BID DOCUMENTS**

BN.C13   **CONTRACTORS INQUIRES**
BN.C13a   Inquiries
BN.C13b   Requests for Approvals of Substitutions
BN.C13c   Approvals and Substitutions Log

BN.C14   **ADDENDA**

PHASE: CONTRACT ADMINISTRATION

CA.CC.   **PROJECT DATA (miscellaneous)**

CA.C15   **SHOP DRAWINGS AND SAMPLES LOG**

CA.C16   **SHOP DRAWINGS FILE**

CA.C17   **INFORMATION REQUESTS**

CA.C18   **SUPPLEMENTAL INSTRUCTIONS AND LOG**

CA.C19   **PROPOSAL REQUESTS AND LOG**

CA.C20   **CONSTRUCTION CHANGE AUTHORIZATIONS AND LOG**

CA.C21   **CHANGE ORDERS AND LOG**

CA.C22   **REQUESTS FOR APPROVALS OF SUBSTITUTIONS**
CA.C22a   Substitution Log

CA.C23   **REQUEST FOR PAYMENT**

CA.C24   **FIELD REPORTS**
CA.C24a   Architectural
CA.C24b   Structural
CA.C24c   Mechanical
CA.C24d   Electrical
CA.C24e   Other

CA.C25   **TEST REPORTS**
CA.C25a   Concrete
CA.C25b   Welding
CA.C25c   Soils
CA.C25d   Other

CA.C26   CONSTRUCTION PROGRESS SCHEDULES

CA.C27   **PROJECT CLOSEOUT**
CA.C27a   Punchlists, etc.
CA.C27b   Project Closeout Schedules

CA.C28   **PHOTOGRAPHS (and Negatives)**

Progress Reports

Each month, the Project Architect should prepare a progress report to accompany the billing. It should conform to the format shown on the following page.

Project Name:

Architect's Project Number:
Date:
For the period from:

1. **Current status of the project and schedule**

2. **Information/action needed (outstanding decisions/information required from the client)**

3. **Actual or anticipated problem areas**

This report summarizes the status of the work for the above project. Please review it and make note of any items which may concern you, or which may require a response or action from you.

126

Meeting Etiquette

Sometimes, as we get busier and busier, it is easy to overlook some of the basic courtesy that is so important to having productive meetings. Here are some reminders:

1. **Write down your appointments:**

   - Keep your calendar with you, and write down appointments on the spot. Do not rely on your memory to do it later. You'll forget.
   - Make sure you reserve the Conference Room.

2. **Be punctual.**
   - In business, there is no such thing as being "stylishly late."
   - Wait for the other guy if you must, but do not make him or her wait for you.
   - Take some work with you in case you need to kill time. Plan to do some correspondence, or keynotes, or spec sections, or something.
   - Observe this courtesy for everyone, not just clients. This means consultants, other people from our own office, even sales people.
   - Start on time, even if it means starting before everyone shows up.

3. **Prepare an agenda.**
   - Have a clear purpose in mind for the meeting, and be sure you need a meeting to achieve it.
   - Inform everyone who needs to be there of the time and place. Give each of them as much notice as possible. Let them know what issues on the agenda they should be prepared to address.
   - If someone else calls the meeting, find out what *you* should be prepared to discuss.
   - Publish the agenda and distribute copies to everyone who attends.
   - Try to limit the number of people (4-6).
   - Don't invite anyone who doesn't need to be there, but be sure to send them minutes.

4. **Take notes.**
   - Select a team member to take good notes. Use a copy of the agenda as an outline. Record the names, company, and telephone number of everyone there. Also, record the topic of discussion, any decisions made, and any follow-up necessary. Make sure the person responsible for the follow-up is clearly identified.

5. **Be prepared**
   - Make sure you have any prints you will need, and decide whether they should be tacked up or laid out on the table.
   - Have enough chairs placed in the Conference Room.

6. **Don't let yourself be interrupted**
   - Don't take telephone calls, even if it is long distance. As soon as one person takes a call, everyone else does too. You will never recapture the momentum you lose by doing this.

7. **Schedule meetings at optimum times**
   - Monday mornings and Friday afternoons are the worst. Mornings are best. Try for an hour to an hour and half before lunch, so you will have a natural ending.

8. **Keep yourself focused**
   - Don't get off on tangents that are not on the agenda, and don't participate when someone else does it.
   - If you are leading the meeting, try something like this to keep the meeting on course: "That's an excellent point, Harry. I'll be glad to discuss it after we have addressed all the items on our agenda, if we have time."

9. If you're having a "power breakfast," it is okay to have the breakfast salad, as long as you eat it with your fingers, and your sleeves are rolled up.
   - To maintain your power position, you choose the time. If your co-meeter suggests 7:00 a.m., you say "How about 6:30 a.m.?". If your co-meeter suggests 6:30 a.m., you say that you won't be finished with your triathlon until 7:00 a.m.

Remember, meetings can be fun. Meetings are your friends. Make a friend for life.

Meeting Minutes

Meeting minutes are to be taken at every meeting, and especially at meetings where an owner, owner's agent, or consultant is present. The Project Architect is responsible for taking general notes at each meeting which (s)he attends, but another member of the design team will be selected at the kick-off meeting to record all of the discussion taking place at the meeting. When a Partner or Project Architect attends a meeting without someone to take notes, (s)he will bear the responsibility for getting the information recorded and distributed.

Meeting minutes should follow the format shown in the attached sample, and should include the following information:

- Project Name
- Project Number
- Date
- A list of those in attendance at the meeting; if there are many people present, it may be helpful to pass out a sign-up sheet where individuals can list their names and the companies they represent.
- Old Business
  Review the minutes from the last meeting, if applicable. Identify any questions which were not answered, and any items requiring action. Report to the group any answers received or action taken since the last meeting. Have those present report on any action required from them at the last meeting.
- New Business
- A list of new business items should be prepared in advance and put on the agenda for the meeting. Send the agenda to anyone attending the meeting in advance, if possible. The items from the agenda can be transcribed into the minutes along with any discussion and decisions. If any action is required, state what the action is, who is required to do it, and when it must be done.

Send copies of the minutes to the owner, everyone present at the meeting, and other interested parties—such as consultants—who were not present. The time frame for this should be established at a meeting with the owner, and will depend on the meeting interval. However, meeting minutes should always be distributed within a week.

Name of Project:
Project Number:
Date:

MEETING MINUTES

These meeting minutes summarize the discussion at our meeting held on the date indicated below. If this summary is not consistent with your recollection, please advise this office in writing within five days.

MEETING

    Date:
    Location:
    Purpose:
    Minutes By:
    Meeting Number:

PRESENT:

    (List the names and respective firms of all those in attendance at this meeting)

COPIES TO:

    All Present
    (List any other individuals who should receive copies of these minutes)

DISCUSSION:

    (List each item of discussion, and any decisions made. If any item requires further action, add an additional paragraph with the heading "Action Required:", and assign responsibility for this action. Also indicate a date by which this action must be completed.)

NEXT MEETING TIME AND DATE:

END OF DISCUSSION

Telephone Logs

All project-related telephone conversations are to be recorded in a daily telephone log. Information recorded should include the following:

- Date
- Time
- Who initiated the call
- Name of the person talked to
- That person's telephone number (if needed for future reference)
- Company name and address of the person talked to (if needed for future reference)
- Content of the discussion

A format for the telephone log is available in the bins in the support staff area, but they are provided only as a convenience. You may elect to use a different format.

If you are working on more than one job at a time, keep a separate phone log for each project. Keep your logs in separate file folders near your phone. Each month, file code your logs, and give them to the support staff for filing. If you would like to keep copies at your desk, be sure to make these copies before submitting them to be filed. Begin each week on a new page so that the logs from other members of your team may be filed together with yours in some coherent manner.

Transmittal forms exist in our computer data base as "macros." This means that the form has been created, and the macro will lead you through each line, prompting you for the required information. However, transmittals should be prepared by the support staff, who will be familiar with this process. If you find yourself with a need to create your own transmittal, make sure you don't do something to delete the macro itself.

To access the transmittal macro, you must be in a WordPerfect document (preferably a blank one). Press the *Alt* key and the *F10* key simultaneously. This will display a prompt at the bottom of the screen: *Macro:* Type *Transmit* after this prompt, and the macro will be activated.

Blank transmittal forms can be found in the bins in the support staff area. They can be redlined for subsequent text entry by support staff.

Any job-related item being sent out of the office must be accompanied by a transmittal, and the transmittal should be typed. Only in the rarest of situations should a hand-written transmittal be used.

If you have not already created a macro for transmittals in your computer system, consider doing it now. It is an excellent way to streamline and accelerate an otherwise tedious and time-consuming activity.

ADDITIONAL SERVICES REQUEST FORM

We use AIA Document G604 to request written authorization from the owner to proceed with additional work.

This form should be prepared by the Project Architect, and then reviewed and signed by the Principal in Charge.

This form should be completed and signed by the owner before we start any additional work.

Blank copies of this form are available in the support staff area, and the necessary information should be redlined on these blanks. The support staff will then either type this information directly on an original AIA document, or it will be incorporated into a computer format which will then allow us to print computerized text directly onto the forms.

Please keep in mind that when we are using AIA documents, we should respect the copyright, and use our computer as a convenient text editor. We should not recreate the entire form in our computer.

(Insert AIA Document G604 Professional
Services Supplemental Authorization or your
office standard here)

Small Drawings

We use 8½ x 11 and 11 x 17 sizes for our small drawings. We have had title-blocks printed on Mylar in these sizes. Examples of these titleblocks are attached. Please limit your choice of sizes to these two.

Small drawings can get mangled or lost if they are kept in the flat files, so we have created a special storage system to keep them in. There are hanging files and envelopes there for your use. Be sure to label both with the project name and number.

Small Drawings
Continued

Insert your office examples of small drawings
formats for 8½ x 11 and 11 x 17 sheets here

Project Wrap-up Meeting Agenda

As soon after the completion of the working drawings phase as practicable, a project wrap-up meeting should be scheduled. All members of the team should be present.

The primary purpose of the wrap-up meeting is to discuss the things that went well, the things that could have gone better, and to make suggestions that can benefit other teams.

The Project Architect should conduct the project wrap-up meeting.

A second meeting should be scheduled after construction is completed. Feedback should be provided from the contract administration team to the original members of the design team. The purpose of this meeting is to provide a forum for lessons learned during construction to be communicated to all members of the team.

The intent of the following outline is to encourage **productive discussion** about the project development process that you've just completed. The outline can be expanded upon as either the Project Architect or Principal in Charge deems necessary. Once the wrap-up meeting has been completed, the Project Architect should answer all questions within the outline and input suggested comments from the meeting.

PART A: GENERAL PROJECT INFORMATION

1. Name of Project: _____

2. Date of meeting: _____

3. Estimated Construction Cost: _____

4. Project phases that are completed:

   _____ Planning   _____ Construction Documents
   _____ Schematic Design   _____ Bidding and Negotiations
   _____ Design/Development   _____ Construction Administration

5. Was the project a phased project?   Yes   No

6. List project team members: (show the approximate % allocation of each member's time)

   Principal in Charge _____   _____
   Project Architect _____   _____
   Job Captain _____   _____
   Others _____   _____

PART B: ADMINISTRATIVE ISSUES

1. Was CAD utilized in any way on this job? If so, how?

2. Did proper CAD maintenance and filing occur? [ ] Yes   [ ] No

3. Do you have any suggestions as to how to improve maintenance or CAD use on a similar project?

4. Have any drawings been tubed?   Yes   No

5. Have the files been boxed?   Yes   No

PART C: FINANCIAL ISSUES

1. Was the fee(s) based on drawings and manhours it would take to complete them?

   Yes   No

2. Was the project appropriately staffed?

   Yes   No

3. What impact did the project schedule have on the project with respect to the fees received?

4. What are some suggestions that would make projects similar to this one more profitable?

PART D: GENERAL ISSUES

1. List several items that went *right* with the project (include team comments).
   a.
   b.
   c.
   d.
   e.
   f.

2. List several things that could be improved upon (include team comments).
   a.
   b.
   c.
   d.

3. Did the project present any special challenges? If so, how did this impact the project?

PART E: TEAMWORK ISSUES

1. Were the roles of the individual team members clearly defined? (If not, provide suggestions as to how to improve them).

2. Did team members clearly understand what was expected of them in their roles? (How could this be improved?)

3. Did your team members feel they had adequate information to fulfill their responsibilities? (How could this be improved?)

4. Was communication with consultants adequate? If no, how could this be improved?

5. Was a specifications consultant used? Was it productive?

6. Were any consultants used that impacted the project in a measurable way (good or bad?)

7. Did a *sense of teamwork* exist on your project? Explain.

8. Was the Interiors Department utilized in the development process? Why or why not?

9. Was the work environment conducive to completing the project (*i.e. grouping teams together*)?

PART F: PERSONAL DEVELOPMENT

1. Did the team utilize the office resources for problem solving? (How can we encourage this?)

2. Did the team find office resources adequate?   Yes   No
   Explain

3. Were individuals appropriately challenged with their responsibility?　　Yes　　No
   Explain

4. Who on the team had the responsibility to perform a majority of the code research?

5. Were there any areas of technical weakness on the team? If so, what were they and how can they be corrected?

6. Did team members create personal "things to do" lists that facilitated their effort to complete their responsibilities?

The Project Architect should chart the course for producing a set of working drawings. He or she should determine key points in the progress of the drawings when coordination sets should be printed and exchanged with our consultants. Each consultant should receive a complete set of drawings, and he or she should coordinate his or her work with each of the other disciplines.

Internally, we should do a systematic check and coordination of our drawings to correspond with our consultant coordination. The Job Captain, the Project Architect, and the Partner-in-Charge should all share in the checking and coordination process, and the Director of Quality Control should also be notified when these sets become available. Together, the Project Architect and the Job Captain will perform a comprehensive check of the drawings and will coordinate the work of the consultants. They should discuss the checking requirements in advance so that each knows who is responsible for a given portion of the checking. The checking responsibilities should follow these broad guidelines:

Job Captain:	Building Data (code related)
	Dimensions
	Keynotes (to confirm that the correct numbers have been used)
	Drawing numbers, titles, scales
	Cross-referencing
	Grid line designations
	Room names and numbers
	Partition types
	North arrow
	Overlay checking of consultant's drawings

Project Architect:
Both the Project Architect and the Job Captain should check the drawings using the Working Drawings Checklist as a guide.

The Project Architect should review the Code Search Checklist prior to checking. He or she should give special attention to the fire-resistive requirements, exiting, area separations, occupancy separations, doors, floor and ceiling assemblies, and other code related issues.

The Project Architect should plan the coordination checking using the Coordination Checklist in Part Three. Make sure consultants are aware of their responsibilities for coordinating their work with the architectural drawings, as well as other disciplines. Coordination checking responsibilities can also be assigned using the checklist, but the Project Architect should plan on doing most or all of this type of checking.

The Project Architect should also review the drawings with the Partner-in-Charge for compliance with the program. Meeting Minutes should be reviewed to ensure that the drawings reflect any decisions made during meetings with the Owner.

The Job Captain should check the items listed above, even though the Project Architect may duplicate this effort.

Principal-in-Charge:
The Principal-in-Charge should also review all aspects of the drawings. However, this in no way relieves the Job Captain or the Project Architect from their responsibilities to perform a thorough and exhaustive check of their own.

In preparing a redline set, we use colors to distinguish different kinds of information; they are as follows:

Red   Red is reserved exclusively for comments, additions or changes which must be incorporated (generally verbatim) in the original drawings.

Green   Green is for questions or comments raised by the checker which should be reviewed and resolved before the drawings are changed. Always make sure the checker has received answers to his or her questions before you proceed. Red may also be used for this purpose, but it should be clouded or otherwise differentiated from redlines, which must definitely be incorporated in the drawings.

Blue   Blue highlighters are used by checkers to highlight all information that has been checked and is correct as is.

Transferring the redlines to the originals

Yellow   Yellow highlighters or pencils are used to color over all redlines and green questions once they have been transferred to the drawings, or otherwise resolved.

Transferring redlines to the original is admittedly a dull and tedious task. Nevertheless, it is an essential part of the working drawing process. You bear the ultimate responsibility to make sure that all redlines get picked up, and get picked up accurately. If you have a question, ASK it. There should be no need for a checker to recheck the drawings to see if all of the redlines were accurately picked up.

Redline/Check Sets
Continued

Because redlines can be complex or fragmented, it is important for you to be very systematic in your methods for making sure the job is done correctly. Before you yellow something out, DOUBLE-CHECK to make sure you really did it. Yellow out each redline separately, double-checking as you go. Don't simply circle drawings with yellow to indicate that you've finished picking up redlines in those areas.

The drawings should be 100% complete before the final check and coordination set is printed—**no exceptions.** Incomplete drawings make it difficult for our consultants and ourselves, and result in extra time for rechecking and coordination. Be sure that the schedule allows sufficient time at the end to do a thorough check and picking up of redlines.

One technique which we have used successfully to manage the redline process is for the Project Architect to keep a check set at his or her desk. Redline (and green) remarks are added to this set on a continuing basis. Periodically these redlines are picked up by one of the team members and the corrected sheet is then inserted in the check set, replacing the old one. This method seems to work very well in managing corrections and changes made to a set of drawings prior to the final check.

FIELD VERIFICATION GUIDELINES AND PROCEDURES

GOALS:

The purpose of all field verification activities is to gather (and record) enough information about an existing project to allow a responsible design and documentation effort to result. In renovation projects, many decisions are driven by the feasibility of modifying existing features of the building. In order to make informed decisions, the existing conditions must be clearly understood. Since we cannot always anticipate how the design may evolve, we must prepare as complete and as accurate a record as we can in order to assess the impact on design issues that were not known at the time of the verification work. In order for our verification work to be successful, we should:

> Verify existing materials
> Verify existing configurations
> Photographically document interior spaces and exterior conditions for future reference
> Measure existing walls (only where required to coordinate with new work)
> Identify areas requiring more extensive verification

METHODS:

Neatness and clarity in your field verification notes are very important.

Use Schematic Design drawings as the redline set. Consolidate redlines into a Master redline set, which will be kept at the Project Architect's desk. For field purposes, xeroxes of partial plans may be most convenient.

Verify room configuration (measure as required to verify).

Do not get bogged down in detail unless the effort seems needed to you. If you have questions, ask your Project Architect.

Photograph walls, ceiling conditions, and special problems for areas affected by new construction. No photos needed for rooms that will not be altered.

Identify photos by date, room number, and initials of photographer. The room numbers shall correspond to Schematic drawing numbers wherever possible. If the room number comes from the existing drawings, indicate so on the photograph.

Keep notes that correspond to the photos (if it seems necessary).

Compare existing drawings to actual materials—note discrepancies.

Drawings shall be marked to indicate existing materials (including finishes).
In some areas, xeroxes of existing drawings may be required to understand the area—especially for demolition.

When you return from the project site, you will be responsible for organizing the photos and transferring their information onto the Master redline set.

Photos will be organized in notebook form to accompany the redline set. Keep the photos and negatives in specially made plastic sleeves. Negatives should be kept in the project files.

Note significant equipment (panel boards, fan units, cabinet heaters, life safety equipment, hose cabinets, pull stations, etc.) and photograph large units.

Pay particular attention to location of expansion joints and covers.

The degree of accuracy reflected in your measurements is important, but keep in mind that a measurement between two walls that are slightly out of plumb could vary by an inch or more, depending on the height at which the measurement was taken. For most purposes, round each measurement to the nearest 1/2". For modular materials, such as concrete block or brick, ignore minor deviations from standard coursing dimensions; minor deviations are presumed when the dimensions are stated with the standard "±" required for all existing dimensions. Therefore, record them as typical coursing dimensions. Any deviation from standard coursing dimensions greater than an inch could mean that bricks were cut, and should be recorded accurately, rounding to the nearest 1/2". If we know we are going to have to accommodate a specific piece of furniture or equipment, increase the level of accuracy to 1/8".

TOOLS:

     Measuring tapes
     Hard hat
     Note pad
     Clip board
     6" scale
     Camera and plenty of film
     Pencils, with regular eraser (include red pencils)
     Backpack (day pack) to carry gear
     Flashlight
     Appropriate dress—hard sole shoes, perhaps jeans

TEAMS/AREAS OF RESPONSIBILITY:
(Identify areas of the building which will have to be verified, and the teams assigned to each area).

TEAM MEMBERS:
(Identify the members assigned to each team).

Timing and Tasks:
(Indicate dates for various verification activities).

Field Measurement Graphics:

1. Standard nomenclature for dimensioning is: 8'-1.

2. Use standards set by office for dimension lines, dashed above, dashed below, centerlines, tenant lease lines, property lines, etc.

3. Sketches to be done in consistent media; preferably graphite on graph paper.

4. On the sketch itself, the following should be indicated:
   - Date sketch was made
   - Indication of floor level
   - Number of sheets used to define the sketch
   - Section, details, and match lines, if necessary

5. Drawings should be sketched with a reasonable sense of scale and clarity.

6. Sketches should be oriented on the sheet in the same orientation as the schematic design drawings.

7. All sketches should be hardlined on trace paper or on CAD.
   • To check for discrepancies
   • To calculate square footage

Drawings should include:
   • Date of original sketch
   • Date of hardline drawings
   • Indication of floor level

CAD Drawings

1. Standard graphic symbols should be used on each drawing.
   • Lines: types—centerlines, lease lines, solid lines, leader lines, symbols
                layers—text, dimensions, partitions, line types
                key plans—titleblocks, attributes

   • Symbols

   • Text: styles
               font files
               layers
               sizes

2. Dimensioning and noting should occur approximately in the same placement and orientation from drawing to drawing.

3. CAD name for drawings should be at the bottom left hand corner of each individual drawing.

4. CAD plotting procedures should be outlined with respect to:
    - Pen sizes
    - Layers and colors
    - Plotting scale
    - Sheet sizes
    - Plotting medium

Specifying Techniques

Drawings and Specs establish a standard of required function, dimension, appearance, and quality.

Specifications accomplish this by using one (preferably) of the following specifying techniques:

Descriptive Specifications
- Detailed description of properties of a product or material.
- Workmanship required for installation.
- Proprietary names are not used.
- The burden of performance is assumed by the specifier.

Example: (Descriptive Specification)

```
Concrete mix of four parts coarse aggregate, two parts
fine aggregate, one part cement, with 0.5 water/cement
ratio.
```

- performance of 3,000 psi at 28 days is implied, but if the concrete did not test out, the contractor could not be held responsible if he provided a concrete mix as described.

Performance Specifications
- Statement of required results

  –all desired end results must be spelled out.

  –criteria for verifying compliance must be included.

Reference Standards
- materials: ASTM
- products: ANSI
- design: ACI
- workmanship: ASTM
- test methods: ASTM
- codes: ANSI/ASME

–reference standards may include words used in a different context than those same words used in the General Conditions.

–inappropriate provisions often appear in Reference Standards.

Specifying Techniques
Continued

Proprietary Specifications
- identification of products manufacturer, brand, model, type, etc.

Closed Proprietary Specifications versus Open Proprietary Specifications
- Open
  - –allows substitutions
  - –named product defines desired properties and level of acceptable quality
  - –substitutions are proposed by contractor
  - –products are reviewed and allowed if approved

MasterSpec language for an open specification is as follows:
"Subject to compliance with requirements, products which may be incorporated in the work include, but are not limited to, the following:"

- Closed
  - –no substitution
  - –may specify one product.
  - –may specify several products as options.

MasterSpec language for a semi-proprietary specification is as follows:
"Subject to compliance with requirements, provide one of the following:".

COORDINATION WITH CONSULTING ENGINEERS

The following form was derived from the Consulting Engineers Council, and summarizes the industry consensus about where certain kinds of information should be shown. It is acceptable to depart from this listing, provided the engineers agree and are informed in advance.

It is important to understand that our consultants are familiar with the Council's standards and conventions, and they typically base their fees and scope of work on this information. If we want to change it, they need to participate in the decision making.

The following standards separate the various construction information to be shown on the drawings of the respective consultants. In some instances, duplication of some information is unavoidable (such as the layout of the structure, the location of fire hose cabinets, etc.), but this should be kept to the necessary minimum.

The use of these standards should achieve the following benefits:
1. Unnecessary drafting is eliminated, thus saving production time.
2. Ease in coordination and checking of documents.
3. Errors caused by inconsistencies in the documents are avoided, and construction change orders are reduced.
4. The consultants have a clear understanding of their scope of work.

General -- All Drawings

1. Use identical drawing sheet size, title, and border arrangement.
   Apply sticky-back titleblock to complete titleblocks on pre-printed mylars.
2. Adhere to drawings standards as shown elsewhere in this manual. This includes drawing titling and sheet numbering.
3 Architectural drawings indicate only dimensions which establish the architectural design. Do not duplicate material thickness dimensions indicated on consultants' drawings.
4. Consultant's drawings dimension only items relating to that specific discipline's design work. Use the same dimensioning system as the architectural drawings.

ARCHITECTURAL DRAWINGS	STRUCTURAL DRAWINGS
1. Grid lines, numbers, and grid dimensions. Floor elevations are to be top of structural floors.	1. Grid lines, numbers, and grid dimensions. Floor elevations are to be top of structural floors.
2. Outline only structural elements where in conjunction with architectural work. Avoid unnecessary duplication of structural elements.	2. Locate and size all structural elements.
3. Locate and dimension all architectural openings in structure, slab depressions, raised floors, and curbs.	3. Show graphically all openings and critical penetrations in structure; locate openings if critical, and coordinate with other consultants. Indicate depths of floor depressions and integral raised floors and curbs.
4. Refer to "Structural Drawings" only when architectural item is defined by structural drawing. Do not refer to specific structural detail.	4. Refer to architectural drawings only in General Notes.
5. Detail miscellaneous metal, including metal stairs. Obtain structural sizes and connections from consultant.	5. Show connections of all miscellaneous metal to structural elements. Submit to architect, and be responsible for all sizes and connections.
6. Fireproofing to structural steel is to be shown on all details where in conjunction with architectural work. (Thickness and rating is established in specifications).	6. For the purpose of establishing the thickness/rating of required fireproofing applied to structural steel and deck, identify girders, beams, columns, etc., as being primary, secondary, etc., members.

ARCHITECTURAL	STRUCTURAL
7. Show elevator shaft and elevator machine beam supports. Locate machine beams supplied by elevator manufacturer.	7. Detail size and locate all elevator shaft and machine beam supports.
8. Outline only of foundation in sections and details.	8. Foundation plan with all dimensions and elevations of tops of footings.
9. Locate and dimension all work outside of building, such as sidewalks, patios, stairs on grade, trenches, etc.	9. Typical detail structural elements of all work outside of building. Show outline only where in conjunction with structural elements.
10. Detail miscellaneous metal including metal stairs, (obtain structural sizes and connections from consultant).	10. Show connections of all miscellaneous metal to structural elements. Submit to architect and be responsible for all sizes and connections.
11. Show below grade membrane (below slab and on walls) in sections and exterior elevations.	11. Show below grade membrane graphically only where in conjunction with structure.

ARCHITECTURAL	MECHANICAL
1. Provide backgrounds of site and building plans; when working transparencies are provided, room names and numbers are to be indicated on separate print.	1. Background to have grid lines and numbers, all structural elements, partitions, door swings, pertinent built-in work, room names, and room numbers. Backgrounds are to be updated as required to reflect final architectural and structural work.
2. Do not show any mechanical elements unless contiguous with an architectural item or part of the architectural appearance or design concept.	2. Identify all mechanical items, coordinate with other consultants. Show sizes of penetrations through structure (locate graphically only).
3. In finished spaces, show outline of equipment only. Show equipment bases and curbs where not part of mechanical work.	3. Locate all mechanical items and detail equipment boxes, curbs, catwalks, concrete pits, roof penetrations, flashings to equipment. Coordinate all reinforced concrete requirements with structural consultants.
4. Locate by dimension non-typical exposed mechanical items for critical architectural appearance.	4 Locate, dimension, and size all typical or standard mechanical items. Show all required access panels. Verify equipment connections to structure, and floor loading requirements with structural consultant. Coordinate mechanical work with other consultants for clearances.
5 Reflected ceiling plan is to show outline of all exposed mechanical items. Reflected ceiling plan, floor plans, elevations, and sections to clearly indicate changes in floor and ceiling levels.	5. Show location of floor and ceiling level changes which affect mechanical work (for clearances) and refer to architectural drawings for specific conditions.
6. Indicate increased wall or partition thickness for mechanical work. Dimension clear openings of shafts and chases.	6. Submit to architect space requirements for all enclosed mechanical work.

ARCHITECTURAL	PLUMBING/SPRINKLER
1. Provide backgrounds of site and building plans. When working transparencies are supplied, room names and numbers are to be indicated on separate print.	1. Backgrounds to have grid lines and numbers, all structural elements, partitions, door swings, pertinent built-in work, room names, and room numbers. Backgrounds are to be updated as necessary to reflect final architectural and structural work.
2. Do not show any plumbing elements unless contiguous with an architectural item, or part of the architectural appearance and design concept.	2. Identify all plumbing items; coordinate with other consultants. Show sizes of penetrations through structure (locate graphically only).
3. Show outline only of all fixtures including floor typical drains, etc. Locate non-typical by dimension.	3. Indicate all plumbing items; give dimensions of all typical locations. Show sizes of penetrations through structure (locate graphically only). Coordinate with other consultants. Show all required access panels. Verify plumbing work connections to structure and floor loading requirements with structural consultant.
4. Locate by dimension non-typical exposed mechanical items for critical architectural appearance.	4. Show locations of sprinkler valves and all sprinkler mains. Coordinate with other consultants for clearances. Where required for architectural appearance, refer specifically to architectural drawings for sprinkler locations.
5. Reflected ceiling plan is to show outline of all exposed plumbing items. Reflected ceiling plan, floor plans, elevations, and sections to clearly indicate changes in floor and ceiling levels.	5. Locate, size, and identify fire hose, cabinets, fire extinguisher, cabinets, etc., and specify.

ARCHITECTURAL	ELECTRICAL
1. Provide backgrounds of site and building plans. When working transparencies are provided, room names and numbers are to be indicated on a separate print.	1. Backgrounds to have grid lines and numbers, all structural elements, partitions, door swings, pertinent built-in work, room names, and room numbers. Backgrounds are to be updated as necessary to reflect final architectural and structural work.
2. Do not show any electrical elements unless contiguous with an architectural item, or part of the architectural appearance or design concept.	2. Identify all electrical items, and coordinate with other consultants. Show sizes of penetrations through structure (locate graphically only).
3. Show electrical panels, surface or recess mounted, on plans. Check partition depths and possible necessary furring.	3. Define and locate all electrical panels. If necessary, indicate all critical clearances around panels and equipment. Verify location of oversize conduits or ducts with structural consultant; if imbedded in structure with architect if critical for architectural appearance and coordination. Detail all reinforced concrete work required for electrical items and coordinate with structural consultant (e.g., trenches, duct banks, concrete pits, equipment bases, etc.).
4. Reflected ceiling plan shall show all ceiling fixture and other electrical items. Locate or indicate by module for critical architectural appearance.	4. Locate graphically all electrical items, and coordinate with other consultants.
5. Locate by dimension non-typical wall outlets and fixtures only if critical for architectural appearance. If locations of floor outlets are critical, issue a "furniture plan" with dimensions for floor outlets.	5 Locate and dimension outlets and fixtures by typical reference only. Refer to architectural drawings for non-typical locations of all electrical items.

Building Code Checklist

There are many forms of building code checklists, and you may use any that you find easy to use and produce a complete investigation into the code requirements for the project.

The attached checklist is provided for your convenience.

SUGGESTED BUILDING CODE CHECKLIST

(For use with 1993 UBC or earlier)
Project Name:
Project Number:
Location:

Applicable Code:
Person Performing Code Check:
Date:

Code check procedure:
First determine zoning restrictions, i.e., permitted uses and uses by right, etc., setbacks, easements, parking ratios, building envelopes, bulk and square footage restrictions.

Warning: Verify exactly which codes have been adopted by all governmental agencies having jurisdiction. Fire districts, state codes, local health district authorities often overlap local government building departments authority. Food preparation, hospitals, swimming pools, and handicapped requirements are frequently in separate code jurisdictions.

Note: For buildings with atriums and/or floor height 75' or more above lowest point of grade at building, see atrium and high-rise building provisions as follows:
    Sec. 1807 and Sec. 1715 (UBC)

1.   Fire Zone: (none in 1979 and later UBC)

2.   Occupancy Classification: (Chapter 5 UBC)
    Mixed Occupancy: Sec 503(a)
    Others (specify): Table (5a) Principal Occupancy:
    Other Occupancies:
-
-
-
-
-

    Go to specific chapters for occupancy type for items such as light, ventilation, and sanitation, location on property, special hazards and fire alarms.

3.   Occupancy Separation Required (Table 5(b))
                  to   =
hours
                  to   =
hours
                  to   =
hours
                  to   =
hours
                  to   =
hours
                  to   =
hours
                  to   =
hours

4.   Construction Type:

    In order to determine the optimum building construction type, you must begin by determining building occupancy and building square footage (based on outside wall dimensions); by floor, for each separate building occupancy group, and for the building as a whole. Basements and cellars may be excluded from this calculation if they do not meet the criteria for a story or the 1st story as defined in Chapter 4.

Next determine if there is more than one major occupancy group (as per Sec. 503 (a). If there is more than one major occupancy group, use the formula in Sec 503 (a) to determine total allowable building area (in conjunction with Tables 5-C and 5-D, and Sec. 505, 506, and 507 as below).

Enter Table 5-C in the appropriate building occupancy group(s) line(s) and starting with the Type V-N column (far right side) find the basic allowable floor area for the occupancy(ies) involved. Verify in Table 5-D if this constructive type is acceptable for number of stories contemplated, and if so, continue as below; if not, move 1- column left in Table and repeat this check.

    This basic allowance may then be increased as per Sec. 505(b) if over 1 story, as per Sec. 506(a) (UBC) for separation on sides, and as per 506(b) and (c) (UBC) for automatic fire sprinklers. If the allowable area calculated as above is equal to or greater than the actual area calculated, then Construction Type V-N should be utilized. If not, move one column left in the table and re-calculate. Continue this process until acceptable construction type is found.

NOTE:
Automatic sprinkler systems throughout cannot be utilized for area
increase purposes in the UBC, if installed as per Sec. 507 for increase in allowable stories, as per Sec. 3802 for Group H-1 and 2, as per Sec. 508 for fire resistive substitution, or as per Sec. 1715 for atriums.

5.   Maximum allowable Basic Floor Area: Table 5-C.
    If surrounded by open space on two or more sides:
        Sec. 506(a) (UBC)
    If over 1 story:
        Sec. 505(b)
    If sprinklered:
        Sec. 506(b) and (c) (UBC)

6.   Maximum allowable basic height:
        Table 5-D and Sec. 507 (UBC)

7.   Fire resistance of exterior wall: (see appropriate Occupancy Type chapter and Construction Type chapter).
        Table 17-A and 5-A and 1705(d) (UBC).

8.   Openings in exterior walls: (see appropriate Occupancy Type chapter and Construction Type chapter)
        Table 5-A (UBC)

9.   Windows required in rooms:
        Sec. 605, 705, 805, 905, 1005, 1204, and 1205 (UBC)
        Window area required: (see sections as above)

10.   Enclosed or semi-enclosed courts - size required:
        Sec. 504(c) and 1206 (UBC)

11.   Minimum ceiling height in rooms: (group B occupancy)
        Sec. 1207(a) (UBC)

12.   Minimum floor area of rooms:
        Sec. 1207(b) (UBC)

13.   Fire resistive requirements:
    Determine fire-resistive requirements for various building elements of building construction type previously selected.

    See also Sec. 508 (UBC) for fire resistive substitution. See also Sec. 1715(a) (UBC) for atriums.

Exterior bearing walls:
Table 17-A; Sec. 1705(d) (UBC)

Interior bearing walls:
Table 17-A;

Exterior non-bearing walls:
Table 17-A

Structural frame:
Table 17-A and Sec. 1702

Permanent partitions:
Table 17-A; Sec. 1705(b) (UBC)

Vertical openings:
Table 17-A and Sec. 1706

Floors:
Table 17-A

Roofs:
Table 17-A

Exterior doors:
Table 5-A (UBC)

Exterior windows:
Table 5-A (UBC)

Inner court walls:
Sec. 504(c) (UBC)

Mezzanine floors (area allowed):
Sec. 1717 (UBC)

Roof coverings:
Sec. 3202(b) (UBC) and Table 32-A

Boiler room enclosure:
Sec. 608, 708, 808, 908, 1008, and 1212 (UBC)

Determine shaft enclosure requirements and exceptions, weather-protection, parapet requirements, bath and restroom requirements, guardrails, and miscellaneous specific requirements.

14. Structural Requirements:
Framework:
Sec. 1801, 1802, 1901, 1902, 2001, 2002, 2101, 2102, 2201, 2202

Stairs:
Sec. 1805, 1905, 2004, 2104, 2204, (UBC)

Floors:
Sec. 1804, 1904 (UBC)

Roofs:
Sec. 1806, 1906, 2005, 2105 (UBC)

Partitions:
Sec. 1801, 1901, 2003(c), 2101, 2103(c) (UBC)

15. Exits:
Determine specific information on occupant loads and general exiting requirements from Chapter 33 Occupancy Load - basis (square feet per occupant):
Sec. 3302 and Table 33-A (UBC)

Number of exits required:
Sec. 3303(a) and Table 33-A (UBC)

Minimum width of exits:
Sec. 3303(b) (UBC)

Exit separation and arrangement:
Sec. 3303(c) (UBC)

Maximum allowable travel distance to exit:
Sec. 3303(d) (UBC)
Allowable exit sequences:
Sec. 3303(e) (UBC)

Exit doors:
Sec. 3304 (UBC)

Minimum width allowed:
Sec. 3304(e) (UBC)

Maximum leaf width allowed:
Sec. 3304(f) (UBC)

Width required for No. of occupants:
Sec. 3303(b) (UBC)

Exit corridors:
Sec. 3305 (UBC)

Minimum allowable width:
Sec. 3305(b) (UBC)

Required to have exit at each end of corridor?
Table 33-A; Sec. 3305(e) (UBC)

Dead end corridors allowed?
Table 33-A; Sec. 3305(e) (UBC)

Wall fire resistance required:
Sec. 3305(g) (UBC)

Doors and frames fire resistance required:

16. Stairs:
Sec. 3306, 3309 and 3310 (UBC)

Minimum width:
Sec. 3306(b), 3303(a) and (b) (UBC)

Maximum riser allowed:
Sec. 3306(c) (UBC)

Minimum tread allowed:
Sec. 3306(c) (UBC)

Are winders allowed?
Sec. 3306(d), (e) and (f) (UBC)

Landings:
Sec. 3306(g), (i) (UBC)

Required height of rails:
Sec. 3306(j), (k) (UBC)

Handrails:
Sec. 3306(j) (UBC)

Stair to roof required?
Sec. 3306(o) (UBC)

Stair to basement restrictions:
Sec. 3306(n) (UBC)

Stair access to roof required?
Sec. 3306(m), (o) (UBC)

Access to roof required?
Sec. 420 and 710(h) (UBC)

Horizontal exit requirements (if applicable):
Sec. 3309 and 3310 (UBC)

Stair enclosure required?
Sec. 3308 (UBC)

Ramps:
Sec. 3307 (UBC)

Exit signs required?
Sec. 3314 (UBC)

Balcony rails?
Sec. 1711 (UBC)

Balusters or intermediate rails required:
Sec. 1711 (UBC)

17. Penthouses (Chapter 36):
    Area limitations:
        3601(b)

    Height limitations:
        601(a)

    Use limitations:
        3601(c)

    Construction requirements:
        3601(d)

18. Parapet walls:
        Chapter 17

    Where required:
        Sec. 1709(a) (UBC)

    Height:
        Sec. 1709(b) (UBC)

19. Fire extinguishing systems (Chapter 38):
    Sprinklers required:
        Sec. 3802 (UBC)

    Dry standpipes required:
        Table 38-A (UBC)

    Location:
        Sec. 3805(c) (UBC)

    Number required:
        Sec. 3805(c) (UBC)

    Number outlets required:
        Sec. 3805(c) (UBC)

    Hose required:
        Table 38-A

    Siamese connections required:
        Sec. 3805(c) (UBC)

    Wet standpipes required:
        Table 38-A (UBC)

Number required (hose run):
    Sec. 3805(d), (e) (UBC)

Location:
    Sec. 3805(d), (e) (UBC)

Fire extinguishers required:
Verify with local fire department or Sec. 3806(e) (Denver), or NFPA 10

20. Toilet room requirements (Chapter 5, Appendix D (UPC)
    Fixture count requirements:
        Appendix D (UPC)

    Showers required?
        Appendix D (UPC)

    Walls:
        Sec. 510(b) (UBC)

    Floors:
        Sec. 510(b) (UBC)

    Compartments:
        Sec. 511(a) (UBC)

    Handicapped requirements: (check state and/or local ordinances)
        Sec. 511 (UBC) Ch.21 (UBC)

21. Skylights (Chapter 34)
        Sec. 5207 (UBC)

    Locations:
        Sec. 5207 (UBC)

    Separation:
        Sec. 5207(a)6 (UBC)

    Maximum size:
        Sec. 5207(a)4 (UBC)

    Maximum aggregate area in room:
        Sec. 5207(a)5 (UBC)

    Curb height:
        Sec. 3401, 5207(a)1 (UBC)

22. Elevators and escalators:
        ANSI 17; Chapter 51, Sec. 1807(h) (UBC)

    Maximum number in each shaft:
        ANSI 17; Sec. 1807(h) (UBC)

    Ventilate penthouse?
        ANSI 17

    Machine room wall construction:
        ANSI 17

23. Use of public property (Chapter 45)
    Doors prohibited from swinging into city property?
        Sec. 4507

    Marquees, canopies, etc.:
        Sec. 4505, 4506

    Support from building?
        Sec. 4505(e) (UBC)

Material restrictions:
    Sec. 4505(e) and 4506(b) (UBC)

Distance above walk:
    Sec. 4505(b) and 4506(d) (UBC)

Maximum distance of extension over walk:
    Sec. 4505(b) and 4506(c) (UBC)

Maximum height:
    Sec. 4505(d) (UBC)

Drainage:
    Sec. 4505(f) (UBC)

Other projections:
    Sec. 4504

24. Fire alarm:
    Sec. 809, 909, 1009, 1202(b), 1210, 1807 (UBC)

25. Emergency lights or power required:
    Sec. 3313, 1807(i) (UBC)

26. Access doors required in exterior walls without openings?
    Sec. 3802(b) (UBC)

27. Requirements for handicapped persons:
    Access to building:
    Sec. 3301(e), Sec. 3304(e), Sec. 1213, Table 33.A (UBC)

    Accessible route requirements:
    Sec. 3303(d), 3304(h), 3305(f), 3315(h), 3306(g), 3307
    (UBC)

There are many forms of drawings and specifications checklists, and you may use any that you may prefer.

The attached checklists are provided for your convenience.

SPECIFICATION WRITER'S CHECKLIST

A. General
1. Recommended Reading: AIA general conditions and contracts.

2. Provisions are to be included in the specifications for a mock-up of any new feature whose final effect is not certain in the designer's mind.

3. Check each division of the specifications for:
   a. Allowances
   b. Unit prices
   c. Warranty-guarantee
   d. Shop drawings
   e. Samples
   f. Inspection and tests
   g. Record drawings
   h. Material bonds
   i. Clean-up

4. New materials used should be checked with the manufacturers representative; their instructions and recommendations should be carefully considered.

5. Electrolytic reaction should be checked where dissimilar metals are used in contact with one another, such as aluminum and ferrous metals.

B. Excavation
1. Pay lines for earth excavation and rock excavation should be established.

2. Site conditions and changes from the borings or contract lines should be provided for and verified by drawings and engineer's approval.

Sub-surface drainage
1. Drain lines in porous fill under concrete slab for all large areas of exterior terrace, etc., should be specified.

C. Site Work
1. Granite or steel curbs are specified for New York City. Check other codes.

2. Department of buildings requires removal of existing bluestone curbs where new sidewalks are specified. Check local requirements.

3. Established curb elevations of Department of Borough Works (or local department) should be checked. Specify resetting curbs to these grades.

D. Landscaping
1. Guarantees for landscaping, other that seeding, should be established.

2. Maintenance contracts for planting should be considered, and if possible, provide an allowance.

E. Waterproofing
1. Check types of waterproofing required.

2. Provide waterproofing under all mat sinkages. Carry to exterior wall and connect to wall dampproofing.

F. Concrete and Cement Finishes
1. Expansion strips for horizontal surfaces such as terraces should be provided.

2. Concrete samples should go directly to the testing laboratory

and reports should go directly to the Engineers. Check New York or other special requirements.

3. Floor hardening and sealing should be checked for drying time, special installation requirements, etc.

4. Construction joints in slabs should not be placed within ten feet of any expansion joint. Contractor should prepare a plan for engineer's approval, locating all construction joints.

5. Large terraced areas of concrete should be provided with minimum 6 x 6 mesh reinforcement, stone base course, expansion joints and under floor drainage tile.

6. Rough textured surfaces should be provided on sidewalks at entrances.

7. Construction joints in concrete slabs should never be placed in the vicinity of mat recesses.

G. Masonry
1. Face brick cost per "M" not lump sum allowance. Quantity to be provided by general contractor.

2. Acoustical isolation for interior rooms should extend above suspended ceilings to the underside of the slab above.

H. Slate and Stonework
1. Sealer on interior slate floors should be specified.

2. Caulk all joints in copings; also flat stone surfaces where foot traffic doesn't occur.

3. Anchorage for copings and stonework shall be thoroughly described in the specifications.

4. Limestone and other soft or porous stones are not to come in contact with the earth, nor platforms or terraces where water can collect and be drawn up by capillary action.

5. Sidewalk surfaces: use rough textured non-slip finish.

6. Smooth surfaced floors should not be used in vestibules as they wear rapidly and are very slippery.

7. Do not use soft stones on heavily traveled stairs.

I. Roofing and Sheet Metal
1. Check for flashing under stone or masonry sills made of more than one piece.

J. Furring and Lathing
1. Furring, lath, and plaster should enclose all pipes, ducts, etc. which would otherwise be exposed in finished areas regardless of whether furring is shown or indicated on architectural drawings.

2. Base screed (or casing bead) should be used with cement base.

3. Casing bead should be used where plaster abuts any other surface.

K. Plastering
1. When a plaster finish is set flush with a ceramic tile wainscot, there should be shown on the drawings a "V" joint at their point of intersection.

L. Terrazzo
1. Rough textured non-slip surfaces should be specified on sidewalks at entrances.

2. Terrazzo floors are not advisable in toilet rooms and slop sink closets, as this material is more absorbent than tile.

M. Ceramic Tile

1. Provide expansion joints for ceramic tile and setting bed for all tile expanses exceeding 16' vertically and/or horizontally wherever construction and expansion joints occur.

N. Resilient Flooring

1. In all alteration work, a paragraph should be added to the specifications stating how work is to be done in area where floor is marked "patch and level floor to receive resilient tile." It should be clearly stated that this means the floor of the entire room shall be patched and uniformly level throughout.

O. Miscellaneous and Ornamental work

1. When specifying metal or glass entrance doors remember that no matter what the material is, push and pull plates should be included, lettered with "push" and "pull."

2. Note: specification writer should keep items in alphabetical order to facilitate checking.

3. Check: area gratings, access trench covers, angle frames in wood flooring, anchorage for exterior carved stone work, astragals; frame anchors, cast iron bumper on loading platform, clean out doors, chimney cap, corner guards, catwalk in roof spaces, cupola, ceiling framing, catch basin gratings, curb angles, supports for concealed expansion joints; driveway curb guards; exterior railings, expansion joints and covers, electric service supports; framing at floodlights, floor plates in boiler rooms; grilles; house trap pit covers, hood over kitchen ranges; interior lintels, interior stairs; kick plates (special).

Where weatherstrips are used on same doors as kickplate, detail carefully; ladders, ladder rungs and handholds, masons ironwork, metal saddles, manhole covers, pipe railings, pipe handrails, projection room equipment; reinforcing steel for exterior walls; steel angle bases, steel wheel guards at overhead garage doors, step nosings, steel sidewalk doors, supports for interior stone trim, supports for folding partitions, supports for column hung bookcases, steel angle curbs at overhead garage doors, supports for folding doors, steel work to support electric service cables, steel plate supports for handrail brackets; leader sleeves, wire mesh partitions, weatherstripping

P. Carpentry

1. Verify with the designers whether wood items indicated are to be veneers or solid.

2. Exterior wood trim should be prime coated in the shop. All cuts made in the field which expose bare wood shall be painted in the field before being set in place.

3. Carpentry specs should include the following: workmanship shall be of the highest grade, and only mechanics especially skilled in this kind of work shall be employed. All work shall be accurately set in place plumb, true, even and in perfect alignment and be securely fastened.

4. Accurately and carefully fit, cut, shim, or block all work, so that adjoining surfaces in the same plane will finish flush, straight, and true.

5. Finished surfaces shall be free of all tool or machine marks and other objectional features. Surfaces shall be finished equivalent to hand sandpapered work.

6. Wood interior doors shall be 1-3/4" minimum thickness in institutional and commercial work.

7. Fiber board for cabinet doors should be limited to sizes smaller than 2' x 3'; in larger sizes the material economy doesn't equal its lack of durability.

Q. Weatherstripping

1. All exterior doors must be weatherstripped.

R. Glass and glazing

1. Glass shall be cut with proper clearance to take care of deflection or temperature changes in wood on metal frames. This is especially critical for dual panes. Adhere to manufacturer's stated clearances.

S. Painting and Finishes

1. Provide protection behind drinking fountains if tile walls are not specified.

2. Luminous ceilings: paint all surfaces, hangers, ducts, pipes, etc., above light strips off-white color for good reflectance and even illumination.

3. Multi-colors: when used in more than a few rooms, specifications should state that multi-colors are to be frequently used throughout the building.

4. Note that walls and base are to be painted as required behind radiators, convectors, etc. On alteration jobs it should also be noted that these items are to be specifically removed before painting takes place.

5. Allowance should be made for lettering of doors. Check if in addition to the following, other rooms should receive door numbers and or room names: toilet rooms, floor numbers in stair and elevator shafts.

6. Base (—inches high) painted in contrasting color wherever wall material extends down to floor.

7. Check whether painted dadoes of contrasting color will be wanted in any spaces.

8. Convector enclosures, etc., should be painted black behind grilles to hide pipes, fins, etc.

T. Hardware

1. Specify coordinator where panic bolt is required on both leaves of double door with astragal or rabbited edge.

2. Whenever using door closers, avoid using closers that employ brackets.

U. Heating and Ventilating

1. If a piece of mechanical equipment such as an air conditioning unit does not completely fill opening in an exterior wall the remaining space shall be fully insulated.

V. Electrical

1. Specify an allowance for special electrical fixtures, such as chandeliers.

2. Check if lighting protection is required; if so, specifications should call for the earliest possible installation and completion of lightning arrestors.

3. Luminous ceilings shall be suspended and supported in strict accordance with manufacturer's instructions, and with all applicable codes. Check details for possible conflicts in trade jurisdiction.

W. *Alterations*

1. Existing openings to be closed or new openings to be made should be checked for matching of existing finishes. Same for floors and bases.

2. Cutting and patching should be carefully noted on drawings and covered appropriately in the specifications.

3. Allowances for replacement of plaster and other finishes should be checked.

ARCHITECTURAL WORKING DRAWING CHECKLIST

A. All Drawings
1. Title
2. Scale
3. North arrow on plans

B. Site or Plot Plan

1. Property lines, property location, city, street names, lot and block number, property line angles and dimensions, markers.

2. Building location, set backs, zoning and clearances, ground floor elevations, future additions, grades at buildings, dimensions, dimensions of all projections beyond building line such as steps, corners, copings, canopies, window sills, etc.
3. Easements (electric, water, gas, sewers).

4. Paving: show existing and contract paving, parking plan, parking bumpers, walks, platforms, steps, drives, paths, terraces, signs, flagpoles, playfields, playground equipment, drinking fountains.

5. Fences and stone walls, retaining walls, areaways, pools.

6. Existing structures, cellars, trees, shrubs, etc. to remain or be removed, structures to be relocated, underground voids to be filled.

7. Storm drainage and catch basins, road drainage.

8. Contract limits.

9. Work not included in contract.

10. Footing drains.
11. Legend: show all indications and materials used on site plan.

12. Contours: existing and new, contour elevations.

13. Datum, bench marks, monuments, etc.

14. Utilities: sewer, water, electricity, telephone, gas hydrants, sewage disposal.

15. Survey date, name and address of surveyor.

16. Borings and their location. Boring contractor's name and address.

17. Details of construction of site contract items.

18. Curbs: check that elevations conform to those established by authorities having jurisdiction; also that materials comply with such requirements.

19. Landscaping: show unless covered by others: indicate existing to be protected, show new trees and significant plants.

20. Temporary fences and gates, temporary toilets and shanties.

21. Material storage area.

22. Orientation: true north and reference symbol.

23. Project sign location.

24. Protection of existing work

25. Paving patterns: scoring and parking markings, traffic markings, expansion joints, striping, wheel stops.

26. Curb and gutter elevations, unless covered by Civil.

27. If applicable, show required sequencing or phasing of parts of project.

28. Demolition: show extents.

C. Architectural Floor Plans
1. Dimensions: overall, column center, building breaks and set backs, masonry dimensions. Tie room dimensions into column centers if possible.

2. Rooms: name and number, finish codes, reference to large scale plans, sections and details.

3. Floors: floor elevations, floor patterns, joint patterns in tile, stone, or other floor finishes,mat recess, changes in materials, ramps, curbs, bases, gutters.

4. Walls: material indication, fire ratings, pipe and duct spaces, recessed convectors; electric panels.

5. Ceilings: calling breaks, change in height or material, skylights, tile patterns showing lights and diffusers.

6. Door swings and numbers. Show saddle if required. Note all fireproof self-closing openings.

7. Windows: indicate mullions; schedule types where applicable.
8. toilet rooms: plumbing fixtures, compartments, floor drains, reference to large scale layouts

9. Stairs: dimensions to stair well; show traffic direction; indicate number of risers, handrails. Reference to large scale layout and details.

10. Miscellaneous items: casework, fire extinguisher cabinets, access doors, drinking fountains, expansion joints, folding partitions, gratings and pit covers, ladders, lockers, shelving, special trenches, corner guards, special convector enclosures, telephone booths, roof leaders, dwarf walls, chalkboards, tackboards, folding gates, wardrobes, railings.

11. Finishes: Clearly indicate extents of finishes, showing where they start and stop. Confirm that they are clearly indicated in schedules, plans, interior elevations, details, and specifications.

D. Architectural Roof Plan
1. Dimensions: indicate overall dimensions of building and roof surface; indicate and dimension overhang; show canopies.

2. Drainage: indicate roof drains or gutters and leaders. Show pitch to drains. Show pitch and expansion joints in gutter. Show high point and low point on flat roofs.

3. Materials: indicate type of roofing and cornice materials; note when face brick is required.

4. General: label high and low roofs where they occur; show copings and indicate joints and material. Indicate column center, chimneys and crickets, skylights, scuttles, hatches and bulkheads, fans and other equipment located on roof. Indicate expansion joints and reference to typical details. Indicate railings or other guards, 3" minimum railings at roofs used by public.
5. Miscellaneous: ladders, steel stairs to bulk heads, splash blocks, ridges, eaves, decks, roof walkways, parapets, special lighting fleches, ventilators, flagpoles, special flashing conditions, snow guards, snow melting equipment, check verification of roof spaces.

E. Exterior Elevations

1. Key plan: indicate elevations, location; show north arrow.

2. Materials: note and indicate; show joint patterns.

3. Windows and doors: show all window and door openings. Dimension height only and relate to floor lines; indicate type for each opening, do not over delineate by drawing in every window of the same type; indicate operating sash on hooper or projected vents.

4. Dimensions: indicate column centers. Show only vertical dimensions and planes. Indicate floor levels. Indicate brick courses and brick ledge locations and elevations. Show grade elevations.

5. Miscellaneous Items: ladders, louvers or other openings, railings, vents, roof slopes, access openings, leaders and sizes, leader boots, conductor heads, splash blocks, gutters and size, leader straps, chimneys, sidewalk levels, curbs, ramps, ridges, eaves, decks, penthouses, parapet, trenches, beams, footings, low points, water outlets, fire plugs, hose bibbs, siamese connections, fresh air intakes, meter boxes, section lines, projections and set backs (sunken or raised), panels, pilasters, columns, railings, inscriptions, street names, numbers, awnings, electric outlets, cornerstones, dormers, gables, hoods, entrances, balconies, flashing, counter flashing, roof scuttles, fleches, skylights, ventilators, snow guards, flag poles and holders, gates, bumper blocks at loading platforms, clocks, plaques, lightning protection.

6. Check dimensions.

7. Check fine grades with site plan.

8. Check detail references with the details.

9. Check elevations, column indications, etc.

10. Check for penthouse, cooling towers, large fans, and other such roof structures which should be on elevation. Also check for exterior ladders on stairs to penthouses.

11. Check for unusual footing conditions which should be shown on the plans.

12. Check plaster and masonry control joints, including fascias and soffits.

F. Wall and Roof Sections

1. Dimensions: show vertical dimensions relating floor, ceiling and roof to top of steel or concrete slab. Relate foundation building face column centers to each other.

2. Section identification: in addition to identifying numbers and key plan, describe typical sections or details by titles.

3. Materials: note and indicate all materials.

4. Technique: limit details to show different conditions only. Avoid repetition, use outlines and refer to typical details. Use adequate scale to show what must be shown, but don't use large scale details to fill up a sheet.

G. Longitudinal and Cross Sections, Interior Elevations

1. Dimensions: show vertical dimensions relating floor, ceiling, and roof to top of steel or concrete slab.

2. Section identification: in addition to identifying numbers and key plan, describe typical sections or details by titles.

3. Materials: note and indicate all materials. Use general terms such as metal, hardwood, softwood, plywood, beam joint, brick, concrete block, etc. when material or item is described in schedules or specifications, or shown on structural or mechanical drawings.

4. Interior elevations: include special rooms, such as chapels, lobbies, typical classrooms, typical bedrooms, corridors, auditoriums, gymnasiums, etc.

5. Miscellaneous items: cabinets base and wall doors, drawers, shelves, stock numbers. Chalkboards: size, joints, map hooks, trim, chalk tray. Closets: doors, clothes poles, mirrors, shelves. display cases: size, shelves, brackets, and standards. Lockers: height and standards. Shelving: shelving width, brackets and standards. Skylights: note location and size. Tackboards: size, surface material, trim. Telephone recess: acoustic materials, shelves. Wardrobes: doors, base, coat hooks, dividers, shelves, overhead bracing.

6. Mechanical Items: note, indicate and locate: access doors, bell, chimes, clocks, convector and enclosures and covers, drinking fountains, fire extinguishers, lighting fixtures, louvers and grilles, speakers, switches, telephones, thermostats, unit ventilators.

7. Check finishes with finish schedule.

H. Interior Details

1. Concrete masonry, concrete bases: height, width, sleeper, facing. Concrete stairs: riser, tread, nosing, finish. Fireplace: size, hearth, damper, lintel, facing. Mat recesses: size, depth, edge strip.

2. Millwork: detail the following except stock items: cabinets, counters, doors, drawers, shelves, stock numbers. Chalkboards: size, chalk tray, map hooks, trim, blocking. Closets: doors, hardware, clothes poles, mirrors, shelves. display cases: size, doors, shelves, brackets and standards. Lockers, built-in: height, width, base, trim. Tackboards: size, surface material, trim, back-up blocking. Telephone recess: surface material, trim, shelves, insulation. Wardrobes: doors, hardware, basecoat hooks, dividers, shelving.

3. Miscellaneous metal. Catwalks: width, railing, suspension. Ladders: spiral, vertical, 60 degree. Pass window: stock item, relate to counter. Railings: size, method of anchoring. Stairs: balustrade, handrail, tread and riser materials, platform, stairs to floors, stair soffit.

I. Detail Plans

1. Spaces: make 1/4" scale plans of the following: kitchen, serving and dishwashing. Typical classrooms: show only equipment in contract. Home arts, science, etc.: detail these only if equipment is in contract. Lobbies and stairs: detail plans as required. Toilets and locker rooms: generally 1/4" scale plans are adequate.

2. Check details for practicability of fabrication and installation.

3. Check finishes against finish schedule.

4. Check materials against specifications. Make sure the materials are properly identified (refer to drafting room manual).

5. Where structural members are indicated, do not indicate size of member.

6. Note any details needed for further clarification, window details (usually show), materials, size, frames, glazing, transoms, sills stools, rough bucks, caulking, etc.

J. Windows

1. Window sizes and types: refer to exterior and interior eleva tions or make 1/4" scale elevations of all window types. Dimension window types. Note when some types have several sizes.

2. Window details: when practical to save drafting, show on wall sections, otherwise make details of all conditions. Relate windows to masonry or porcelain panels. Show method of securing windows to building. provide reinforcing for large windows. Check method of operating vents.

3. Consider the following: screens, reinforcing for attachment, washing of windows. Check method of operating vents.

4. Interior venetian blinds. Square head sash for double hung circular headed windows. Arrangement of stools for grilles, convectors, etc. Consider height of sills for safety, 3'-0" minimum where above first floor. Consider hospital type bottom rails for double hung windows in bedrooms, etc. Window operators for high windows. Wire mesh guards in gymnasium, etc. Coordinate window coverings operation with window hardware, such as casement levers. Confirm sufficient stacking space for draperies.

5. Weatherstripping, type of glass: schedule.

6. Check the following: a. window size to provide equivalent of 1/10 floor area of room. b. cover strips at window mullions where marble stools are used. c. window stops, caulking. d. painting of screens when frames are non-ferrous. e. punching of angles inlets for securing metal lath at heads of windows. f. blocking or solid construction at heads of windows provided for securing venetian blinds, shades, drapery tracks, etc., window sizes and types against details, and against plan and elevations. g. proper glass indication. h. lateral bracing for strip windows.

K. Stairs

Note: In offices where a similarity of work so warrants, standard details of stairs are used. It is important that adequate stair plans and sections be prepared to check headroom, structural clearance, code requirements and dimensions.

1. Check the following: materials, width of treads, number of risers and heights. Stair numbers and line of travel against scale plans. Newels: show caps and drops. Handrails: provide intermediate brackets that may be required, check minimum finger clearance. Elevations of stair landings and platform. Safety treads for cement stairs. Check details of railing anchorage.

2. Exterior steps: a. width of treads. b. pitch. c. end of buttresses or ramps. d. checks of buttresses. e. anchoring of railings, handrails. f. stagger joints for stone steps. g. cast iron or other inset nosings on cement steps where required. h. materials. i. verify stone depth with spec: dimensions, number and dimensions of treads and risers, headroom clearance.

L. Ceilings

1. Show reflected ceiling plans of principal rooms. Consider soffits of beams, location of lights, grilles, drapery track, access openings to mechanical equipment. Consider access opening, catwalks, etc. for re-lamping from above, access to dampers, mechanical equipment scuttles, skylights and for inspection of roof and plumbing leaks.

2. Check the following: a. clearances of structure and ducts where light fixtures are recessed lights. b. coordination of mechanical equipment. c. acoustical treatments, plaster borders, cornices, control joints, cove lighting. d. arched ceiling supports. e. furring of bathroom ceilings to conceal plumbing pipes. f. low ceilings, furred soffits to conceal piping, ducts,

etc. g. structural supports for special ceilings, catwalks, folding doors, testers, special lighting fixtures, equipment, etc. h. rela tion to partitions, piers, columns, etc. with ceiling beams, features such as skylights, coves, etc. i. finish schedule. j. mechanical and electrical plans for correct location of ceiling diffusers, lighting fixtures, sprinkler heads and access panels. k. ceiling patterns with design. Check whether design relates to window mullions or other wall patterns.

3. Show control joints in gypsum board ceilings and soffits; show expansion joints.

4. Show: paging annunciators, smoke detectors, fire alarms, exit signs, corridor mirrors, lights, diffusers, returns, sprinkler heads, curtain tracks.

M. Schedules

1. Doors are usually covered by schedules. It should be noted that in offices where similarity of the work so warrants, standard details of doors and bucks are used. This permits the various types to be delineated for reference. Where a door schedule is used, it should show size, type, opening, location material, frame, glazing, louvers, transoms, panels, saddles, undercuts, legal requirements, and special features.

2. Hardware requirements are usually considered separately, but consideration should be given to space for door check clearance, and electric strike with panic bolts.

3. Check trim clearances where doors are close to each other at right angles. Consider electric switch locations.

4. Note when hatchway doors and bucks are part of a separate elevator or dumbwaiter contract. Note and specify that general contractor shall leave openings in masonry as required for setting bucks.

5. Check building code and multiple dwelling law on size of glass and louvers in various types of fireproof doors.

6. Where fireproof structures are built in areas not governed by building coed, the recommended practice is to provide doors in accordance with the National Board of Fire Underwriters as follows:

7. Check exterior doors for weather stripping and caulking; check with specs. Also check saddle types whether interlocking or not, etc. Check weatherstrip detail where kick plates are used

8. Meeting stiles of doors should be checked whether bull nosed or beveled. Exterior doors grooved for astragals with hardware.

9. Check codes for: a. actual width required for 3'-0" and 3'-8" stall doors. b. all interior doors such as fire prevention self closing doors to public halls should be 7'-0" high to allow clearance below door closer brackets where same are required. c. all exterior doors should be 7'-0" high where they swing out and require door closer brackets.

10. Door schedule should show types of glass required.

11. Weatherstrip plenum room doors.

12. See that transoms above doors are covered on drawings and specifications. If floor hinges are used, check granite and concrete floor for cutout for box, and saddle-coordinate. Detail door head conditions where carrying partition.

13. Check the following: a. door numbers and all items in schedules against door numbers on plans. b. door type against

graphic schedule. c. mechanical for louvered and/or undercut doors. d. proper labeling of fire doors.

14. Finish schedules: interior finishes are usually covered by schedules. It should be noted that in some offices where a similarity of the work so warrants, typical details of floor construction, base, and other features are covered by typical details. this permits various types to be delineated and referred to in schedules.

15. Schedule of interior finishes usually shows materials, heights, types, etc. Particular care should be taken that all notes on plans and details conform to this schedule and specification.

16. Schedule or indicate on details the following: floor trim, plinths, base (type in schedule); check screeds. Note paneling in schedule drawing to be referred to. Schedule types and height of chair rails, check window stools. Wainscot: painted or otherwise for flush-type wainscots.

17. Note on drawings: covers, cornices, plaster reveals, floor borders and patterns (note thickness and locate terrazzo strips), slope for floors, pitch of floors. Consider drainage, mark highpoint, lowpoint, and elevation of porches, areas, terraces, and saddles.

18. Note on schedule rooms as toilets, showers, kitchen, etc. that are to have membrane waterproofing.

19. Marble thickness, graining, quirks, anchors, reinforcement should be shown on details.

20. Where marble stools are used, check convector heights.

21. Show plaster corner guards on plans.

22. Ceilings: reflected plan should show beam soffits; cornices, panels, etc. Lighting layout should be studied especially where flush type lights may be in conflict with structural members or piping.

23. Check mechanical and structural work for all furred or hung ceiling requirements.

24. Determine accurate heights of tile and structural facing tile wainscots.

25. Schedule or note window stools: marble, slate, wood, tile, etc.

26. Prepare interior studies, name, color of materials. Use samples in office and get client approval information to be incorporated in specification.

27. Check the following: a. room names and numbers in the finish schedule against room names and numbers indicated on the floor plans. b. finish schedule with interior elevations. c. finishes with design, graphics and coordinator.

N. Procedure for Job Captain Checking of Completed Working Drawings.

Architectural Drawings

1. The architectural job captain should make a line for line check of the architectural working drawings and a cross check of the structural, mechanical, electrical and civil drawings with reference to dimensions, clearances, interference and conformance to architectural requirements. This check is to be made after completion of all working drawings, and before issuing for bidding.

2. Refer to drafting room manual for drafting standards.

3. Review the working drawing check list which has been maintained during progress of the work.

4. Check the following: a. sheet index against sheet titles, and against sheet index in specifications. b. title blocks and revision blocks. c. north arrows. d. general notes on all drawings for spelling, clarity and general usage. e. all dimensions on architectural plans. f. cross references between small scale plans and large scale details.

Structural, Mechanical, and Electrical Plans

5. Check the architectural plans against the structural plans for: a. column identification. b. all dimensions c. slab openings. d. slab depressions.

6. Compare architectural, structural, mechanical, plumbing, and electrical plans for agreement on location and size of openings.

7. Compare the architectural and structural drawings with the mechanical drawings for possible impaired headroom.

8. Check the architectural, mechanical, and electrical plans for proper location of motors, fans, pumps, compressors and other equipment.

9. Check the architectural plans and the mechanical plans with the electrical plans: a. location and size of switches, panel guards, telephone equipment. b. locate water heaters and drinking fountains on architectural plans.

10. Check the architectural, mechanical, and electrical plans to make sure wall and furred spaces have sufficient clearances for pipes, ducts.

11. Check the architectural drawings with the plumbing drawings for locations and number of roof drains, downspouts, sprinkler risers, vents through roof, toilet fixtures, etc. Access panels must be noted. Check number of toilet fixtures with code requirements.

12. Check the architectural and structural drawings with the mechanical drawings for location of equipment, ducts, air inlets, exhausts, etc. Check for proximity of exhaust and intakes to wall openings. Check that any large equipment has proper structural support. Look for possible beam interference.

The renovation checklist is a collection of general notes that should be considered for every renovation project. Not all of them will apply in every situation, but those that do should be included.

Pay particular attention to the note regarding the presence of asbestos. Either the presence of asbestos (or other hazardous materials, such as lead-based paint, PCBs, etc.) has been verified by the owner, or it has not. The note should reflect the proper condition.

Add other notes as necessary to respond to the actual conditions of the project.

RESPONSIBILITIES OF THE GENERAL CONTRACTOR
WITH REGARD TO EXISTING CONDITIONS

A. GENERAL

1. Information contained on these drawings with regard to existing conditions of construction is provided for the convenience of the General Contractor in executing the work. Every attempt has been made to provide complete and accurate representations of such existing conditions. This interpretation has been taken from record sets of "as-built" drawings on file at and has as been further supplemented by extensive field-measurement and observations. The Architect cannot and does not guarantee the accuracy of any such information and assumes no liability therefore.

2. The information contained on these drawings with regard to existing conditions of construction in no way releases the General Contractor from the responsibility for verifying completely all field conditions relating to and affecting the execution of the work, as described in these contract documents.

3. It is the responsibility of the General Contractor to field verify and document all existing dimensions, elevations and benchmarks, materials and methods of construction that may affect or be affected by new work, and to coordinate such field verification with the contract documents and the execution of the work. Discrepancies and/or conflicts involving anticipated existing conditions shall be brought to the Architect's attention immediately.

4. Field-verification of existing conditions related to specific portions of the work shall be undertaken in advance to allow for the timely identification of existing conditions that may affect the scheduled installation of new work as designed and detailed, and to avoid undue and unreasonable delays to the project should such conditions be discovered. Timely identifications of such conditions shall provide for a minimum period of ten (10) working days during which time the Architect will evaluate the conditions and make recommendations for accommodating new work.

5. It is the responsibility of the General Contractor to assist the Architect in making their evaluations and recommendations by providing in a timely manner, at no additional cost to the Owner, accurate and complete drawings, sketches, and photographs sufficient to clearly describe discrepancies, conflicts, and concealed or otherwise unanticipated existing conditions affecting new construction.

6. The General Contractor shall further assist the Architect by providing in a timely manner prepared solutions to unanticipated existing conditions.

7. The Architect has endeavored to identify as completely as possible in the drawings and specifications existing items of equipment and construction that are required to be removed or otherwise demolished so as to allow the execution of new work. This information is provided for the convenience of the General Contractor, and is in no way intended to mean that demolition is limited only to those items specifically identified. It is the General Contractor's responsibility to execute demolition work as required to allow the execution of new work.

8. All areas above or on the existing ceiling that are affected by installation of new work shall be repaired completely with materials and products to match existing installation and fire-rated assemblies.

9. All items indicating contract limits and lines of demarcation are shown of the convenience of the General Contractor, and are not to be taken literally. Actual contract limits are to be determined by the General Contractor prior to bid openings by field verification. The General Contractor is responsible for ensuring proper interface between existing and new work.

10. The General Contractor must be aware that construction in some areas surrounding the limits of this contract is currently in progress. For this reason, actual existing conditions may vary from conditions indicated on these drawings. All such discrepancies shall be accurately and thoroughly recorded by the General Contractor and promptly reported to the Architect.

11. The General Contractor is responsible for identifying all signage and other assemblies that may be affected by demolition or installation of new work. Such project elements shall be removed and stored prior to the performance of any work. The Contractor is responsible for cataloging each element and its location in the building, and is responsible for reinstalling each element in its original location after all work in the area has been completed.

12. The General Contractor is responsible for identifying any unfinished wall areas that may be exposed as a result of adjusting finished ceiling heights. The Contractor is responsible for finishing these areas to match existing adjacent finished areas and fire-rated assemblies.

13. The General Contractor and affected subcontractors shall visit the project site prior to submitting a proposal. The Contractor shall become generally familiar with the project, and with the impact of the new work on the existing conditions. Any areas of concern shall be brought to the attention of the Architect prior to submitting a proposal. No additional charge to the Owner will be approved which is attributable to the Contractor's failure to do this.

14. The project is currently occupied, and must remain completely operational during normal business hours (7:00 a.m. to 6:00 p.m. weekdays). Coordinate with the Owner any construction activities which may impede normal operations, including any activity which operates excessive noise, airborne dirt, or which disrupts the normal functionality of the space. Protect any adjacent space with dust partitions or curtains from activities which will create dust. Notify any occupants of the building of any construction activities which may affect their ability to operate normally.

15. ASBESTOS LOCATION AND ABATEMENT—The Architect has been made aware that others have determined the presence of asbestos in the premises. The Architect understands that others have prescribed or may prescribe procedures for location and abatement of asbestos. These plans and specifications do NOT contain information from which asbestos may be located nor have they been prepared in contemplation of asbestos removal. Before any work is performed under these plans and specifications, the contractor performing the work should become fully aware of the location of asbestos and abatement procedures, if any, for asbestos. The Architect undertakes no responsibility to provide such information or guidance, and the contractor should contact the Owner directly with respect to asbestos location and abatement.

B. BUILDING ACCESS, AND CAPACITY OF EXISTING BUILDING STRUCTURE

1. It is the responsibility of the General Contractor to identify points of access to the building and to verify minimum clearances available for use in transporting necessary construction machinery, equipment, materials, and components into the building. Use of such points of access shall be approved by the Owner.

2. It is the responsibility of the General Contractor to identify existing components and assemblies within the building that are constructed as fire-rated assemblies and to determine their hourly fire rating.

When the execution of new work requires that these assemblies be disturbed, the contractor shall undertake to repair the existing work so that the required fire rating is maintained.

C. EXISTING LIFE SAFETY AND EMERGENCY SYSTEMS

1. Existing life safety and emergency systems may not be shown on the drawings in their entirety.

2. The General Contractor is responsible for field-verification of location and extent of these systems (including but not limited to fire sprinkler systems, smoke detection systems, emergency lighting systems) as they may be affected by new work. The General Contractor is responsible for accommodating these systems when affected by new work so that all applicable code requirements are satisfied.

D. PHOTOGRAPHS OF EXISTING CONDITIONS.

1. Photographs of existing building conditions are included on portions of these drawings. Information contained on these photographs is provided for the convenience of the General Contractor. Existing conditions may vary from what these photographs show. It shall be the responsibility of the General Contractor to verify all field conditions prior to the time of the bid and alert the Architect to any discrepancies between existing conditions and what the photographs show.

2. The general condition of the building, including the conditions of the finished surfaces and materials, shall be inspected, photographed, and recorded by the General Contractor prior to beginning any work. Any change to these conditions which occurs after making this record will be attributed to construction operations, and it shall be the responsibility of the General Contractor to restore any part of the project to the condition shown in the record.

E. CONTRACTOR'S PROJECT RECORD DOCUMENTS

1. Maintain at the job site one copy of all drawings, specifications, addenda, approved shop drawings, field orders, and other contract modifications, and other approved documents submitted by the Contractor in compliance with various sections of the Specifications.

2. Each of these Contractor's Project Record Documents shall be clearly marked "Project Record Copy," maintained in good condition, available at all times for observation by the Architect, and not used for construction purposes.

3. Mark on the most appropriate Documents to show significant changes made during the construction process, and significant detail not shown in the original Contract Documents. The information given shall include, but not be limited to:

   a. The location of underground utilities and appurtenances referenced to permanent surface improvements.

   b. The location of internal utilities and appurtenances concealed in the building structures, referenced in visible and accessible features of the structures.

4. Upon completion of the work, the General Contractor shall provide the Owner one complete set of documents marked "Project Record Documents" showing changes to be original documents.

Coordination Checklist

COORDINATION CHECKLIST

The Coordination Checking Checklist provided here is to be used to clarify which discipline is responsible for checking what things in which other disciplines. You will see duplication of this responsibility, which is intentional.

Use the boxes after each item to record the specific discipline responsible for coordinating that particular item, and then forward copies to each discipline. Some consultants are reluctant to take responsibility for coordinating their work with other consultants, but this should never be permitted. As the architect, we have responsibility to coordinate the work of all disciplines, but this does not relieve the consultants of the responsibility for coordinating their work with any discipline that might be affected, or that might affect their work.

The following Coordination Checklist was taken (in part) from the REDICHECK checklist authored by William T. Nigro. It is used here by permission; however, permission for use is limited to in-house checking and coordination of drawings. Third-party use, such as by coordination consultants, is expressly prohibited.

	A	S	M	E
1. Verify that property line dimensions on survey or civil site plans match architectural.				
2. Verify that building is located behind setback lines.				
3. Verify that locations of columns and bearing walls, and overall building dimensions match structural.				
4. Verify that existing and new work are clearly identified on site plans.				
5. Verify that building elevations match floor plans; in particular, check roof lines, window and door openings, louver openings, exterior light fixtures, and expansion joints.				
6. Verify weep hole elevations with site grading.				
7. Verify that building sections match elevations and plans.				
8. Verify that wall sections match architectural and structural building sections.				
9. Verify that sizes of openings for windows and doors match structural; verify window glass types with specifications.				
10. Verify that expansion joints are continuous throughout building.				
11. Verify that large scale partial floor plans match small scale floor plans.				
12. Verify that reflected ceiling plans match architectural floor plans to ensure no variance with wall locations. Include room numbers on RCPs.				
13. Verify that locations of mechanical registers/diffusers and electrical fixtures on mechanical and electrical plans do not conflict with locations shown on reflected ceiling plans.				
14. Verify that room finish schedule information matches plan and elevation information, including room numbers, names of rooms, finishes, and ceiling heights. Look for omissions and inconsistencies.				
15. Verify that door schedule information matches plan and elevation information, including sizes, types, labels, etc.; look for omissions and inconsistencies. Coordinate straight frames in curved walls. Note differences when "similar" conditions are referenced.				
16. Verify that appropriate roof membrane protection has been provided for window washing system.				

17. Verify that items to remain and items to be demolished are shown clearly in both plan view and section or elevation. Make sure that notes regarding salvage of items to be removed are consistent with owner's wishes.

18. Verify that concrete scoring patterns, and control and expansion joints are clearly shown.

19. Coordinate vertical masonry coursing with opening locations and sizes. Verify coursing control points when interfacing new masonry with existing. Coordinate locations of lintels, brick ledges, and special coursing with structural.

20. Verify that head and jamb details provide adequate space for hinges, closers, astragals, push bars, etc.; confirm that all finishes for builders hardware has been specified and coordinated.

21. Verify that landscape irrigation vacuum breaker location has been concealed or located in an inconspicuous location.

22. Verify that transitions between guardrails and handrails have been addressed.

23. Review floor finish thicknesses at doors and material transitions; confirm clearances for doors and accessibility for wheelchairs.

24. Verify that owner-provided equipment has been coordinated in plan view and interior elevations. Make sure that it is clear which party furnishes and which party installs each piece of equipment (furnished by owner, installed by general contractor? Furnished and installed by general contractor?) Verify any items of equipment that must be recessed (such as control and alarm panels). Make sure there is adequate length, height, and **depth.** Keep recessed items out of rated walls whenever possible.

25. Verify that locations of fire rated walls matches the locations of fire and/or smoke dampers on mechanical plans. Verify mechanical and electrical equipment clearances.

26. Verify that cabinets, water coolers, fire extinguishers and hose cabinets, toilet room accessories, etc., will fit in available space and partition thicknesses. Verify that electrical outlets on cabinet walls are the correct height. Coordinate heights and locations of casework with electrical, telecommunications, plumbing, and mechanical. Allow adequate filler strips at each end. Coordinate computer and electrical cabling and equipment security requirements with owner. Plan grommets and raceways for cabling.

27. Verify that flashing materials, gauges, and construction methods match between drawings and specifications.

28. Verify that sealant types shown on the drawings are the same as those specified.

	A	S	M	E
29. Verify that the locations of flag poles, dumpster pads, and landscaping have been coordinated with other discipline site plans.				
30. Verify that all assemblies terminate as required by code at adjacent wall conditions.				
31. Verify that design patterns in wall and floor finishes are coordinated with required joints, such as control joints in gypsum board walls and soffits.				
32. Confirm the content and spelling of all notation, titles, labels, etc.				
33. Verify that the sheet index accurately reflects the actual drawing numbers, names, and sequence.				
34. Verify that cross-references (building section references, wall section references, detail references, interior elevation references, etc.) are complete and correct.				
35. Verify that all partitions are identified with a partition type designation, and that the fire ratings indicated by partition types match ratings shown on RCPs.				
36. Verify that room names and numbers are consistent between/among plans and room finish schedule.				
37. Verify that keyed notation identifies the proper materials.				
38. Verify that new work is easily distinguishable from existing work (remodel projects)				
39. Verify that the titleblock is correct and is consistent with the identifying information shown elsewhere on the floor plan sheets.				
40. Verify that the drawing title, scale, drawing number, north arrow, and key plan are provided on all plan sheets.				
41. Verify that all partitions, partition offsets, alcoves, etc., are dimensioned.				
42. Verify that changes in floor elevations have been addressed with spot elevation marks, and that railings are provided where necessary.				
43. Verify that door locations and door swing directions permit wheelchair access and exit egress. Check hardware schedule for closers, coordinators, stops.				
44. Confirm that details do not show dissimilar materials with different construction tolerances to be in alignment with each other without a reveal.				

	A	S	M	E
45. Check for consistency between large-scale details and the smaller scale drawings from which they were referenced.				
46. Verify that control joints are shown in large areas of drywall.				
47. Verify that all surfaces are shown to receive paint or other finish.				
48. Verify that insulation is contiguous.				
49. Verify that alternates are clearly defined and differentiated from base bid conditions.				
50. Make sure fire-rated corridors maintain the continuity of the fire rating.				
51. Verify that fire-rated corridors or rooms have fire-rated ceilings, or that the perimeter walls extend to structure. Verify that the ceiling/roof assembly is adequate to maintain the fire rating.				
52. If fire rated ceilings are used, verify that the specifications include a section on fire-rated ceilings.				
53. Confirm that all light fixtures in rated ceilings are tented with drywall, if necessary.				
54. Confirm that fire-safing is called out on partition types, details, or general notes.				
55. Confirm that UL numbers are shown on partition types, and that the UL design matches the design shown.				

SPECIFICATIONS -- Plan Check Coordination	A	S	M	E
1. Check that bid items explicitly state what is intended.				
2. Check specifications for phasing of construction.				
3. Compare architectural finish schedule to specification index.				
4. Check major items of equipment and verify that they are coordinated with contract drawings				
5. Verify that items specified "as indicated" or "where indicated" in the specifications are in fact indicated on the drawings.				
6. Verify that all specifications are in the index, and that related specification sections are identified.				
7. Try to avoid indicating thicknesses or quantities of materials in the specifications.				
8. Verify that specifications are tailored to the project.				
9. Avoid duplications between specifications sections.				
10. Make sure specifications include Schedule of Alternates.				
11. Specified desired finishes in mechanical, electrical, and storage spaces.				
12. Confirm that performance specifications thoroughly address specific design requirements.				
13. Include thorough mock-up requirements in specifications.				
14. Verify that sealant colors have been considered and specified accordingly. Indicate joint width tolerances.				
15. Verify that a custom color is specified where it is desired.				
16. Verify that attachment systems for rigid and batt insulation are specified, and that the systems will work for all applications, especially unsupported horizontal installations.				

CIVIL-- Plan Check Coordination	A	C	M	E
1. Verify that new underground utilities have no interferences • power • telephone • water • sewer • gas • storm drainage • fuel lines • grease traps • fuel tanks		●		
2. Verify that existing power/telephone poles, guy wires, street signs, drainage inlets, valve boxes, manhole covers, etc., do not interfere with new driveways, sidewalks, or other site improvements.		●		
3. Verify that limits of construction, clearing, grading, sodding, grass, or mulch are shown, and are consistent with other disciplines.		●		
4. Verify that fire hydrants and street light poles do not conflict with other above ground items.		●		
5. Verify that profile sheets show underground utilities and avoid conflicts.		●		
6. Verify that horizontal distances between drainage structures and manholes match scaled dimensions and stated dimensions on both plan and profile sheets.		●		
7. Verify that all existing and proposed grades are shown.		●		
8. Verify that all tie-ins from roof drains and perimeter drains are shown connected to storm drains.		●		
9. Confirm that civil engineer is providing coordination with city and utility service providers.		●		
10. Verify that civil drawings are graphically and dimensionally consistent with architectural and other discipline drawings.		●		
11. Verify that site lighting does not conflict with lighting on adjacent sites.		●		
12. Coordinate utility penetrations through retaining walls and site features. Indicate retaining wall elevations.		●		
13. Identify use of adjacent site areas for soil storage and detention during construction.		●		
14. Verify that survey completely ties existing buildings and facilities to property lines on all sides.		●		

STRUCTURAL -- Plan Check Coordination	A	S	M	E
1. Verify that column grid lines on structural and architectural match.		●		
2. Verify that column locations are the same on structural and architectural.		●		
3. Verify that perimeter slab on structural matches architectural.		●		
4. Verify that depressed or raised slabs are indicated and match architectural.		●		
5. Verify that slab elevations match architectural.		●		
6. Verify that foundation piers are identified and sized on a schedule or plan.		●		
7. Verify that foundation beams are identified and sized on a schedule or plan.		●		
8. Verify that locations of roof framing column lines and columns match foundation column lines and columns.		●		
9. Verify that structural perimeter roof line matches architectural roof plan.		●		
10. Verify that columns, floor beams, and roof beams are listed in column and beam schedules.				
11. Verify that length of columns in column schedules matches the length shown in the sections and the elevations shown on plans.		●		
12. Verify that sections are properly labeled.		●		
13. Verify that expansion joint locations match other disciplines.		●		
14. Verify that dimensions match architectural.		●		
15. Verify that drawing notes do not conflict with specifications.		●		
16. Coordinate interior movable partition locations and plumbing fixture locations to avoid conflicts with locations of structural elements.		●		
17. Consider sequencing. Coordinate penetrations for terrazzo, pedigrid, etc., with architectural.		●		
18. Verify that structural steel and deck finishes have been coordinated with fireproofing requirements.		●		
19. Verify that structural drawings identify "primary" and "secondary" or "unrestrained" members, since fireproofing requirements are generally stipulated according to these classifications.		●		
20. Verify that structural drawings include a note referring subcontractors to the architectural drawings for all miscellaneous steel. All miscellaneous steel should be shown on the architectural drawings, but sizes should be provided by structural engineer. Structural drawings should show details of connections of miscellaneous steel to structural members.		●		

	A	S	M	E
21. Verify that appropriate structural supports have been provided for window washing systems.		●		
		●		
		●		
		●		
		●		
		●		
		●		
		●		
		●		
		●		
		●		
		●		
		●		
		●		
		●		
		●		

MECHANICAL and PLUMBING-- Plan Check Coordination	A	S	M	E
1. Verify that plumbing floor plans match architectural floor plans.			●	
2. Verify that new gas, water, sewer, etc., lines connect to existing or new utilities on civil drawings.			●	
3. Verify that plumbing fixtures match fixture schedules and architectural locations.			●	
4. Verify that roof drain locations and roof slopes match architectural roof plan.			●	
5. Verify that pipes are sized sensibly and that drains are connected and do not interfere with foundations.			●	
6. Verify that wall chases are provided on architectural to conceal vertical piping.			●	
7. Verify that sanitary drain system pipes are sized and all fixtures are connected.			●	
8. Verify that HVAC floor plans match architectural.			●	
9. Verify that sprinkler heads are in appropriate rooms and do not interfere with other ceiling items.			●	
10. Verify that mechanical/plumbing ducts and pipes do not conflict with architectural features or structural members.			●	
11. Verify that adequate ceiling height exists at worst case duct intersections or largest beams.			●	
12. Verify that structural supports required for mechanical equipment are indicated on structural drawings.			●	
13. Verify that dampers are indicated at smoke and fire walls.			●	
14. Verify that diffuser locations match architectural reflected ceiling plans.			●	
15. Verify that openings for roof penetrations (ducts, fans, etc.) are indicated on structural roof plans.			●	
16. Verify that ductwork is sized logically.				
17. Verify that notes are referenced.			●	
18. Verify that air conditioning units, heaters, and exhaust fans match architectural roof plan locations.			●	

	A	S	M	E
19. Verify that mechanical equipment will fit in spaces allocated and that there is room for maintenance, such as removing filters or tubes.				
20. Verify that horsepower ratings, phases, and voltages of major items of equipment on mechanical and electrical drawings and specifications match.				
21. Verify that thermostat locations have been coordinated with architectural drawings; thermostats should not be located in the center of walls which may receive artwork.				
22. Coordinate exterior mechanical pad locations and loads with soils report recommendations.				
23. Verify that sound isolators are adequate for size and location of mechanical equipment.				
24. Refer to architectural drawings for locations of devices which are visible in finished areas.				
25. Verify that outside dimensions have been considered for pipes and ductwork (for clearances with other work), and not just inside dimensions used in design.				
26. Verify that slopes have been considered for roof and sewer drains, and that pipes do not run below ceilings.				
27. Make sure that damper requirements are indicated on partition types on the architectural drawings.				
28. Confirm that horizontal rated ductwork is detailed on the mechanical drawings.				
29. Verify that items requiring service or maintenance access are in areas with accessible ceilings, or that access panel locations have been coordinated with architectural design.				

ELECTRICAL -- Plan Check Coordination	A	S	M	E
1. Verify that electrical floor plans match architectural and mechanical; check that the location of floor mounted equipment is consistent between disciplines.				●
2. Verify that the location of light fixtures matches architectural reflected ceiling plan and that light fixtures do not conflict with the structure or mechanical HVAC system.				●
3. Verify that major pieces of equipment have electrical connections and that horsepower ratings, phases, and voltages are consistent with other disciplines schedules.				●
4. Verify that locations of panel boards are consistent with architectural, mechanical, and plumbing floor plans, and that the panel boards are indicated on the electrical riser diagram.				●
5. Verify that notes are referenced.				●
6. Verify that there is sufficient space for electrical panels to fit.				●
7. Verify that electrical panels are not recessed in fire walls.				●
8. Verify that exterior electrical equipment locations are coordinated with site paving, grading, and landscaping.				●
9. Verify that structural supports are provided for rooftop electrical equipment.				●
10. Verify that locations of electrical conduit runs, floor trenches, and openings are coordinated with structural floor plans.				●
11. Verify power requirements for all mechanical equipment.				●
12. Refer to architectural drawings for locations of devices which are visible in finished areas.				
13. Confirm that light switches, outlets, cover plates, etc., are the appropriate color or finish for the design.				●
14. Confirm that lightning rod locations and aircraft warning light locations have been coordinated with architectural drawings.				●
15. Make sure that architectural interior elevations show thermostats, switches, intercoms, phone and electrical outlets, etc., and that the locations are coordinated with both architectural and mechanical drawings.				●
16. Confirm that light fixture lamp types have been coordinated with owner standards or requirements.				●

There are some very simple but important procedures we must follow during bidding.

Typically, we are responsible for issuing the drawings to prospective bidders.

- All sets of drawings should be numbered, and the Owner, our consultants, and ourselves should receive a numbered set.

- Names, addresses, and phone numbers for everyone who receives a bid set should be recorded in the "Register of Bid Documents," which should be kept in a separate file folder in the central files.

- When the specifications require it, a deposit should be collected from all prospective bidders before drawings are released to them. Drawings may be issued to anyone willing to pay a deposit, provided restrictions are not placed on this by the Owner. When the Owner limits the number of sets available for deposit, sets may be purchased by interested parties.

- Partial sets should not be issued. Too often a supplier's work is affected by other work shown elsewhere in the drawing set. The specifications require the Contractor to provide a complete project based on all the drawings. However, if we issue partial sets, a sub or a supplier could make a claim that we should have known what drawings he would need, and should have provided them even if he didn't ask for them. Don't do it.

- Frequently, a select group of bidders will be invited by the Owner to bid on the project; when this is the case, a limited number of sets is usually made available (for deposit) to each bidder.

When drawings are issued for competitive bidding, there is some very important protocol that we must follow to ensure that we are not responsible for giving a competitive advantage to any bidder.

- First, all of our specifications should include a time frame for receipt of all questions (for example, 72 hours before the bid opening).

–   Some projects may warrant a requirement for all questions to be in writing, but more commonly, we allow questions to be asked over the phone.

–   Our specifications should also state a point in time prior to the bid after which no further clarifications can be issued (for example, 48 hours prior to the bid). Sufficient time must be allowed for all bidders to receive the addendum before they must submit bids.

*   It is very important that no questions be answered over the telephone, even if you think you know the answer.

–   All questions should be carefully recorded in your telephone log, and answers or clarifications should be issued in written or graphic form through appropriate channels to all plan holders. Plan holders are listed on the AIA document "Register of Bid Documents," with addresses and telephone numbers.

–   We have an addendum format on floppy disk for the word processor, a copy of which is included later in this manual.

(Insert AIA Document G804 Register of Bid Documents
or your office standard here)

Addenda

Addenda are changes made to the drawings anytime after the drawings are formally issued for bidding and before a contract is signed between the Owner and the Contractor.

- Occasionally, drawings may be issued formally prior to the Bid Issue; for example, drawings may be issued to the Building Department or to the Owner before they are issued for bidding.

  - Any changes made to the drawings after a formal issue of any kind must be recorded.

  - If these changes are made prior to issuing the drawings to a contractor for pricing, an addendum is not necessary. However, the changes should be "clouded" on the originals, and a revision symbol included at each change. The revision symbol (delta) should have a number, and the revision number should be dated in the titleblock. All revisions issued on the same date should have the same number. Usually a description or "title" of the revision is also included on the sheet in a conspicuous location.

- Questions invariably come up during bidding that must be answered prudently and promptly (see the section on "BIDDING").

  - Addendum dates should be scheduled at the time the drawings are issued, usually allowing weekly intervals for each addendum spread out over the bid period. Do not issue any Addendum later than 72 hours prior to bid opening.

  - Addenda should be issued on our standard Addendum form.

  - Addenda are numbered sequentially, beginning with "Addendum #1."

  - Addendum items that are described verbally must be given an item number. This number begins with "AD" and the addendum number, followed by the item number (AD1- 01).

  - Addendum items should be sequenced to follow the same order as the drawings which they modify. Items which modify the specifications should be first, and should also be sequenced in numerical order.

– Addendum drawings should be listed in the verbal portion of the addendum, and should be given a number in numerical sequence.

– Addendum drawings that modify one of the original drawings should be identified with the addendum number and the number of the drawing. The first change to a given drawing should be labeled "a," the second "b," etc. (for example, AD1- A3.1a).

– Any new drawings which do not modify one of the original drawings are labeled as follows:
  AD1.01
  AD1.02
  etc.

– Addendum drawings should be issued on 8½ x 11 titleblock wherever possible. When this is not possible, use 11 x 17 title block. When neither of these sizes will work, use 24 x 36 or 30 x 42 (whichever size the original drawings were produced on).

Usually the specifications require that requests for substitutions for any products must be made during the bid period. Requests should come through the architect and be distributed to consultants if necessary.

• All such requests should be duly recorded and either approved or rejected.

– Requests for substitutions should be recorded in a format similar to the AIA shop drawing log. This should facilitate tracking the status of each submittal.

– All approved requests for substitutions should be indicated in the addenda; any item which is not approved should be disapproved for "cause"; that is, you should have a good reason for disapproving it. "Cause" may be that the item does not compare favorably with some significant specification requirement, or it may even be that insufficient information was received on which to make a determination. Typically we do not include items which are not approved in our addenda; we prefer to communicate disapproval as an act of omission in order to avert confrontations or accusations from manufacturers.

- Any changes made to the drawings by way of addendum should be recorded on the stick set for reference. See the section "STICK FILES/RECORD SETS".

  - If changes must be made after bids are received, it is very important that an addendum be issued to the apparent low bidder so that he or she may have an opportunity to modify the bid before signing a contract.

  - The Owner should also receive all addenda, along with an explanation of why changes are necessary.

  - We should clarify distribution of Addenda to contractors, subcontractors, consultants, building departments, to make certain that everyone understands how important it is that all concerned parties receive all addenda.

  - Changes may be made after bids are received and a contract is signed, if this is the method preferred by the Owner. It will then become a Change Order.

We use our own standard addendum format, which is patterned after the AIA Change Order document.

This form should be prepared by the Project Architect, and then reviewed and signed by the Principal in Charge.

Blank copies of this form are available in the support staff area, and the necessary information should be redlined on these blanks. The support staff will then incorporate it into a computer format.

PRECONSTRUCTION CONFERENCE AGENDA

The preconstruction conference serves the same purpose for the members of the construction team (owner, architect, consultants, and contractor) that our in-house kick-off meeting serves for the design team. Roles, procedures, performance standards, communications, and the like are spelled out in advance so there will be a minimum of misunderstanding.

This agenda should be prepared by the Project Architect in advance of the meeting. It may be altered to suit the requirements of the project or the client.

A copy for each member of the team who will be in attendance should be prepared prior to the meeting, and distributed several days in advance if possible. The agenda may also be used as a place to record discussion and decisions so that the record of the meeting can be distributed to all concerned parties later.

PRECONSTRUCTION CONFERENCE AGENDA

I. Introduction of Key Personnel

A. Owner's Personnel
   1. Owner
   2. Owner's Representative

B. Architect's Personnel
   1. Partner in Charge
   2. Project Architect
   3. Structural Engineer
   4. Mechanical Engineer
   5. Plumbing Engineer
   6. Electrical Engineer
   7. Landscape Architect
   8. Any other consultants who will be reviewing submittals or visiting the job site

C. Contractor's Personnel
   1. Project Manager
   2. Project Engineer
   3. Superintendent

II. Authority and Responsibilities of Key Personnel

A. Define Roles
   1. Owner's Representative
   2. Architect
      a. Partner-in-Charge
      b. Project Architect
   3. Contractor
      a. Project Manager
      b. Project Engineer
      c. Superintendent

B. Chain of Command
   1. Architect/Contractor
      a. Owner's Representative
      b. Architect's Consultant
      c. Subcontractors

III. Review of Scope of Work

    A. Review of work in contract documents
    B. Review of work under separate contracts
    C. Review of work beyond property lines
        1. New pavement, curb, and gutter
        2. New sidewalks
        3. New landscaping
        4. New drainage ditches
    D. Review of any special requirements of specifications sections

IV. Project Procedures

    A. Submittals (shop drawings, product literature, samples)
        1. Review and stamp by General Contractor
        2. Indication of time when Architect's review must be complete
            a. Review by Architect's consultants
        3. Necessary changes which are discovered during submittal review
        4. "Action" required
            a. No Exception Taken
            b. Make Corrections Noted
            c. Revise and Resubmit
            d. Rejected
            e. Submit Specified Item

    B. Clarifications requested by Contractor
    C. Architect's Supplemental Instructions
    D. Requests for Proposal
        1. Establish a time frame for Contractor and Owner response
    E. Construction Change Directives
    F. Change Orders
    G. Applications for Payment
        1. Pencil copy
        2. Cover letter
        3. Lien waivers
        4. Submittal date
        5. Turnaround time
        6. Payment date
        7. Payment for materials stored off-site
        8. Method of payment for general conditions
    H. Requests for Substitutions
    I. Methods for resolving conflicts in the Contract Documents
    J. Methods for handling unsatisfactory work
    K. Record Drawings

Preconstruction Conference Agenda
Continued

V. Time and Order of the Work

    A. Construction Time
        1. Date of Issuance of Building Permit
    B. Liquidated Damages
    C. Progress Schedule
        1. Periodic Updates
        2. Architect has the right to review schedule and order changes
    D. Job Site Meetings
        1. Frequency
        2. Location
        3. Who attends

VI. Special Concerns

    A. Areas requiring special attention to workmanship
    B. Field-constructed mock-ups

Applications for Payment

Applications for Payment (aka Pay Requests) are a contractor's lifeline; they are more important to him than anything else on the job. When the Application for Payment is received, it should be processed as quickly as possible. It should not be delayed for any reason. A delay in the processing of a pay request can lead to a claim for extra time (and money), and the Architect can be held responsible for that delay. Besides that, it will make the contractor even grumpier than usual, and none of us wants that.

The time allowed for us to review the Application for Payment is specified in the General Conditions of the contract documents, and is usually stated as a ***minimum*** of 10 days. In reality and practice, this becomes a ***maximum*** of 10 days. The date of issuance of each progress payment is specified in the Owner/Contractor agreement. Usually, this date is the 15th of the month; that means that the pay request has to be submitted no later than the 5th. That allows the contractor 5 days from the 1st to prepare the information for the pay request, which is based on the previous month's activity, starting on the first day and ending on the last day of the month. If the contractor is late in submitting the pay request, you should warn him that payment may also be late, but don't use that as an excuse to delay processing. Frequently, the specifications require a preliminary pencil version of the Application for Payment. This is reviewed at the regularly scheduled job-site progress meeting closest to the end of the month.

When we review the pay request, we look for several things. First, we must give our opinion as to whether the amount of money requested is in alignment with the amount of work done, as of the end of the period covered by the pay request. This is a judgement call, and should be made by or under close supervision by the Partner in Charge. Part of this assessment is a judgement as to whether the money left unpaid is sufficient to finish the project if the contractor went bankrupt or to jail (both of which have happened) while the project was still under construction. We also check the arithmetic, and we use a computer program to do that for us almost automatically. Updated figures should be plugged in for each successive application.

Generally, the contractor is required to submit a Schedule of Values at least seven days prior to submitting the first pay request. The Schedule of Values breaks the work into several subcategories, and assigns the portion of the contract sum allocated for each portion of the work. This will make it easier for you to judge completeness of the work. Look at the Schedule of Values when you receive it; if you don't think the breakdown is detailed enough, ask the contractor to redo it.

The contract documents commonly require the contractor to submit partial waivers of lien along with the pay request. A lien waiver is a legal document that says the owner has fulfilled that portion of his financial obligation to the contractor represented by the pay request, and the contractor agrees not to put a lien on the property. Make sure the lien waiver is attached when required. The amount stated in the lien waiver should match the amount of the pay request, with retainage subtracted.

The contractor may be uncomfortable or unwilling to submit a lien waiver that is current with the pay request. This is understandable, since he has not yet received payment. If this is the case, the contractor should submit a conditional lien waiver that is subject to payment of the amount requested. Or, with owner approval, lien waivers for the previous month's application may be submitted.

The Supplemental Conditions specify the amount of retainage that should be withheld on each pay application. This could vary, so make sure you understand the requirements. A common arrangement for retainage would be to withhold 10% of each pay request until final payment. Possibly more common would be to withhold 10% until the work was 50% complete, and then not withhold any more. Make sure you know what the retainage requirements are, and verify that the pay request complies.

When the arithmetic is checked and the remainder of the pay request appears to be in order, the Partner in Charge will sign the cover letter for it. It then becomes a Certificate for Payment. It is forwarded to the owner for signature and payment. Make sure the owner understands when he is obliged to make payment. The contractor should submit three copies of the Application for Payment. Keep an unsigned copy for our files until a copy signed by all parties is returned. Make sure the owner knows he should return a signed copy to us. When the contractor, the architect, and the owner have signed all three copies, one copy goes to the contractor, one to the owner, and one to the architect. Sometimes, other parties, such as the lender, will get copies, too. Check the contract documents in the Project Manual.

The Certificate of Payment cover letter is prepared by the Project Architect who is responsible for the contract administration of the project. It must be signed by a Principal in the firm.

We use AIA Document G709 to request a written proposal (price) from the contractor in order to determine in advance the cost of additional work.

This form should be prepared by the Project Architect, and then reviewed and signed by the Principal in Charge.

Approval of all proposals should be obtained in writing from the owner, and then incorporated by reference in a subsequent Change Order. Keep in mind that not all items on a proposal request will be approved. Each item should be numbered sequentially, using the following naming convention:

PR01.12

In this example, the **PR** indicates the document type; in this case, a Proposal Request. The **01** indicates that this is the first Proposal Request for the project, and the **.12** indicates that this is item number 12 of the first Proposal Request.

Blank copies of this form are available in the support staff area, and the necessary information should be redlined on these blanks. The support staff will then either type this information directly on an original AIA document, or it will be incorporated into a computer format which will then allow us to print computerized text directly onto the forms.

Please keep in mind that when we are using AIA documents, we should respect the copyright, and use our computer as a convenient text editor. We should not recreate the entire form in our computer.

All approved proposals (which then eventually become change orders) should be posted in the CA record set of documents.

The scope of work described in a PR should be reviewed by the contractor, and he should confirm that the schedule can accommodate this change. Otherwise, the contractor should indicate the impact of this change on the schedule.

The amount of time the contractor is given to respond to proposal requests should be established at the preconstruction conference.

Proposal Request Log

PROPOSAL REQUEST LOG

This Proposal Request Log is prepared by the Contract Administration (CA) Assistant assigned to the construction phase of the project. Actual data entry may be accomplished by support staff.

Project:
Job Number:

PR Number	DESCRIPTION	DATE ISSUED	STATUS
1			
2			
3			
4			
5			
6			
7			
8			
9			
10			
11			
12			
13			
14			
15			
16			
17			
18			
19			
20			
21			
22			
23			
24			
25			
26			
27			
28			
29			
30			
31			
32			
33			
34			
35			
36			
37			
38			
39			
40			

Requests for Information (RFIs)

REQUESTS FOR INFORMATION (RFIs)

There is no formal document which standardizes Requests for Information (RFIs). These requests originate with the general contractor, and require a response from us. This response may be written or graphic (but they may not be solely oral).

RFIs should be tracked using the attached Log format.

The Project Architect is responsible for completing this form, although this responsibility may be delegated to another member of the contract administration team.

If RFIs result in changes to the documents, they must be posted on the CA record set.

RFIs should be discussed at the preconstruction conference, and it should be determined whether an RFI is an acceptable instrument to effect changes in the work. The AIA provides several other documents for this purpose, and we discourage the use of ASIs (the typical document used to respond to RFIs) to make changes for that reason. There are many pieces of paper required to track activities during construction that cannot be eliminated. We should simplify the tracking procedures wherever and however we can.

Architect's Supplemental Instructions (ASIs)

We use AIA Document G710 to provide written instructions to the contractor for minor changes in the work that do not involve a change in the contract sum or the contract time.

This form should be prepared by the Project Architect, and then reviewed and signed by the Principal in Charge.

Approval of all Supplemental Instructions should be obtained in writing from the owner. Each item should be numbered sequentially, using the following naming convention:

ASI01.12

In this example, the **ASI** indicates the document type; in this case, a Supplemental Instruction. The **01** indicates that this is the first Supplemental Instruction for the project, and the **.12** indicates that this is item number 12 of the first Supplemental Instruction for the project.

Blank copies of this form are available in the support staff area, and the necessary information should be redlined on these blanks. The support staff will then either type this information directly on an original AIA document, or it will be incorporated into a computer format that will then allow us to print computerized text directly onto the forms.

Please keep in mind that when we are using AIA documents, we should respect the copyright, and use our computer as a convenient text editor. We should not replicate the entire form in our computer.

All ASIs should be posted on the CA record set of documents.

(Insert AIA Document G710 Architect's Supplemental
Instructions or your office standard here)

ARCHITECT'S SUPPLEMENTAL INSTRUCTIONS LOG

Project:
Job Number:

ASI Number	DESCRIPTION	DATE ISSUED
1		
2		
3		
4		
5		
6		
7		
8		
9		
10		
11		
12		
13		
14		
15		
16		
17		
18		
19		
20		
21		
22		
23		
24		
25		
26		
27		
28		
29		
30		
31		
32		
33		
34		
35		
36		
37		
38		
39		
40		

Construction Change Directives

We use the AIA Document G714 Construction Change Directive as the formal instrument for changes which may involve a change in the contract sum or contract time, but for which there is insufficient time to solicit a proposal from the contractor and to get the owner's approval in advance.

However, the contractor should not get carte blanche. He must begin immediately to determine any changes in the contract sum or contract time. An agreement should be reached on these issues before the Construction Change Directive is converted into a change order.

The Construction Change Directive replaces the former Construction Change Authorization, which in turn replaced the former Field Order. Both of the prior documents are now obsolete and should not be used.

The Project Architect is responsible for completing these forms, although this responsibility may be delegated to another member of the contract administration team.

Construction Change Directives should be carefully tracked using the CCD Log attached here for your reference.

(Insert AIA Document G714 Construction Change
Directive or your office standard here)

Project:
Job Number:

CCD Number	DESCRIPTION	DATE ISSUED
1		
2		
3		
4		
5		
6		
7		
8		
9		
10		
11		
12		
13		
14		
15		
16		
17		
18		
19		
20		
21		
22		
23		
24		
25		
26		
27		
28		
29		
30		
31		
32		
33		
34		
35		
36		
37		
38		
39		
40		

Change Orders

Change orders are usually originated by the contractor. Our specifications should require that the contractor use the AIA Document G701 for this purpose. Any approved proposal requests should be incorporated into this document.

Change orders should include any changes in the contract time, as well as changes in the contract sum.

Three copies of each change order should be required from the contractor. They should be signed by the contractor before he forwards them to us. We should review them to make sure they include only approved proposals, and that the change order accurately reflects the approved information shown on the proposal. We should then sign it and forward three copies with original signatures to the owner, keeping a non-original copy for our files until a signed copy is returned to us. We should make sure the owner is aware of his responsibility to sign all three copies, and then return one of them to us, and one to the contractor. He should keep one for his own records.

Construction Change Directives should also be incorporated into the change order.

(Insert AIA Document G701 Change Orders or your
office standard here)

While it is the purpose of the working drawings to clearly, completely, and accurately describe and define a project, it is not their intent to function as fabrication drawings for the contractor. Each element of the work is subject to layout and fabrication criteria that are solely in the domain of the contractor and his subs. These layout and fabrication criteria are spelled out in precise detail in the shop drawings, based on what is shown in the working drawings. Shops comprise a fundamental step in translating architectural design into built reality. Whereas construction documents combine the ingredients of architecture to communicate design intent and **one** way of realizing that intent, shop drawings indicate **the** way specific components of a building are to be fabricated and assembled.

Our contracts for professional services usually include provisions requiring us to review shop drawings submitted by the general contractor. This offers us significant opportunities:

- To continue guiding design execution by confirming that our drawings have been correctly interpreted and that proposed materials conform to the requirements of the specifications.

- To further protect ourselves from claims by checking for errors or omissions in the construction documents.

- To learn from exposure to new techniques and materials.

Our office has developed certain submittal standards that should be incorporated in the specifications. You should also be aware of what these requirements are, and why they were established as they were.

Our submittal standards are as follows:
· shop drawings   1 reproducible (sepia) and 3 bluelines
· product literature   1 original and 3 copies
· samples   2 each

Shop Drawings
We will return only the marked up sepia to the contractor. The 3 bluelines are required only to facilitate the review process, but none are returned to the contractor. The typical distribution of these materials is as follows:

–Assuming consultant review is required, send the sepia and one blueline to the primary consultant. This consultant will use the blueline as a worksheet to draft his or her review comments. These comments are then transferred to the sepia, which is returned to us. The primary consultant makes a print of the sepia for his or her own records, and either keeps or discards the worksheet copy.

–When the primary consultant review copy is returned, we then send out the marked-up sepia and another blueline to a secondary consultant, if one is involved. The procedure for the secondary consultant is the same as for the primary consultant. If review by a secondary consultant is not required, the second blueline may be discarded.

–When the secondary consultant has returned the marked-up sepia, we will then perform our review. We will use the third blueline as a worksheet to record drafts of our comments. When our review is completed, we will transfer our comments to the sepia, and then we will make prints for each affected consultant, as well as ourselves. The sepia is then returned to the contractor, bearing an imprint of our rubber stamp indicating the required action. The consultant's stamp should also appear on each submittal. Remember, we should stamp everything that goes through our office, even if it already bears the stamp of our consultant. And by stamping it, we are obligating ourselves to review it, as well. Our "action required" should never be less stringent than the action required by our consultant; however, it may be more stringent. The worksheet blueline should be retained if it contains comments made by the reviewer that are not needed by the contractor, but that might facilitate review of resubmittals.

Product Literature
The original and 3 copies of product literature are to be handled in the same manner as the shop drawings.

Samples
We approve the use of selected materials based upon the qualities exhibited by the samples of those materials as submitted by the contractor. The owner has a right to receive the same level of quality— color, color variation, texture, finish, etc.—that we have observed in the submitted samples. The only manageable way we have to assure the owner of this level of quality is to review and accept two samples of each material. One sample is returned to the contractor, whose job it is to make certain his suppliers provide materials that are comparable in quality to that sample. We use our sample to compare with materials actually installed in the work. If we observe discrepancies, deviations, or significant variations, we should call them to the attention of the contractor, and require replacement of the defective product. Our sample is always retained in our internal CA files until the project is completed.

You may encounter a subcontractor who requests (demands) a blueline copy of a shop drawing or a copy of product literature with a wet ink stamp and our original signature. Sometimes, this sub may request an original wet-stamped print for any number of suppliers, sub-subcontractors, etc. Obviously, this request is the result of some legal entanglement that this sub has experienced. However, we should take a hard line against this. This effort requires much unnecessary extra work that we do not get paid extra to do. The specifications should make it clear what we will do and what we won't. Besides, it should be in the contractor's domain to make copies for his subs. Our owner-architect agreement should always indicate that prints, xerox copies, or other reproductions made of submittals are expenses incurred on behalf of the owner in the interests of the project, and that we will be reimbursed for them, in accordance with the contract language regarding reimbursable expenses.

Theoretically, the responsibility for the content of the shop drawings lies with the general contractor. His agreement with the building owner requires him to provide products, materials, and construction in strict conformance with the contract documents. It also makes him solely responsible for the methods and sequencing of construction. The architect's review (remember, theoretically) is a convenience to the general contractor. The architect looks for conformance with the intent of the construction documents as indicated in the language included in the rubber stamp, which is applied to every submittal:

> CHECKING IS ONLY FOR GENERAL CONFORMANCE WITH THE DESIGN CONCEPT OF THE PROJECT AND GENERAL COMPLIANCE WITH THE INFORMATION GIVEN IN THE CONTRACT DOCUMENTS. ANY ACTION SHOWN IS SUBJECT TO THE REQUIREMENTS OF THE PLANS AND SPECIFICATIONS. CONTRACTOR IS RESPONSIBLE FOR: DIMENSIONS WHICH SHALL BE CONFIRMED AND CORRELATED AT THE JOB SITE; FABRICATION PROCESSES AND TECHNIQUES OF CONSTRUCTION; COORDINATION OF HIS WORK WITH THAT OF ALL OTHER TRADES; AND THE SATISFACTORY PERFORMANCE OF HIS WORK.

The general contractor is responsible for the detailed review of shop drawings. He is to verify that the shop drawings are consistent with the architectural drawings, field conditions, construction tolerances, etc., and he must verify that information shown on one set of shop drawings is fully coordinated with other shops, and with other trades. The contractor indicates that he has completed this review by stamping and signing the submittal and noting any action to be taken. In reality, the procedure varies with each contractor. For this reason, our reviews must be considerably more thorough than for general conformance with design intent.

We review only those submittals (a submittal is a shop drawing, a sample, or manufacturer's literature) that are required by the specifications. Any submittals not required by the specifications should be returned to the contractor unreviewed, with a letter indicating that it was not required and it was not reviewed.

The specifications require the contractor to review submittals before he submits them to you, but this is not done uniformly by all contractors. Be on the lookout for this, to make sure the contractor performs his review. The contractor can look for coordination issues that you may not be aware of. Require the contractor to stamp each submittal, and to approve it before he sends it to you. If he doesn't, return it to him as above. (It should be made clear at the preconstruction conference that we expect thorough checking and stamping by the general contractor. This is for his benefit in coordinating the work).

Do not accept partial submittals. Frequently, a contractor will ask you to begin your review before he can provide complete shop drawings. This is intended to get a preliminary reaction from you on the level of completeness and accuracy of the submittal. It is possible that this could save the contractor time, but it will double your time. Don't do it. Return any partial submittals to the contractor immediately upon receipt, along with an explanation of why you have not reviewed them. Incomplete submittals should be brought to the attention of the contractor. The review period should not begin until complete submittals are received. However, judgment and fairness must be used regarding this.

The specifications should spell out the time we require for review and return of submittals. Keep in mind the review process described above. If a primary and a secondary consultant is involved, we need time to distribute the submittal to each, they need time to review and return it to us, and we need time to review and return it to the contractor. Put in a couple of weekends, and your time could be used up before you even have a chance to look at a given submittal. We like to require a turn-around time of 15 working days, to ensure everyone of the necessary time to do a responsible review. Of course, this will not please the contractor, who will say that every other architects with whom he does work turns shops around in 10 calendar days. Don't buckle. Instead, tell the contractor that you would be more than willing to review selected shops in a shorter time period, if he can convince you that that is necessary. But with only rare exceptions, hold the line on the 15 working days. Be sure to remind the contractor that if his submittals are not timely, the review period may need to be extended.

A submittal schedule (as required and described in the specifications) is to be provided by the general contractor. Where numerous shops are to be submitted at one time, the contractor should indicate which ones are to receive priority.

Dimensions should be checked, and corrected if necessary. A rubber stamp is used to mark the shops, placing full responsibility for correctness of dimensions shown on the contractor, as follows:

> GENERAL CONTRACTOR'S RESPONSIBILITY FOR DIMENSIONS
>
> Dimensions shown on this drawing have been reviewed (and revised, if necessary) by the Architect, solely as a convenience to the General Contractor. This in no way releases the General Contractor from his responsibility for providing correct dimensions on the shop drawings, in accordance with the construction documents, or from his responsibility to coordinate such dimensions with the work of other trades, and any field conditions which may affect the dimensions indicated here.

Our action is to be indicated by stamping the submittal with our shop drawings "ACTION" stamp. Submittals reviewed by consultants must have the consultant's action indicated as well.

We should review and stamp all submittals, even if they clearly pertain to one of our consultant's disciplines. Our review should be for general conformance with the design intent, as indicated in the shop drawings stamp.

Shop Drawings Review
Continued

Prior to receipt of any shop drawing submittals, the reviewer should have the shop drawings log and filing system in place. A sample of the log is included with this handout. It should be filled out as required. The filing system consists of one or more accordion files (11" x 17" minimum size) placed in a file storage box. Organize the files according to CSI Division number (1-16), and use a numerical sequence within each division. The shops log is to be kept in space number one, along with the first submittal.

Upon receipt of a submittal (which should arrive with a transmittal describing the complete contents), check to be certain all items were received as specified. Confirm that the submittal is one that is required by the specifications. Then:

- Use a submittal numbering system to record each submittal. The contractor should indicate which specification section applies to each submittal, and you should use that number to identify each submittal. For example:

  · 03300-1.0   (to identify the first submittal received in section 03300)
  · 03300-1.2   (to identify a resubmittal of the first submittal)
  · 03300-2.0   (to identify the second submittal in section 03300)
  · 03300-2.1   (to identify the first resubmittal of the second submittal)
  · 03300-2.2   (to identify the second resubmittal of the second submittal)
  · etcetera

  Assign a consecutive log number to the submittal. Separate submittals must receive separate log numbers. The log numbers must correspond to the number of the slot in the accordion file in which the submittal will be filed.

- File the transmittal in the central transmittal file.

- Log in the submittal. Fully describe each item included. For example, instead of "Door Hardware," log in "Door Hardware" *and* a description of each specific hardware item submitted. Be sure to record the date on which the submittal was received, and the quantity.

- In logging in a resubmittal, use the same log number as the original submittal, but with a letter suffix added (for example, 23, 23A, 23B).

During the construction phase, the architect typically serves as a central point through which all submittals from the contractor flow. We review those pertinent to our areas of responsibility, and then return them directly to the general contractor. Others relating to the engineering disciplines must be forwarded immediately to the appropriate consultant, checked, and returned to the architect. We review those submittals as well, and stamp them with our shop drawings "ACTION" stamp. We may require more stringent action than our consultants require, but never less. Then we return them to the contractor. A transmittal must accompany the submittal on each leg of its journey.

Shop Drawings Review
Continued

Prepare for review of submittals by reading pertinent specification sections and familiarizing yourself with the applicable portions of the drawings. Review the shop drawings with the Shop Drawings Checklist (attached). Answer each question on the checklist, and make certain the submittal is complete and in order. Then begin a methodical review of the shops. Look for:

- Conformance with approved manufacturers and products

- Consistency with the design intent

- Conformance with specified levels of quality

- Conformance with referenced standards

- Conformance with applicable code requirements

Usually during construction, the temptation will arise to correct a deficiency in our drawings by changing shop drawings. Resist this temptation. No changes to the contract documents should be made in this manner. Always follow the typical procedure for identifying, pricing, and executing changes.

Submittal Log

This Submittal Log is prepared by the Contract Administration (CA) Assistant assigned to the construction phase of the project. Actual data entry may be accomplished by support staff.

(Insert AIA Document G712 Shop Drawing and Sample
Record or your office standard here)

Stick Sets

The office stick files are reserved for complete record sets of drawings for any project in the Bidding/Negotiations or Contract Administration phases.

- This set is available to the Project Architect or the Job Captain (or CA Assistant) for reference in receiving telephone queries about the project.

  - As addenda are issued, notes are made on the stick set referencing a specific addendum number. Each written or graphic change is "posted" to the record set. That is, a copy of the addendum is cut out and pasted or taped to the record set in the appropriate location. New drawings which supersede older ones may be pasted right on top of the older ones, along with the appropriate change reference.

- During construction, further clarifications or changes to the drawings are inevitable.

  - When Supplemental Instructions, Change Orders, Construction Change Directives, and the like are issued, they should also be posted to the record set on the stick file.

  - When drawings in the stick set are changed, copies of the revised version should be taped down over the superseded drawings, where possible. Where this is not feasible, the changed drawing should be marked "Superseded," and reference to the new drawing should be given.

When construction is complete, this record set should be saved in the tube storage system.

Record Drawings

The contractor is frequently required by the specifications to maintain a set of blueline prints at the jobsite, showing all "as-built" conditions. This set should be posted in the same manner in which our office record set is. RFIs, ASIs, accepted PRs, etc., should be cut out and pasted in appropriate locations on the set, or, if adequate space is not available, on the back of the preceding sheet. Other changes should be recorded in red ink in the appropriate locations on the drawings. You should review this set each time you visit the jobsite. This set should be kept clean, undamaged, and legible at all times, because this is the "as-built" set for the project, and it is very, very important. The specifications should indicate that payment may be withheld in the event of the contractor's failure to do this.

However, it is not the "record drawing" set that our contracts often require us to provide. Record sets are generally required to be reproducible on a diazo print machine. But, beyond that, our experience has shown that an accepted industry standard for what constitutes a "record drawing" is very difficult to come by. In the days before CAD, some owners required that architects change the original mylars to reflect all changes in the project. However, this does not permit a realistic way to deal with the myriad kinds of changes recorded throughout the project from a variety of sources (such as the PRs, ASIs, RFIs, etc.). With the increasing popularity of CAD, owners are now requiring that these kinds of changes be done on CAD, and then plot new mylars. This seems to be the wave of the future, even though this method also does not permit a realistic way to deal with all of the changes made to the drawings via other kinds of instruments of change. If you are lucky (very lucky), you may be able to convince your clients that drawings, whether CAD or hand-drawn, are merely instruments of service, and not databases for facilities management purposes. If you are that fortunate, a better way to create "record drawings" would be to make full-size mylar xerox copies of the contractor's as-built drawings. If you are not that fortunate, then you have to make sure you can be compensated for the duplicative (and some might say redundant) effort required to change the original mylars or CAD drawings that were changed once already by some other method. If you have extremely good foresight (and equally good CAD skills), you may be able to change CAD drawings on the fly, to create drawings plotted in small windows to make changes for RFI (etc.) purposes. In that event, you wouldn't have to do it again later, obviously. But the safest way to protect yourself against having to do work that you hadn't negotiated a fee for is to clear all of this up in the contract. That way, at least you have an opportunity to negotiate a fee; whether or not you are successful depends on you.

Another source of potential disagreement is the manner in which changes are documented on the record set. Let's say your original design included a bell tower which was deleted during construction. Your change drawings might cloud the tower, with a note that says "delete." However, your client may feel justified in saying that the tower was not built, and record drawings should be modified so that they no longer show the tower. Again, we could find no industry standard to govern this kind of thing. It is better to include some language in your owner-architect agreement that states specifically what you intend to do. An example might be:

> The architect shall provide the owner with a reproducible set of record drawings for the project. This record set will be in the form of full-size xerox copies on mylar of the contractor's as-built drawings, which shall include all changes made to the project, whether by written or graphic means. Changes to the original mylar drawings or the original CAD files shall be performed as an additional service at the hourly rates outlined in Article __ of this agreement.

Always remember to require a signed return receipt when transmitting either as-built or record drawings to the owner, or anyone else.

The architect has the responsibility during construction to make sure the construction is proceeding in conformance with the contract documents (all of them, not just the drawings). This is done through observation rather than inspection (the design-professional liability insurance people have stricken the word "inspection" from the minds and mouths of modern—and postmodern—architects everywhere), and through review of submittals. This chapter deals with our observation responsibilities.

The time you spend observing construction in-progress is likely to be some of the most educational time you will ever spend in this business. However, the opportunities to do it as part of your job responsibilities are just as likely to be few and far between. You should look for opportune times to visit job sites, even if you have to do it on your own time. The dividends this will pay in your daily work will be enormous.

If you are fortunate enough to be selected to participate in construction observations as one of your assignments, you will also probably be fortunate enough to be selected to write the field report which must follow every visit. Here are some things to keep in mind:

Prepare yourself before visiting the job site.
- Find out what construction activities will be going on during your visit; then, review the drawings and specifications to familiarize yourself with that portion of the work.

- Familiarize yourself with the General and Supplementary Conditions; know your rights and duties in administering the contract. Know also what you are not responsible for.

- Familiarize yourself with the "execution" sections of the specifications in particular; remember that construction methods and techniques are the responsibility of the contractor.

- Be familiar with any standards referenced in the specifications.

Verify that the completed work is consistent with the Application for Payment.
- Generally, this judgment will be made by the Partner in Charge, but your knowledge of the project will make your opinion valuable to him or her.

Keep in mind the purpose of your observations.

• Your purpose is to verify that the construction is proceeding generally according to the contract documents. That doesn't mean you need to measure the distance between caissons, but it does mean that you should see caissons rather than spread footings.

• Think about construction that comes later, and look for some assurance that the contractor is thinking about it too. Sequencing of the work is the contractor's responsibility, but if drywall is going up and there is no backing to receive the shelving standards later, you should query the contractor about it.

• Make sure you get the quality of workmanship the owner deserves. Contractors are touchy about this, so you'll have to be careful about how you present any questions about workmanship. Keep in mind that the first subcontractor on the site sets the standard of performance (and the prevailing mindset) for all those who come later. You may want to choose your battles here carefully. For example, would you rather have footings that were perfectly straight, or would you rather that the joints in the rosewood veneer be perfectly tight and smooth? Remember that you aren't going to find perfection everywhere, just as your drawings aren't going to be perfect. But you do have the right (and the responsibility) to insist on high-quality workmanship.

• While you are at the job site, invariably you will be asked questions seeking clarification of design intent. The architect is the final authority on questions of artistic effect, so wield this power cautiously. Remember that the contractor views you as much the architect (when it serves his purpose) as he does the Partner in Charge. Anything you say can and will be used against you in a kangaroo court. Do not give direction directly to subs; always communicate through the superintendent.

• The architect has the right to reject the work, but this decision rests with the Partner in Charge. Never stop the work unless directed to do so by the owner.

Record your observations, and document them in a report.

• Create standards for documentation; use a three-ring binder for notes, with graph paper for sketches.

• Always check in with the superintendent before touring the site. Try to get the superintendent to accompany you (this will not be difficult), and try to review your observations and comments with him before you leave the site.

• Describe in general the progress and quality of work at the site; avoid being overly detailed.

- Try recording your observations on a hand-held tape recorder. This method will keep you on track in objectively reporting what you see, rather than editorializing, particularly if a 300-pound superintendent is escorting you through the project. Of course, hand-written notes always work, too.

- Follow-up your visit with a report; we use AIA Document G711, printed via computer.

- Note all conversations, including those with the subcontractors.

- Note deviations from the contract documents—be meticulous.

- Note questions from the contractor.

- Always take a camera with you; photograph the general progress of the work, and specific details of interest.

- Include selected snapshots with your report; refer to them specifically in the text of your report when convenient. And remember, they may be very educational for people back at the office.

Our role during construction is to make sure the owner receives the project that is described in the contract documents. Even though we are being paid by the owner, we must always remain objective in interpreting or enforcing the requirements shown in the documents. Obviously, the owner wants the best project possible for the money. And so do we. But we must remain ever mindful of the realities of the construction process. There may a difference between good or acceptable workmanship, and perfection. If the owner is demanding perfection, you may have to express your opinion that the work is of an acceptable level of quality. If the contractor is being a bit sloppy, you must be on top of that as well. But, first and foremost, you must be objective and fair. You are not on the owner's side, and you are not on the contractor's side. You are on the side of the project, and you must do what you have to do to make the project successful.

(Insert AIA Document G711 Architect's Field Report or
your office standard here)

The following punchlist format has been developed and refined over many years of use. Please conform to this format when you create punchlists.

You may find it to be time-conserving to dictate punchlist comments into a hand-held tape recorder. If you do, take a copy of this format along with you so that you will be able to dictate according to the prescribed format.

Often, the contractor will ask you to make a premature punchlist visit. This multiplies our work many times. Resist this temptation. Demand that the contractor complete the work before you make the trip. Also, require the contractor to do his own punchlist before he asks you to come out to the job site. Then use his list for reference when you go. The punchlist should not be used as a "Items to be Finished" list.

Review the schedule several weeks in advance of the punchlist timeframe. Make sure the contractor understands our expectations, and that he allows adequate time, both for us to perform the punchlist activities, and for him to take remedial action on any punchlist items.

Sometimes, the owner will ask us to do a post-punchlist visit. This is a visit to make sure all of the items on the punchlist are satisfactorily addressed. Make sure the general contractor and each affected subcontractor has personally inspected and addressed each item on the list before they ask you to come out. The punchlist format should include a column for each contractor and sub to sign off the work within their area of responsibility.

Certificate of Substantial Completion

CERTIFICATE OF SUBSTANTIAL COMPLETION

We use AIA Document G704 to establish the date of Substantial Completion for the project. The AIA has developed a legal definition of the term *substantial completion*, and this definition should be used to determine the actual date. As a practical matter, the date of substantial completion is usually defined as the date that the client or owner can begin to use the building for its intended purpose. This means that the date will usually occur after final punchlist items have been addressed. Occasionally, the schedule for occupancy of the building demands that this date be interpreted a bit more loosely, and this should be discussed with the Principal in Charge.

This form should be prepared by the Project Architect, and then reviewed and signed by the Principal in Charge.

The Certificate of Substantial Completion should not be issued before the Certificate of Occupancy (or the Temporary Certificate of Occupancy) has been issued by the Building Department.

Once the Certificate of Substantial Completion has been issued, the owner then becomes responsible for operating the building, for maintaining it, and for repairing any damage discovered after issuance. Make sure the owner is comfortable with the status of the work and for assuming these responsibilities.

Blank copies of this form are available in the AIA Handbook. The necessary information should be redlined on these blanks. The support staff will then either type this information directly on an original AIA document, or it will be incorporated into a computer format which will then allow us to print computerized text directly onto the forms.

Please keep in mind that when we are using AIA documents, we should respect the copyright, and use our computer as a convenient text editor. We should not recreate the entire form in our computer.

(Insert AIA Document G704 Certificate of Substantial
Completion or your office standard here)

Project Closeout Checklist

PROJECT CLOSEOUT CHECKLIST

There are many activities going on at the end of a construction project. The owner is highly motivated to move in, the contractor is highly motivated to move out. Important administrative items can easily get lost or forgotten in the skirmish. The following Project Closeout Checklist is provided for your use to help keep track of these things. Share it with the owner and the contractor to make sure everyone is aware of those items requiring their attention.

Project Closeout Checklist

Project:
Architect:
Address:

Phone:

Item	Specification Section	Date Submitted	Date Confirmed	Confirmed By	Request for Additional Data	Date Received	Remarks
Record Documents	1700.1.01						
Schedule A Completed--Receipts for Extra Materials	1700.1.04						
Delivered to Owner	1700.1.04						
Final Application for Payment	1700.1.04						
Consent of Surety	1700.1.04						AIA Form G707A
Contractor's Affidavit of Payment of Debts and Claims	1700.1.04						AIA Form G706
Inspection Certificates	1700.1.05						
Schedule B Completed--Warranties	1700.1.06						
Miscellaneous Keys and Switches	1700.1.07						
Schedule C Completed--Maintenance Manuals and	1700.1.08						
Parts Lists	1700.1.09						
Schedule D Completed--Demonstrations/Tests	1700.1.10					8710.2.01 E,A	
1 Year Maintenance Schedule	1710.1.03						
Final Cleanup	800.2.24						
Advertisement of "Notice of Contractor's Final Settlement"	1700.1.02						
Check of Any Claims for Payment/Amounts to Withhold	1700.1.02						
Issue Final Punchlist and Certificate of Substantial Completion	1700.1.02A						
Process Final Application for Payment							
Final Inspection							
Issue Final Certificate of Payment							

Project Closeout Schedule A--Receipts for Extra Materials Delivered to Owner

Project:

Architect:
Address:

Phone:

Item	Specification Section	Date Submitted	Date Confirmed	Confirmed By	Request for Additional Data	Date Received	Remarks

Project Closeout Schedule B--Warranties

Project:

Architect:
Address:

Phone:

Item	Specification Section	Date Submitted	Date Confirmed	Confirmed By	Request for Additional Data	Date Received	Remarks

Project Closeout Schedule C--Maintenance Manuals and Parts Lists

Project:

Architect:
Address:

Phone:

Item	Specification Section	Date Submitted	Date Confirmed	Confirmed By	Request for Additional Data	Date Received	Remarks

Project Closeout Schedule D--Demonstrations and Tests

Project:
Architect:
Address:

Phone:

Item	Specification Section	Date Submitted	Date Confirmed	Confirmed By	Request for Additional Data	Date Received	Remarks

RECORDS RETENTION SCHEDULE

In order to respond to frequent questions about what things we should keep, where we should keep them, and for how long, and to anticipate as yet unasked questions about these things, we have prepared the following *Records Retention Schedule*, for your reference (and **use**).

This is a living document. The "paperless" office has seemingly produced at least one new piece of paper that we have to find a place for every day. If you discover something not listed here, make a note of it on your copy, and then let's make sure we have made a conscious decision about whether to keep it or not, and for how long.

This schedule will have to be modified to reflect the storage methods and devices in each office, as well as the computer back-up systems available.

Records Retention Schedule

What is it?	Where to Keep it?	Until When?	Then What?	Remarks
Pre-Design				
Project Files	General file storage cabinets	Project closeout	Dead storage	
Planning Submittal Materials	General file storage cabinets	Project completion	Dead storage	
Presentation Materials				
Boards	Studio/Team pod display areas	Project completion	Discard	Discard only after partner consultation
Models	Studio/Team pod display areas	Project completion	Give to Owner	Give away only after partner consultation
Existing Facilities Survey				
Measured Drawings	Flat files	Project closeout	Dead storage	Return originals to Owner
Owner-Supplied Information	Flat files	Project closeout	Dead storage	Return originals to Owner
Record Drawings Received	Flat files	Project closeout	Dead storage	Return originals to Owner
Photographs	Project files	Project closeout	Dead storage	Return originals to Owner
Schematic Design (SD)				
Project Files	General file storage cabinets	Project closeout	Dead storage	
Drawings--Original Mylars	Project Flat File	End of SD	Tubes	
Drawings--Presentation Copy (colored)	Promotion Flat File	End of SD	Tubes	
Drawings--Office Copy Prints for Team Use	Project Stick Files	End of DD	Discard	
Drawings--Office Copy Prints for Reference	Reference Stick Files	Indefinite	Indefinite	
Drawings--Office Copy Redlines	Project Architect	End of SD	Discard	
Drawings--File Server Copy	Project Directory	End of SD	Make tape copy	
Drawings--Tape Backup Copy (system-wide backup)	System Administrator	Daily tape backup	Weekly tape backup	Monthly backups to off-site storage
Drawings--Tape backup (project-specific backup)	System Administrator	Created at end of SD	Stored indefinitely	Tape backup to off-site storage when file server copy is deleted
Specifications--Originals	Project Files	Project closeout	Dead storage	
Specifications--Redline markups	Project Architect	End of SD	Discard	
Specifications--File Server Copy	Project Directory	Project closeout	Make tape copy	
Specifications--Tape Backup Copy	System Administrator	Updated daily	Updated weekly	Monthly backups to off-site storage
Specifications--Office Copy for Team Use	Project Architect	End of SD	Discard	Discard only after partner consultation
Presentation Models	Gallery	Until further notice	Pod display areas	Confirm with PIC
Study Models	Studio/Team pod display areas	Project closeout	Discard	Discard only after partner consultation
Model Photographs	Marketing Coordinator	Indefinite	Indefinite	
Presentation Boards	Owner or Studio/Team pod	Project closeout	Discard	Discard only after partner consultation
Design Development (DD)				
Project Files	General file storage cabinets	Project closeout	Dead storage	
Drawings--Original Mylars	Project Flat File	End of DD	Tubes	
Drawings--Presentation Copy	Promotion Flat File	End of DD	Tubes	
Drawings--Office Copy Prints for Team Use	Project Stick Files	End of CDs	Discard	
Drawings--Office Copy Prints for Reference	Reference Stick Files	Indefinite	Indefinite	
Drawings--Office Copy Redlines	Project Architect	End of DD	Discard	
Drawings--File Server Copy	Project Directory	End of SD	Make tape copy	
Drawings--Tape Backup Copy (system-wide backup)	System Administrator	Daily tape backup	Weekly tape backup	Monthly backups to off-site storage
Drawings--Tape backup (project-specific backup)	System Administrator	Created at end of DD	Stored indefinitely	Tape backup to off-site storage when file server copy is deleted
Specifications--Originals	Project Files	Project closeout	Dead storage	
Specifications--Redline drafts	Project Architect	End of DD	Discard	
Specifications--Office Copy for Team Use	Project Architect	End of DD	Discard	
Specifications--File Server Copy	Project Directory	Project closeout	Make tape copy	
Specifications--Tape Backup Copy	Office Administrator file cabinet	Updated daily	Updated weekly	Monthly backups to off-site storage
Presentation Models	Gallery	Until further notice	Pod display areas	Confirm with PIC
Study Models	Studio/Team pod display areas	Project closeout	Discard	Discard only after partner consultation
Model Photographs	Marketing Coordinator	Indefinite	Indefinite	
Presentation Boards	Owner or Studio/Team pod	Project closeout	Discard	Discard only after partner consultation

Records Retention Schedule

Construction Documents (CDs)

Project Files	General file storage cabinets	Project closeout	Dead storage	
Drawings--Original Mylars	Project Flat File	End of CDs	Tubes	
Drawings--Presentation Copy	Promotion Flat File	End of CDs	Tubes	
Drawings--Office Copy Prints for Team Use	Project Stick Files	End of CDs	Discard	
Drawings--Office Copy Prints for Reference	Reference Stick Files	Indefinite	Indefinite	
Drawings--Office Copy Redlines	Project Architect	End of CDs	Discard	Discard only after partner consultation
Drawings--File Server Copy	Project Directory	End of CDs	Make tape copy	
Drawings--Tape Backup Copy (system-wide backup)	System Administrator	Daily tape backup	Weekly tape backup	Monthly backups to off-site storage
Drawings--Tape backup (project-specific backup)	System Administrator	Created at end of CDs	Stored indefinitely	Tape backup to off-site storage when file server copy is deleted
Specifications--Originals	Project Files	Project closeout	Dead storage	
Specifications--Office Copy for Team Use	Project Architect	End of CDs	Relocate to Reference Spec	
Specifications-Redline drafts	Project Architect	End of CDs	Discard	Discard only after partner consultation
Specifications--File Server Copy	Project Directory	Project closeout	Make tape copy	
Specifications--Tape Backup Copy	System Administrator	Updated daily	Updated weekly	Monthly backups to off-site storage
Reference Samples	Project Architect	Construction samples are received	Generally discard; save special samples in samples	Review selections to retain with PIC
Presentation Models	Gallery	Until further notice	Pod display areas	Confirm with PIC
Study Models	Studio/Team pod display areas	Project closeout	Discard	Discard only after partner consultation
Model Photographs	Marketing Coordinator	Indefinite	Indefinite	
Presentation Boards	Owner or Studio/Team pod	Project closeout	Discard	Discard only after partner consultation

Bidding/Negotiation (B/N)

Bid Sets	Bidders	End of Bidding	Owner/Contractor	
Addenda--Originals	Project files	Project Closeout	Dead storage	
Addenda--Copies	Bidders	End of Bidding	Owner/Contractor	

Construction Administration (CA)

Project Files	General file storage cabinets	Project closeout	Dead storage	
Shop Drawings and Product Literature	Accordion Files/CA Assistant	Project Closeout	Dead storage	
Samples	Studio CA staging area	Project closeout	Discard	Discard only after partner consultation
CA Record Set	CA Architect or Assistant	Record drawings are complete	Tube	
CA Record Specifications	CA Architect or Assistant	Record drawings are complete	Relocate to Reference Specifications	
Reproducible record drawings	Flat files	Record drawings are complete	Give to Owner	

Bibliography and Suggested Reading

PURPOSE

The following list of titles includes all the resources we have used to prepare the information in this manual, as well as others we have found useful in our own practice of architecture. These are time-honored references that have been explaining "how to do it" for many years. Any of these books would be good reading, and all of them deserve a place on your library shelf. If there is any you are not familiar with, get it from you library or bookstore.

PROPOSITION

The following list can be used to conduct research to find the information that is not included in this manual.

Ambrose, James, ed. *Construction Details.* New York: John Wiley & Sons, 1992.

Callendar, John Hancock, ed. *Time-Saver Standards for Architectural Design Data.* New York: McGraw- Hill, 1974.

Callendar, John Hancock, ed. *Time-Saver Standards for Building Types.* New York: McGraw- Hill, 1973.

Ching, Frank. *Architectural Graphics.* New York: Van Nostrand Reinhold Company, 1975.

Ching, Francis. *Building Construction Illustrated.* New York: Van Nostrand Reinhold Company, 1975.

Detailing for Building Construction - Designer's Manual of Standard Details. Boston: Butterworth Architecture, 1988.

Handbook to the Uniform Building Code. Whittier, CA.: International Congress of Building Officials, 1991.

Hoke, John Ray, ed. *Architectural Graphic Standards.* New York: John Wiley & Sons, 1988.

James, Gregory, and Versen, Michael *Site Details.* New York: Van Nostrand Reinhold Company, 1989.

Liebing, Ralph, and Paul, Mimi Ford. *Architectural Working Drawings.* New York: John Wiley & Sons, Inc., 1977.

O'Connell, William *Graphic Communications in Architecture.* Champaign, IL: Stipes Publishing Co., 1972.

POP Manual - Recommended Standards on Production Procedures. by Committee on Production Office Procedures Northern California AIA, 1980.

Reznikoff, S.C. *Interior Graphic and Design Standards.* New York: Whitney Library of Design, Watson-Guptill, 1986.

Rush, Richard, ed. *Building Systems Integration Handbook.* Boston: Butterworth–Heinemann, 1986.

Stitt, Fred. *Systems Drafting.* New York: McGraw–Hill, 1980.

Stitt, Fred. *Systems Graphics.* New York: McGraw–Hill, 1984.

Sutherland, Martha. *Lettering for Architects and Designers.* New York: Van Nostrand Reinhold Company.

Wiggins, Glenn. *Construction Details for Commercial Buildings.* New York: Whitney Library of Design, 1988.

This Appendix contains ready-to-use examples of documents discussed in the body of this manual. They may be copied on the office xerox machine and used as they are, or they may be modified and adapted for the specific uses of the office in which you find yourself. Many of the documents included here are ready to be applied directly to your mylar drawings. If you are producing your drawings on the computer, you may wish to replicate these documents on the computer, rather than the xerox machine.

ABBREVIATIONS

AFF	Above Finish Floor	M.O.	Masonry Opening
ARCH	Architect(ural)	(N)	New
BLDG	Building	NIC	Not in Contract
CJ	Control Joint	NOM	Nominal
CLG	Ceiling	NTS	Not to Scale
CONC	Concrete	O.C.	On Center
CONT	Continuous	O.D.	Outside Diameter
C.T.	Ceramic Tile	OPG	Opening
DIA	Diameter	OPP	Opposite
D.S.	Downspout	(P)	Paint
DWG	Drawing	PR	Pair
(E)	Existing	R	Riser
EA	Each	(R)	Remove
EJ	Expansion Joint	Re:	Refer (to)
ELEC	Electrical	REQD	Required
EL	Elevation	R.D.	Roof Drain
EQUIP	Equipment	R.O.	Rough Opening
EWC	Electric Water Cooler	S.C.	Solid Core
F.D.	Floor Drain	SF	Square Feet
F.O.C.	Face of Concrete	SIM	Similar
F.O.F.	Face of Finish	SPEC	Specifications
F.O.S.	Face of Stud	S.S.	Stainless Steel
F.R.	Fire-Retardant	STD	Standard
GA	Gauge or Gage	STR	Structural
GC	General Contractor	S.A.C.	Suspended Acoustical Ceiling
G.I.	Galvanized Iron	T	Tread
GYP. BD.	Gypsum Board	T.O.B.	Top of Beam - Steel
H.C.	Hollow Core	T.O.C.	Top of Concrete
H.M.	Hollow Metal	T.O.W.	Top of Wall
HORIZ	Horizontal	TYP	Typical
HT	Height	UNO	Unless Noted Otherwise
I.D.	Inside Diameter	VCT	Vinyl Composition Tile
JT	Joint	W/	With
LAV	Lavatory	WC	Water Closet
MAX	Maximum	WR	Water Resistant
MECH	Mechanical	WWF	Welded Wire Fabric
MFR	Manufacturer		
MIN	Minimum		

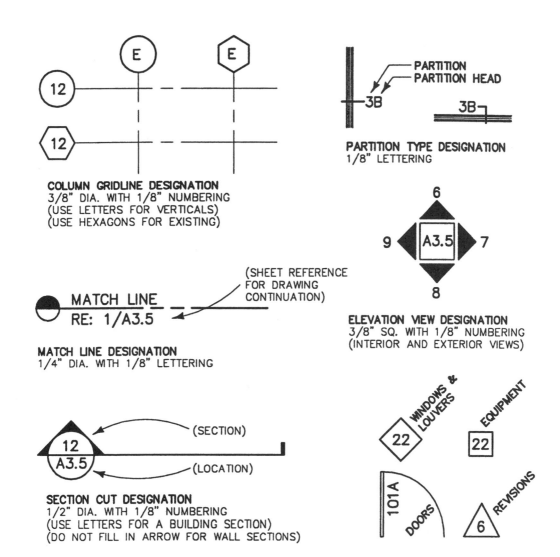

COLUMN GRIDLINE DESIGNATION
3/8" DIA. WITH 1/8" NUMBERING
(USE LETTERS FOR VERTICALS)
(USE HEXAGONS FOR EXISTING)

PARTITION TYPE DESIGNATION
1/8" LETTERING

MATCH LINE
RE: 1/A3.5

(SHEET REFERENCE FOR DRAWING CONTINUATION)

MATCH LINE DESIGNATION
1/4" DIA. WITH 1/8" LETTERING

ELEVATION VIEW DESIGNATION
3/8" SQ. WITH 1/8" NUMBERING
(INTERIOR AND EXTERIOR VIEWS)

(SECTION)
(LOCATION)

SECTION CUT DESIGNATION
1/2" DIA. WITH 1/8" NUMBERING
(USE LETTERS FOR A BUILDING SECTION)
(DO NOT FILL IN ARROW FOR WALL SECTIONS)

WINDOWS & LOUVERS
EQUIPMENT
DOORS
REVISIONS

Standard Symbols

The symbols on this page are suggested for adoption by your office. They were selected for their recognizability as industry-accepted standards, for their simplicity, and for their ability to make drawings easier to read. The above information may be copied onto adhesive-backed material and applied directly to the cover, title, or data sheets of your working drawings. Or, if you prefer, the symbols may be replicated on your CAD system for use on title, cover, or data sheets.

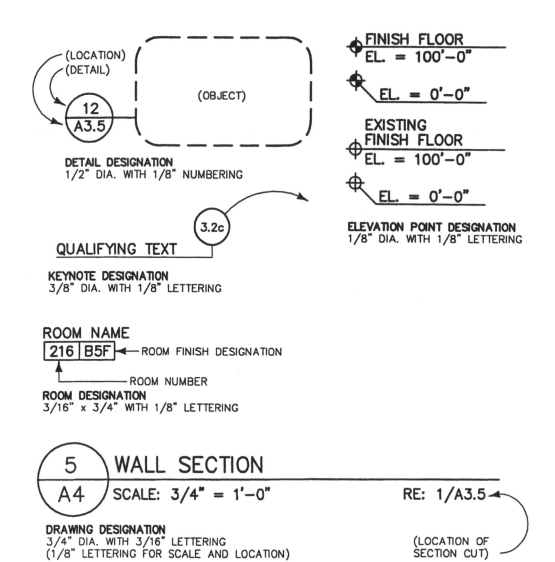

DETAIL DESIGNATION
1/2" DIA. WITH 1/8" NUMBERING

KEYNOTE DESIGNATION
3/8" DIA. WITH 1/8" LETTERING

ELEVATION POINT DESIGNATION
1/8" DIA. WITH 1/8" LETTERING

ROOM DESIGNATION
3/16" x 3/4" WITH 1/8" LETTERING

DRAWING DESIGNATION
3/4" DIA. WITH 3/16" LETTERING
(1/8" LETTERING FOR SCALE AND LOCATION)

Standard Symbols

The symbols on this page are suggested for adoption by your office. They were selected for their recognizability as industry-accepted standards, for their simplicity, and for their ability to make drawings easier to read. The above information may be copied onto adhesive-backed material and applied directly to the cover, title, or data sheets of your working drawings. Or, if you prefer, the symbols may be replicated on your CAD system for use on title, cover, or data sheets.

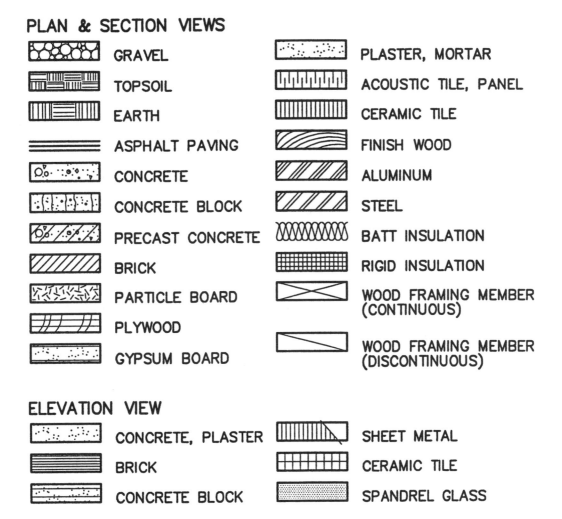

PLAN & SECTION VIEWS

GRAVEL

TOPSOIL

EARTH

ASPHALT PAVING

CONCRETE

CONCRETE BLOCK

PRECAST CONCRETE

BRICK

PARTICLE BOARD

PLYWOOD

GYPSUM BOARD

PLASTER, MORTAR

ACOUSTIC TILE, PANEL

CERAMIC TILE

FINISH WOOD

ALUMINUM

STEEL

BATT INSULATION

RIGID INSULATION

WOOD FRAMING MEMBER
(CONTINUOUS)

WOOD FRAMING MEMBER
(DISCONTINUOUS)

ELEVATION VIEW

CONCRETE, PLASTER

BRICK

CONCRETE BLOCK

SHEET METAL

CERAMIC TILE

SPANDREL GLASS

Standard Materials Indications

The materials indications on this page are suggested for adoption by your office. They were selected for their recognizability as industry-accepted standards, for their simplicity, and for their ability to make drawings easier to read. The above information may be copied onto adhesive-backed material and applied directly to the cover, title, or data sheets of your working drawings. Or, if you prefer, the symbols may be replicated on your CAD system for use on title, cover, or data sheets.

24 X 36

1/8" FLOOR PLANS

The following Work Plan should be used as guide for developing the 1/8" plan working drawing sheets. While some flexibility will be necessary, follow the sequence shown as closely as possible. Complete each item of the work plan before going on to the next; don't complete the entire work plan in one area of the drawing and then go on to the same thing in another area of the drawing, for example. Make sure you understand the CAD layering conventions that should be used, to facilitate making backgrounds for consultants, as well as the architectural reflected ceiling plans.

1. If the sheet size has not already been determined, propose a sheet size that will allow the entire floor plan to fit on one sheet, if possible. If the plan must be divided into parts, propose a division of the plan for review by the Project Architect.

   • When possible, locate match lines in corridors; draw approximately an inch of the floor plan information beyond the match line for ease of reference between drawings.

2. Together will the Project Architect, determine whether the drawings should be drawn on matte polyester film (Mylar), vellum, or some other medium.

   • Determine how the title block information will be put on the sheet (will it be done on CAD, pre-printed, or applied as sticky-back material); confirm the project name, number, address.

3. Establish the drawing area on the sheet.

   • Set aside space for the drawing title, scale, the title block, general notes, and keynotes legend.

4. Determine which direction will be north on the sheet.

   • North should point up on the sheet whenever possible, and to the right for most other situations.

5. Locate the plan near the center of the drawing area unless the plan is small enough to allow other drawings (such as details) to appear on the same sheet.

   • Allow approximately 3" at the bottom of the sheet for the title, scale, and north arrow.
   • Allow space on the drawing in the lower right hand corner for a key plan, if applicable.
   • Allow a 3-1/2"-4" zone next to the titleblock for the keynotes legend

6. Allow zones around the actual plan for:

   • Cross-referencing symbols (1fi" all around)
   • Dimensions (2" all around)
   • Grid identification bubbles (1" all around)

7. Draw structural grid lines and identification bubbles first, on the back of the sheet. Since the grid lines should rarely change, it is better to have them on the back of the sheet where they will not be erased when making changes to other parts of the drawing.

8. Turn the sheet over (and do not put any other information on the back of the sheet, not even poché). Put on the drawing title, the scale, and the north arrow.

9. Draw the structural elements, such as columns, bearing or foundation walls, shear walls.

10. Remember, when drawing floor plan information, show only information inside the building; use the site plan to show exterior improvements, including sidewalks that come right up to the face of the building. Exterior features shown on the floor plan will only clutter the drawing when dimensions and cross-referencing symbols are added, and could easily conflict with site plan information.

11. Add other concrete or masonry walls.

12. Draw the stud walls. Define the thickness of the walls very accurately with thin, light pencil lines first; then when you darken the wall outlines, keep your pencil or pen thickness entirely inside the guidelines. Show a change of material line between stud walls and masonry concrete. Show a change of material line between concrete and masonry as well. When laying out walls and partitions in CAD, use the actual (or nominal for masonry) dimensions for wall thicknesses, to the 1/8 of an inch. This will allow you to use the automatic dimensioning feature of the CAD system when the time comes.

13. Show windows, storefront, borrow lights, and other openings. Be sure to show mullions accurately spaced and drawn to scale.

14. Show stairs and handrails; show handrails extending 18" beyond the risers and returning to the wall to comply with code requirements; show number of risers. Use an arrow that begins on the first riser and ends on the last riser to show the direction of travel.

15. Add door swings and jambs. Doors should be shown open at 90 degrees, using a double line to indicate thickness. Use a thin line to indicate the door swing arc. Use a circle template with a circle of the same radius (to scale) as the door swing itself.

16. Show plumbing fixtures, such as water closets, urinals, lavatories, sinks and mop sinks.

17. Show match lines. If the project is a renovation project, show contract limits.

18. Show countertops, shelves, built-in casework, vanities, partial height walls, and toilet partitions.

19. Show changes in floor materials, floor patterns, changes in floor elevations, floor recesses, ramps, curbs, floor drains, floor outlets.

20. Show toilet room accessories (unless a larger scale plan is provided), electrical panels, water coolers, telephones, mail boxes, refrigerators, ice makers, disposers

21. Show ceiling soffits, plane changes, or other features (such as skylights) with a dashed line.

22. Show equipment (dash in if not in contract).

1/8" FLOOR PLANS (continued)

23. If you are drawing the plans manually, pull them now to make sepias for the reflected ceiling plans.

24. Make a print for pre-planning the dimensions.

25. Add dimensions (see Section 3.3 on Dimensioning).

25. Add room names, numbers, and finish codes. Use "100" series of numbers for the first floor, "200" series for the second floor, etc.

26. Add cross-referencing symbols, including section marks for building sections, wall sections, larger scale plans, plan details, interior elevations, door marks or numbers, partition types, frame or window marks. Information such as partition types and door numbers should be shown only on the 1/8" plans, so users of the plans have only one place to look for this kind of information. Avoid the temptation to duplicate this information on the larger scale versions of the plans, and do not leave it off the 1/8" plans in the areas of the plan blow-ups with the intention of showing it on larger scale plans.

27. Indicate fire-rated partitions only on the reflected ceiling plans, using special pattern tapes, applied to the back of the sheet (unless these patterns can be replicated using CAD).

28. Add keyed notation, general notes.

29. Add miscellaneous items such as fire extinguisher cabinets, access doors, expansion joints, ladders, lockers, shelving, hanging rods, corner guards, roof drain leaders, chalkboards, tackboards, projection screens.

30. Add materials indications (poché) for walls and tile or masonry floors. Concentrate poché at corners and intersections. Do not poché the entire lengths of walls.

SITE PLAN

1. If the sheet size has not already been determined, propose a size that will allow the site plan, in its entirety, to fit on one sheet. If the sheet size has been determined, propose a scale that will allow the entire site plan to fit on the sheet for review with the project architect.

2. Together with the project architect, determine whether the drawings should be drawn on matte polyester film (mylar), vellum, or some other medium.

   • Determine how the title block information will be put on the sheet; confirm the project name, number, and address.

3. Establish the drawing area on that sheet.

   • Set aside space for the drawing title, the title block, general notes, and keynotes legend.
   • Develop a vicinity plan and set aside space for this drawing.

4. Determine which direction will be north on the sheet.

   • North should be the point up on the sheet whenever possible, and to the right in most other situations.

5. Locate the plan near the center of the drawing area unless the drawing is small enough to allow other drawings to appear on the same sheet.

   • Allow approximately 3" at the bottom of the sheet for the title, scale, and north arrow.
   • Allow additional room on the sheet for the vicinity plan.

6. Layout the property lines and any elements that are off but directly adjacent to the site (such as streets, sidewalks, and lighting).

7. Show the limits of the work if only a portion of the site is to be improved.

8. Show all setback lines and easements. If a civil engineer is not involved on the project, show all utilities (including sewer, water, gas, electric, and telephone). Locate transformer vaults, exterior lighting, public telephones, fire hydrants, and catch basins.

9. Locate the building on the site. Draw the building "footprint" on the site plan; the footprint is the plan of the building at ground level (not a roof plan). Add structural gridlines at the extremities of the plan, for reference; intervening gridlines are not necessary.

10. Layout all curbs and paved areas (parking lots, streets, and sidewalks). Show the control joints in concrete paving. If intricate paving patterns exist, show them schematically and refer to an enlarged plan for further detail. Show all parking and street striping.

11. Show drainage patterns including swales, road drainage, and sidewalk drainage.

12. Locate all free-standing walls, retaining walls, fences, and areaways.

13. Show all temporary structures and facilities (including fences, gates, guardhouses, signs, and trailers).

14. Show all structures and facilities that are to be demolished.

15. Draw all miscellaneous architectural items, such as bicycle racks, flag poles, mailboxes and signs.

16. Show datum elevations at building entrances and periodically at sidewalks, curbs, and gutters. Indicate finished floor elevation for the first floor and relate to datum elevation. If no civil engineer is involved on the project, datum elevations need to be shown at all catch basins, retaining walls, intersections of roadways, and corners of buildings.

17. Show all landscaped areas and trees. If a landscape architect is not involved on the project, another site plan may have to be developed which shows the type and location of the trees, shrubs, ground cover, irrigation systems, and other landscape features.

18. Dimension all property lines, buildings, streets, parking lots, sidewalks, walls, retaining walls, fences and lighting poles.

LARGE SCALE FLOOR PLANS

1. Together with the project architect, determine whether the drawings should be drawn on matte polyester film (mylar), vellum, or same other medium.

   • Determine how the title block information will be put on the sheet; confirm the project name, number, and address.

2. Establish the drawing area on the sheet.

   • Set aside space for the drawing title, the title block, general notes, and keynotes legend.

3. Locate the plans in the drawing area. Most sheets are large enough to accommodate several plans; plans should be arranged so that equal amounts of white space lay between them.

   • Allow enough space between each row of sections for the title and scale.

4. Allow zones around each plan for:

   • Dimensions
   • Grid identification bubbles
   • Cross-referencing symbols

5. Draw structural grid lines and identification bubbles first, on the back of the sheet. Since the grid lines will rarely change, it is better to have them on the back of the sheet where they will not be erased when making changes to other parts of the drawing.

6. Turn the sheet over (and do not put any other information on the back, not even poche). Show the drawing title, the scale, and the north arrow.

7. Draw the structural elements, such as columns, bearing or foundation walls, and shear walls.

8. When drawing the enlarged plans, show only information that is in need of more detail than is shown on 1/8" scale plans. Do not duplicate information which is more appropriately shown on the 1/8" plans, such as the partition types cross-reference symbols, door marks, and the like.

9. Draw stud walls. Show a change of material line between stud walls and masonry or concrete. Show a change of material line between concrete and masonry as well. Show wall furring.

10. Show windows, storefront, borrow lights, and other openings. Be sure to show mullions accurately spaced and drawn to scale.

11. Draw stairs and handrails; show number of risers. Use an arrow that begins on the first riser and ends on the last riser to show the direction of travel.

12. Add door swings and jambs. Doors should be shown open at 90, using a double line to indicate thickness. Use a thin line to indicate the door swing arc.

13. Show plumbing fixtures, such as water closets, urinals, lavatories, sinks and mop sinks.

14. Show counter tops, vanities, partial height walls, and toilet partitions.

15. Draw ceiling soffits, plane changes, or other features (such as skylights) with a dashed line.

16. Show equipment (dash in if not in contract).

17. Make a print for pre-planning the dimensions.

18. Add dimensions (see Section 3.3 on Dimensioning).

19. Show room names, numbers, and finish codes.

20. Add cross-referencing symbols, including section marks for building sections, wall sections, larger scale plans, plan details, interior elevations, door marks.

21. Add keynotes or systems notes. Note each material or item at least once on each elevation.

22. Poche floor materials, Do not overpoché!

BUILDING ELEVATIONS

1. If the sheet size has not already been determined, propose a sheet size that will allow all of the elevations in their entirety, to fit on one sheet, if possible. If the elevations must be divided into parts, propose a division of the plan for review with the Project Architect.

2. Together will the Project Architect, determine whether the drawings should be drawn on matte polyester film (Mylar), vellum, or some other medium.

   • Determine how the title block information will be put on the sheet; confirm the project name, number, address.

3. Establish the drawing area on the sheet.

   • Set aside space for the drawing title, the title block, general notes, and keynotes legend.

4. Locate the elevations in the drawing area. Most sheets are large enough to accommodate several rows of elevations; elevations should be arranged so that equal amounts of white space lay between each row of elevations.

   • Allow enough space between each row of elevations for the title and scale.

5. Allow zones around the actual building elevation for:

   • Elevation markers
   • Vertical dimensions
   • Grid identification bubbles
   • Cross-referencing symbols

6. Draw structural grid lines and identification bubbles first, on the back of the sheet. Since the grid lines will rarely change, it is better to have them on the back of the sheet where they will not be erased when making changes to other parts of the drawing.

7. Turn the sheet over (and do not put any other information on the back of the sheet, not even poche). Show the drawing title and the scale.

8. Block out massing of the building. Draw the major building components, including the ground line, corners, cornices, ridges, dormers, parapets, chimneys, roof lines, setback lines, penthouses, balconies, ramps, stairs, columns, pilasters, and beams.

   Show footings, foundation walls, grade beams, and drilled piers; use a dashed line for any work below grade. Show steps in footings and brick ledges. Brick ledge elevations should be shown only on the structural drawings.

9. Draw all of the glazed and unglazed openings, including windows, doors, skylights, barrel vaults, ridged vaults, roof scuttles, colonnades, and arcades.

10. Show all waterproofing members, such as coping, gutters, leaders, scuppers, conductor heads, splash blocks, and flashing.

11. Draw all mechanical equipment, such as cooling towers, vents, louvers, grilles, flues, hose bibs, and siamese connections.

12. Locate all electrical equipment, such as lighting, meters, transformers, and alarm panels.

13. Show all elements that allow for structural movement, such as expansion, seismic, and control joints and reveals.

14. Show all directional elements, including signs, plaques, clocks, and street names and numbers.

15. Draw all miscellaneous architectural items, such as bicycle racks, flag poles, ladders, railings and mailboxes.

16. Draw elevation markers to the left or right side of the elevation. These elevation markers should mark elements, such as floor lines, roof lines, parapets, top and bottom of windows, break lines, and tops of arches, lintels, or any major horizontal elements.

17. Add vertical elevations of major elements that are not marked by elevation markers (see Chapter on Dimensioning).

18. Add cross-references symbols, including section marks for building sections and wall sections, elevation marks, and detail marks.

19. Add keynotes or system notes. Note each material or item at least once on each building section.

20. Poche all materials. Show major horizontal and vertical materials, including brick coursing and horizontal and vertical siding. Do not overpoché!

WALL SECTIONS

1. If the sheet size has not already been determined, propose a size that will allow the sections, in their entirety, to fit on one sheet. If the sections must be divided into parts, propose a division of the sections for review with the project architect.

   Determine the appropriate scale (1/2" or 3/4" = 1'-0); frequently, wall sections drawn at 3/4" will reduce the need for details later.

2. Together will the Project Architect, determine whether the drawings should be drawn on matte polyester film (Mylar), vellum, or some other medium.

   - Determine how the title block information will be put on the sheet; confirm the project name, number, address.

3. Establish the drawing area on the sheet.

   - Set aside space for the drawing title, the title block, and keynotes.

4. Locate the sections in the drawing area. Most sheets are large enough to accommodate two rows of wall sections; sections should be arranged so that equal amounts of white space lay between each row of sections.

   - Allow enough space between each row of sections for the title and scale.
   - If the wall sections are stacked to allow two rows to appear on the sheet, line up the outside of the wall for all sections, above and below.
   - All wall sections should be cut so that the outside of the building is oriented the same way on each drawing.

5. Allow zones around the actual plan for:

   - Elevation markers
   - Vertical dimensions
   - Grid identification bubbles
   - Cross-referencing symbols
   - Notation

6. Draw structural grid lines and identification bubbles first, on the back of the sheet. Since the grid lines should rarely change, it is better to have them on the back of the sheet where they will not be erased when making changes to other parts of the drawing.

7. Turn the sheet over (and do not put any other informa tion on the back of the sheet, not even poche). Show the drawing title and the scale.

8. Block out the portion of the building that is to be cut. Draw the major building components, including the ground line, footings, foundations, brick ledges, floors, walls, ceilings, roofs, parapets, penthouses, balconies, ramps, and stairs. Wall sections should generally be cut through door or/and window openings; this will allow the maximum number of conditions to be addressed in one drawing; if the scale is large enough, additional details may not be necessary.

9. Draw all of the glazed and unglazed openings in section and in elevation, including windows, doors, skylights, barrel vaults, roof scuttles, colonnades, and arcades.

10. Show all room names and numbers in rooms that have been cut.

11. Show all waterproofing members, such as coping, gutters, leaders, scuppers, conductor heads, splash blocks, and flashing in section and elevation.

12. Draw all mechanical equipment, such as cooling towers, ducts, boilers and chillers, vents, louvers, grilles, flues, drinking fountains, toilet room fixtures, and siamese connections in elevation.

13. Draw all electrical equipment, such as lighting, meters, service panels, transformers, thermostats, and alarm panels in elevation.

14. Draw all miscellaneous architectural items, such as casework, counters, shelves, chalkboards, and tackboards, display cases, fire extinguisher cabinets, mirrors, toilet partitions, and accessories, ladders, railings and mailboxes in section and elevation.

15. Draw elevation markers to the left or right side of the elevation. These elevation markers should mark elements, such as floors, ceilings, roofs, parapets, top and bottom of windows, arch break lines and top of arches, lintels, or any major horizontal elements. Allow plenty of space (2-3") between vertical dimension strings and the section drawing itself; place notation within this space so leader lines will not have to cross vertical dimension lines.

   Show (and dimension) vertical masonry coursing, including special coursing, such as rowlocks, headers, belt courses, stone sills or accents, etc.

WALL SECTIONS (continued)

16. Add vertical elevations of major elements that are not marked by elevation markers (see Chapter on Dimensioning).

17. Add cross-references symbols, including section marks for wall sections and details.

18. Add keynotes or system notes. Note materials on a typical section at the lower right portion of the drawing sheet. Do not repeat typical materials notes or dimensions unless clarity is suffering. Add a note indicating that materials and dimensions are similar on other sections, unless noted otherwise.

19. Poche all materials. Show major horizontal and vertical materials, including brick coursing and horizontal and vertical siding. Do not overpoché!

BUILDING SECTIONS

Building sections should be diagrammatic; their intent is to convey a general sense of the vertical dimensions and forms of the building, and to provide a place to cross-reference larger scale wall sections, which show the detail. Show as little detail as possible in building sections. Do not use building sections to show interior elevations of walls beyond; show room names and numbers only when necessary for clarity. Show a profile of the portions of the building exposed by the section cut. Do not show joists, beams, insulation, etc. that is better shown in a wall section or a detail. Use building sections to reveal portions of the building that need to be shown in elevation (such as the walls surrounding an interior courtyard) that do not appear in the normal building elevations.

1. If the sheet size has not already been determined, propose a size that will allow the sections, in their entirety, to fit on one sheet.

2. Together will the Project Architect, determine whether the drawings should be drawn on matte polyester film (Mylar), vellum, or some other medium.

   • Determine how the title block information will be put on the sheet; confirm the project name, number, address.

3. Establish the drawing area on the sheet.

   • Set aside space for the drawing title, the title block, and keynotes.

4. Locate the sections in the drawing area. Most sheets are large enough to accommodate several rows of sections; sections should be arranged so that equal amounts of white space lay between each column.

   • Allow enough space between each column of sections for the title and scale.

5. Allow zones around the actual section drawing for:

   • Elevation markers
   • Vertical dimensions
   • Grid identification bubbles
   • Cross-referencing symbols

6. Draw structural grid lines and identification bubbles first, on the back of the sheet. Since the grid lines should rarely change, it is better to have them on the back of the sheet where they will not be erased when making changes to other parts of the drawing.

7. Turn the sheet over (and do not put any other information on the back of the sheet, not even poche). Show the drawing title and the scale.

8. Block out all building sections. Draw the major building components of the section, including the ground line, footings, foundations, floors, walls, ceilings, roofs, parapets, penthouses, balconies, columns, beams, ramps, and stairs.

9. Draw all of the glazed and unglazed openings in section and in elevation, including windows, doors, skylights, barrel vaults, roof scuttles, colonnades, and arcades.

10. Show members, such as copings, gutters, leaders, scuppers, conductor heads, splash blocks, and flashing in section and elevation, where applicable.

11. Draw all mechanical and electrical equipment

12. Draw elevation markers to the left or right side of the elevation. These elevation markers should mark major building elements, such as floors, ceilings, roofs, parapets, top and bottom of windows, arch break lines and top of arches, lintels, or any major horizontal elements.

14. Add vertical elevations of major elements that are not marked by elevation markers (see Chapter on Dimensioning).

15. Add cross-references symbols for wall section locations.

16. Add keynotes or system notes. Notation should be minimal; materials indications and notations should generally be shown on the wall sections. Materials shown in elevation should be noted in the same way as the building elevations.

17. Poche all materials. Show major horizontal and vertical materials, including brick coursing and horizontal and vertical siding. Do not overpoché!

MISCELLANEOUS DRAWINGS

1. Vertical Circulation

    Detail elevators, stairs, dumbwaiters, chutes.
    Draw stair sections through near run looking at opposite run.
    Draw elevator section through front and back elevator walls.
    Detail elevator sill and special elevator cab features.
    Detail architectural features including special features, nosings, guardrails, handrails.
    Detail ladders, ramps.
    Verify building code and handicap code (ADA) compliance.

2a. Building Details

    Detail building corners,heads, sills, parapets.
    Detail storefront, entrances, curtainwall, and windows.
    Detail changes in wall material, construction or geometry.
    Detail expansion joints and crack control joints.
    Detail louvers.
    Detail roofing flashings, scuppers, equipment supports, pipe penetrations, and expansion joints.
    Detail roof hatches, skylights.

2b. Finish Details

    Detail column enclosures and unusual wall intersections.
    Detail special fire assembly closures.
    Detail changes in finish materials.
    Detail custom millwork, acoustical treatments, special wall finishes.
    Detail special lighting assemblies.
    Detail floor mats.
    Detail wall heads to accommodate deflection as applicable.
    Detail special requirements for fixtures and equipment.
    Detail toilet partition hangers.

Consider alternative methods for scheduling doors, room finishes, and for handling interior elevations. Projects with only a few different kinds of doors that repeat many times throughout the project should have a numbering and scheduling system showing only those few types, rather than having a unique number for each door. Toilet room accessories may be better handled using a few typical elevations (of just the accessories), showing typical mounting heights, rather than drawing elevations of all the toilet room walls. Casework types with typical dimensions may make many interior elevations unnecessary. Think about the most appropriate way to communicate the information, and then choose the simplest and least time-consuming method that gets the job done.

3. Openings

    Schedule door and window openings indicating door and frame elevations, materials, sizes, finishes, hardware, fire ratings, glazing, and detail references.
    Detail heads, jambs, and sills.
    Identify screens and window coverings.
    Coordinate specified hardware with details.
    Provide identification of latches/locks, exit devices, push/pull plates, hinges, closers, door operators, stops, kickplates, weatherstripping, smoke seals, thresholds, and mail slots.
    Coordinate all electrical documents for electronic locks, magnetic holds, and for door operators including overhead door operators and gates.

4. Interior Elevations, Casework

    Draw interior elevations for all walls not clearly understandable from plan information.
    Show materials if there is more than one or if colors or textures vary.
    Show special tile patterns or paneling patterns.
    Show wall mounted equipment such as chalkboards, tackboards, clocks, fire hose cabinets, and fire extinguishers.
    Show doors and windows.
    Show mechanical diffusers and louvers.
    Show electrical fixtures and outlets.
    Show casework and furnishings that are in the contract.
    Reference casework details or keynote casework by type.
    Show toilet accessories and toilet partitions.
    Show plumbing fixtures.
    Show mirrors.
    Show ceiling height changes and soffits viewed in elevation.
    Show thermostats, light switches, outlets, controls.
    Detail special trim conditions.
    Detail custom millwork showing specifics of construction and special components.
    Dimension wall items from the floor. Dimension wall items horizontally if plan dimensions have not been identified else where.

5. Room Finishes

    Schedule room finishes to identify the substrate and the finish material for each room surface.
    Schedule room number, room name, materials and finishes for floors, base, walls, and ceilings.
    Indicate paint, paint sheen, wall coverings, paneling, tile, and material colors or product numbers.

MISCELLANEOUS DRAWINGS (continued)

6. Wall Types

    List each wall type to be designated.
    Group wall types by construction type (frame, masonry, concrete), and designate wall types within each group using the same letter designation (A1, A2, A3...).
    List the components for each wall assembly in sequence from exterior to interior.
    Coordinate with specification language for the proper nomenclature to identify component materials.
    Indicate fire assembly ratings, sound transmission coefficients, and testing laboratory design designations.
    Indicate walls that extend vertically to structure above, walls which extend just a few inches above the ceiling plane, and walls which terminate at the ceiling.
    Indicate special wall construction for acoustics.
    Indicate HVAC fire damper requirements for fire-rated walls.

	DOOR SCHEDULE													
	DOORS						**FRAMES**							
				SIZE						**DETAILS**			Fire Rating	Hdw. Group	
Door #	TYPE	MAT.	FIN.	WIDTH	HEIGHT	THICK	TYPE	MAT.	FIN.	JAMB	HEAD	SILL			REMARKS

Door Schedule

The door schedule on this page is suggested for adoption by your office. It was selected for its recognizability as an industry-accepted standard, for its simplicity, and for its ability to make drawings easier to read. The above information may be copied onto adhesive-backed material and applied directly to your working drawings. Or, if you prefer, the symbols may be replicated on your CAD system.

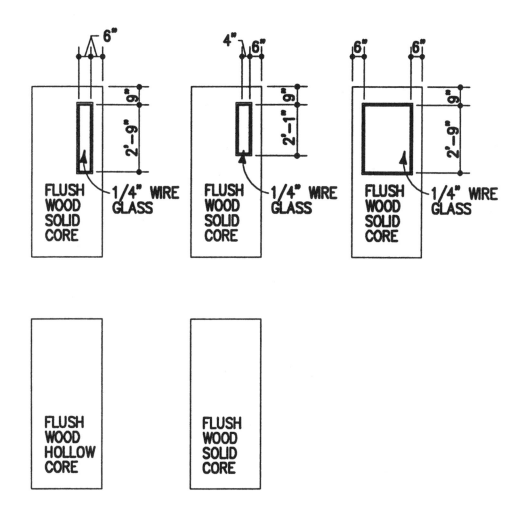

Door Types

The door types on this page are provided as the beginning elements of a more comprehensive library of door types that will eventually be prepared by your office. They are included here to suggest a standardized, stylistic approach for communicating this information, and are suggested for adoption by your office. They were selected for their recognizability as industry-accepted standards, for their simplicity, and for their ability to make drawings easier to read. The above information may be copied onto adhesive-backed material and applied directly to your working drawings. Or, if you prefer, the symbols may be replicated on your CAD system.

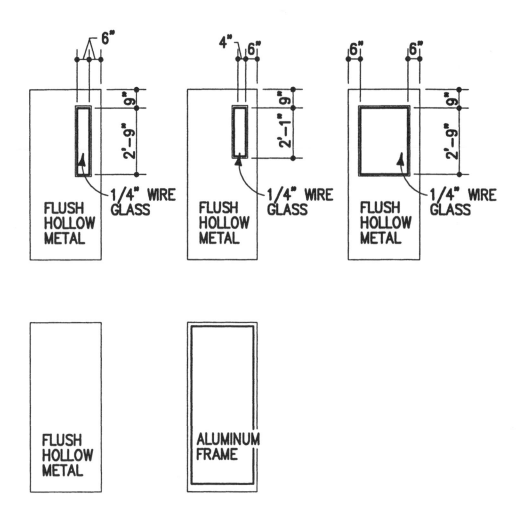

Door Types

The door types on this page are provided as the beginning elements of a more comprehensive library of door types that will eventually be prepared by your office. They are included here to suggest a standardized, stylistic approach for communicating this information, and are suggested for adoption by your office. They were selected for their recognizability as industry-accepted standards, for their simplicity, and for their ability to make drawings easier to read. The above information may be copied onto adhesive-backed material and applied directly to your working drawings. Or, if you prefer, the symbols may be replicated on your CAD system.

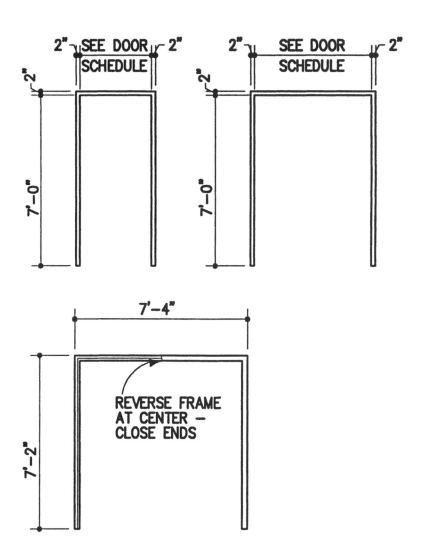

Frame Types

The frame types on this page are provided as the beginning elements of a more comprehensive library of frame types that will eventually be prepared by your office. They are included here to suggest a standardized, stylistic approach for communicating this information, and are suggested for adoption by your office. They were selected for their recognizability as industry-accepted standards, for their simplicity, and for their ability to make drawings easier to read. The above information may be copied onto adhesive-backed material and applied directly to your working drawings. Or, if you prefer, the symbols may be replicated on your CAD system.

FINISH SCHEDULE

ROOM #	NAME	FLOOR	BASE		North Wall		East Wall		South Wall		West Wall		Ceiling	Ceiling Height	REMARKS
			FINISH	MAT.	FINISH	MAT.	FINISH	MAT.	FINISH	MAT.	FINISH	MAT.			

Finish Schedule

The finish schedule on this page is suggested for adoption by your office. It was selected for its recognizability as an industry-accepted standard, for its simplicity, and for its ability to make drawings easier to read. The above information may be copied onto adhesive-backed material and applied directly to your working drawings. Or, if you prefer, the symbols may be replicated on your CAD system.

FINISH SCHEDULE							
ROOM #	NAME	FLOOR	BASE	WALLS	CEILING	Clg. Height	REMARKS

Finish Schedule

The finish schedule on this page is suggested for adoption by your office. It was selected for its recognizability as an industry-accepted standard, for its simplicity, and for its ability to make drawings easier to read. The above information may be copied onto adhesive-backed material and applied directly to your working drawings. Or, if you prefer, the symbols may be replicated on your CAD system.

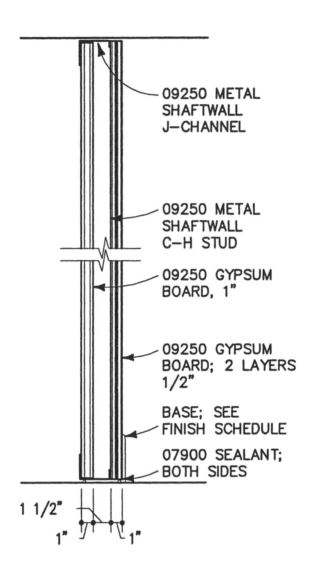

09250 METAL
SHAFTWALL
J-CHANNEL

09250 METAL
SHAFTWALL
C-H STUD

09250 GYPSUM
BOARD, 1"

09250 GYPSUM
BOARD; 2 LAYERS
1/2"

BASE; SEE
FINISH SCHEDULE

07900 SEALANT;
BOTH SIDES

1 1/2"
1"   1"

Partition Types

The partition types on this page are provided as the beginning elements of a more comprehensive library of partition types that will eventually be prepared by your office. They are included here to suggest a standardized, stylistic approach for communicating this information, and are suggested for adoption by your office. They were selected for their   simplicity, and for their ability to make drawings easier to read. The above information may be copied onto adhesive-backed material and applied directly to your working drawings. Or, if you prefer, the symbols may be replicated on your CAD system.

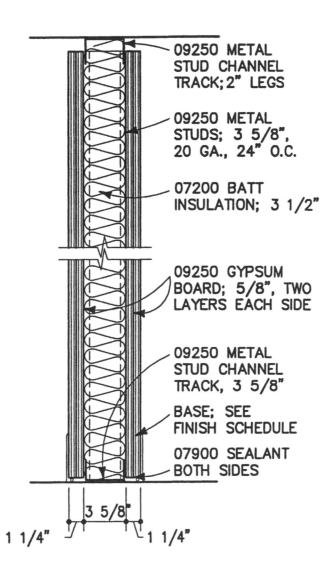

09250 METAL
STUD CHANNEL
TRACK; 2" LEGS

09250 METAL
STUDS; 3 5/8",
20 GA., 24" O.C.

07200 BATT
INSULATION; 3 1/2"

09250 GYPSUM
BOARD; 5/8", TWO
LAYERS EACH SIDE

09250 METAL
STUD CHANNEL
TRACK, 3 5/8"

BASE; SEE
FINISH SCHEDULE

07900 SEALANT
BOTH SIDES

3 5/8"

1 1/4"   1 1/4"

Partition Types

The partition types on this page are provided as the beginning elements of a more comprehensive library of partition types that will eventually be prepared by your office. They are included here to suggest a standardized, stylistic approach for communicating this information, and are suggested for adoption by your office. They were selected for their simplicity, and for their ability to make drawings easier to read. The above information may be copied onto adhesive-backed material and applied directly to your working drawings. Or, if you prefer, the symbols may be replicated on your CAD system.

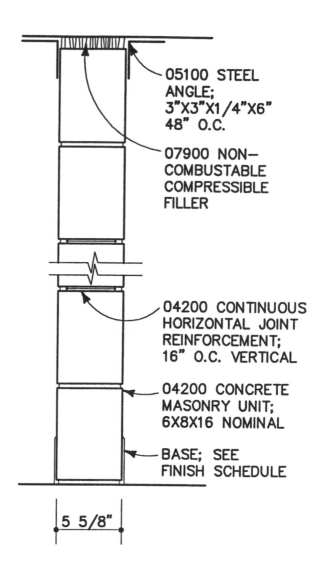

05100 STEEL
ANGLE;
3"X3"X1/4"X6"
48" O.C.

07900 NON—
COMBUSTABLE
COMPRESSIBLE
FILLER

04200 CONTINUOUS
HORIZONTAL JOINT
REINFORCEMENT;
16" O.C. VERTICAL

04200 CONCRETE
MASONRY UNIT;
6X8X16 NOMINAL

BASE; SEE
FINISH SCHEDULE

5 5/8"

Partition Types

The partition types on this page are provided as the beginning elements of a more comprehensive library of partition types that will eventually be prepared by your office. They are included here to suggest a standardized, stylistic approach for communicating this information, and are suggested for adoption by your office. They were selected for their   simplicity, and for their ability to make drawings easier to read. The above information may be copied onto adhesive-backed material and applied directly to your working drawings. Or, if you prefer, the symbols may be replicated on your CAD system.

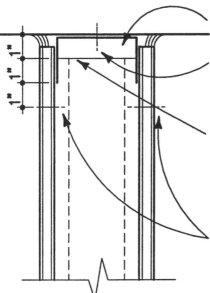

1" CLEAR SPACE ABOVE TOP OF STUDS

RUNNER TRACK W/ 2" FLANGES – ANCHOR TO CONC. W/ POWER DRIVEN FASTENERS, 2'-0" O.C. MAX.

AT FIRE RATED PARTN'S, FILL ALL GAPS AT TOP OF GYP. BD. W/ FINISHING COMPOUND. AT PARTN'S W/OUT FIRE RATING, STOP GYP. BD. 1" BELOW STRUCTURE.

DO NOT ATTACH GYP. BD. TO RUNNER TRACK. LOCATE HIGHEST SCREWS THROUGH GYP. BD. 1" MIN. BELOW BOTTOM OF RUNNER FLANGES.

PROVIDE LATERAL ANCHORAGE FOR STUDS AT PARTITION INTERSECTIONS & CORNERS AND AT JAMBS OF FRAMES BEFORE GYP. BD. IS APPLIED. SPLIT RUNNER FLANGES AND FOLD BACK AGAINST EACH SIDE OF STUD OR FASTEN STUD TO RUNNER WITH ONE SCREW. APPLY GYP. BD. ON OPPOSITE SIDE AND THEN REMOVE SCREW.

Partition Types

The partition types on this page are provided as the beginning elements of a more comprehensive library of partition types that will eventually be prepared by your office. They are included here to suggest a standardized, stylistic approach for communicating this information, and are suggested for adoption by your office. They were selected for their   simplicity, and for their ability to make drawings easier to read. The above information may be copied onto adhesive-backed material and applied directly to your working drawings. Or, if you prefer, the symbols may be replicated on your CAD system.

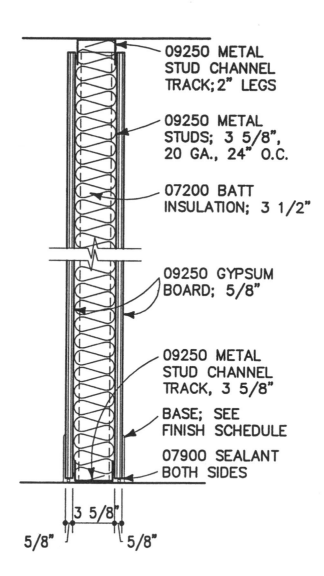

09250 METAL
STUD CHANNEL
TRACK; 2" LEGS

09250 METAL
STUDS; 3 5/8",
20 GA., 24" O.C.

07200 BATT
INSULATION; 3 1/2"

09250 GYPSUM
BOARD; 5/8"

09250 METAL
STUD CHANNEL
TRACK, 3 5/8"

BASE; SEE
FINISH SCHEDULE

07900 SEALANT
BOTH SIDES

3 5/8"

5/8"   5/8"

Partition Types

The partition types on this page are provided as the beginning elements of a more comprehensive library of partition types that will eventually be prepared by your office. They are included here to suggest a standardized, stylistic approach for communicating this information, and are suggested for adoption by your office. They were selected for their   simplicity, and for their ability to make drawings easier to read. The above information may be copied onto adhesive-backed material and applied directly to your working drawings. Or, if you prefer, the symbols may be replicated on your CAD system.

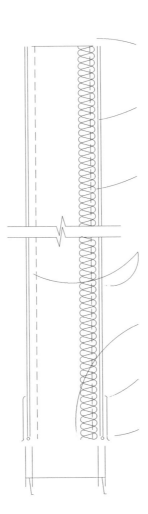

Partition Types

The partition types on this page are provided as the beginning elements of a more comprehensive library of partition types that will eventually be prepared by your office. They are included here to suggest a standardized, stylistic approach for communicating this information, and are suggested for adoption by your office. They were selected for their simplicity, and for their ability to make drawings easier to read. The above information may be copied onto adhesive-backed material and applied directly to your working drawings. Or, if you prefer, the symbols may be replicated on your CAD system.

TOILET AND BATH ACCESSORIES SCHEDULE

LOCATION	RECESSED							SURFACE MOUNTED																	REMARKS
	TOILET PAPER DISPENSER	PAPER TOWEL DISPENSER	TRASH RECEPTACLE	COMBINATION PAPER TOWEL/TRASH	SANITARY NAPKIN DISPENSER	SANITARY NAPKIN DISPOSAL		TOILET PAPER DISPENSER	PAPER TOWEL DISPENSER	TRASH RECEPTACLE	COMBINATION PAPER TOWEL/TRASH	SANITARY NAPKIN DISPENSER	SANITARY NAPKIN DISPOSAL		MIRROR	ROBE HOOK	TOWEL BAR	SOAP DISPENSER	CURTAIN ROD	SHELF	GRAB BAR	MEDICINE CABINET	TOILET SEAT COVER DISPENSER		

Toilet and Bath Accessories Schedule

The toilet and bath accessories schedule on this page is suggested for adoption by your office. It was selected for its recognizability as an industry-accepted standard, for its simplicity, and for its ability to make drawings easier to read. The above information may be copied onto adhesive-backed material and applied directly to your working drawings. Or, if you prefer, the symbols may be replicated on your CAD system.

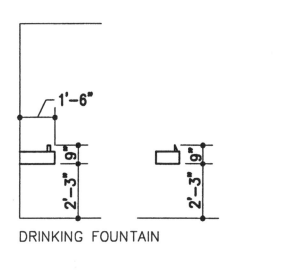

DRINKING FOUNTAIN   PHONE

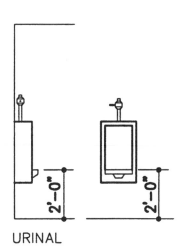

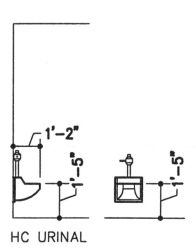

URINAL   HC URINAL

Toilet and Bath Elevations

The toilet and bath elevations on this page are provided as the beginning elements of a more comprehensive library of toilet and bath elevation drawings types that will eventually be prepared by your office. They are included here to suggest a standardized, stylistic approach for communicating this information, and are suggested for adoption by your office. They were selected for their simplicity, and for their ability to make drawings easier to read. The above information may be copied onto adhesive-backed material and applied directly to your working drawings. Or, if you prefer, the symbols may be replicated on your CAD system.

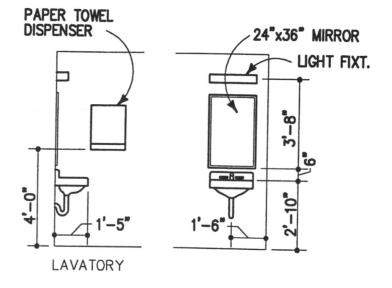

LAVATORY

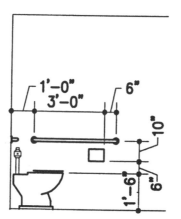

TYPICAL HANDICAP TOILET STALL

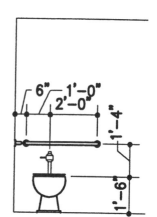

Toilet and Bath Elevations

The toilet and bath elevations on this page are provided as the beginning elements of a more comprehensive library of toilet and bath elevation drawings types that will eventually be prepared by your office. They are included here to suggest a standardized, stylistic approach for communicating this information, and are suggested for adoption by your office. They were selected for their simplicity, and for their ability to make drawings easier to read. The above information may be copied onto adhesive-backed material and applied directly to your working drawings. Or, if you prefer, the symbols may be replicated on your CAD system.

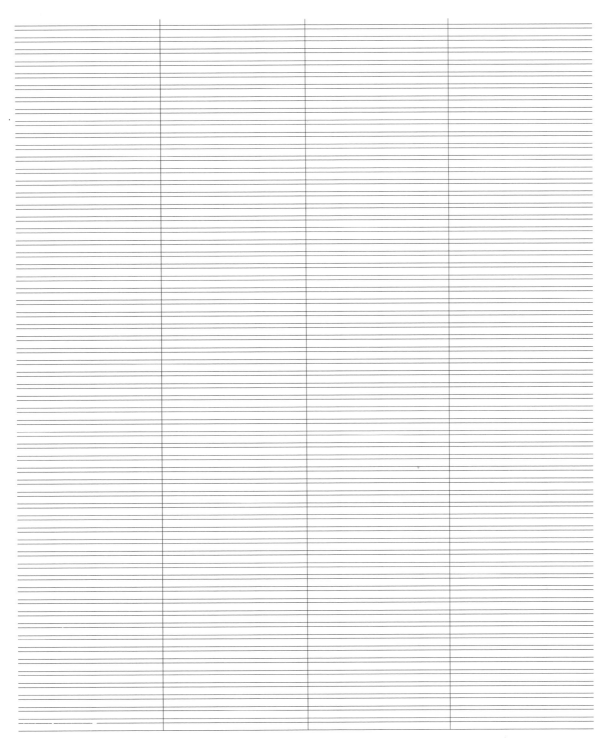

Lettering Guidelines

The lettering guidelines provided here are for use as an underlay in doing hand lettering. With the use of this underlay, it should not be necessary to draw lettering guidelines.

Index

Index

About the Author

Larry Jenks AIA, is a principal with Klipp Colussy Jenks DuBois Architects, P.C., a Denver architectural firm. His responsibilities include oversight and direction of the firm's training and development program, which has twice received national recognition for excellence from the American Institute of Architects. As the firm's Principal in Charge of Technical Operations, Larry provides leadership in the areas of technical design and documentation strategies. He was recruited by the Denver Chapter of the American Institute of Architects to chair the Office Practice Committee to guide the creation of this manual of standard office practices and procedures.